Literature and the Continuances of Virtue

Literature and the Continuances of Virtue

Warner Berthoff

PRINCETON UNIVERSITY PRESS

PRINCETON, NEW JERSEY

Copyright © 1986 by Princeton University Press
Published by Princeton University Press, 41 William Street,
Princeton, New Jersey 08540
In the United Kingdom: Princeton University Press,
Guildford, Surrey

ISBN 0-691-06688-4

Publication of this book has been aided by a grant from
The Andrew W. Mellon Foundation
This book has been composed in Linotron Sabon

Clothbound editions of Princeton University Press books
are printed on acid-free paper, and binding materials are
chosen for strength and durability

Printed in the United States of America
by Princeton University Press
Princeton, New Jersey

For Ann

Contents

Preface

This book takes its shape from a number of contributing impulses that may seem at times to be pushing off in different directions; accordingly it may be helpful to outline briefly and in sequence what is to follow. In the opening chapter I argue for a particular conception of imaginative literature's essential subject matter—a conception broached in the main title—and go on to explore certain theoretical and interpretive considerations currently at issue in any such inquiry. I hope it will be clear from the start that no full-dress theory of literature is on offer, only a theory of meaning and of the valuations at work in the attribution of force of meaning, weight of meaning, level and direction of meaning, as distinct from any particular content of meaning (or theme). The second chapter traces out the key property of *virtue* in its historical descent from classical texts to those of our era. Four additional chapters treat in detail the figuring of this judgment-framing property in a variety of literary works and bodies of work each of which has the supplementary advantage of remaining a live focus of critical conjecture and dispute. Of course if the main argument has merit, many more exemplifications might be attached; instead I would simply invite those interested to try out its perspectives for themselves, with any literature they know and value.

I hope too—especially in the opening chapter, and in an Afterword which the theory-minded might turn to as a second introduction—that a slight polemical edge the proceedings take on at moments will not be automatically read as expressing hostility to theory as such. We are all theory-tethered; sound root-of-the-matter speculation is always at a premium; and the confusions nourished by a fresh deluge of theoretical adventuring (confusion itself being always with us) can make their own contribution to a renewed speculative alertness. Yet I ought to acknowledge that twenty years along in the latest migration of European *nouvelle critique* to the ever-porous American strand my own day-to-day concern with theory is more and more that it not get in the way of an appropriate enjoyment, an openness to any genuine act of imaginative renewal. Correspondingly a first premise in every part of the book will be that the acts constituting the continuum of literature are always a potential augmentation of self-reflective life, and are worth having and worth encouraging precisely as they claim space for themselves within a semiologic world that casually frustrates every purifying or totalizing design; a world, the one we all conspire in, where dreamed-of transformations into an absolute fitness in every cognitive or associative relationship are always and irremediably "not here, not yet."

If this book does no more than, in its later chapters, send readers back with renewed expectancy to the writings treated, it will have served its principal purpose.

Grateful acknowledgment is made to the following for the use of copyrighted material: The Putnam Publishing Group of New York and Martin Secker and Warburg Limited of London for passages from *The Man Without Qualities* by Robert Musil, tr. Eithne Wilkins and Ernst Kaiser, copyright © 1953 by Coward-McCann Inc. and copyright © 1953, 1954, 1960 by Martin Secker and Warburg Limited; Macmillan Publishing Company of New York and Michael B. Yeats and Macmillan London Limited for selections from *W. B. Yeats: The Poems*, ed. Richard J. Finneran, copyright © 1919, 1928, 1933 by Macmillan Publishing Company, renewed 1947, 1956, 1961 by Bertha Georgie Yeats, and copyright © 1940 by Georgie Yeats, renewed 1968 by Bertha Georgie Yeats, Michael Butler Yeats, and Anne Yeats; City Lights Books of San Francisco for selections from *Lunch Poems* by Frank O'Hara, copyright © 1964 by Frank O'Hara; Alfred A. Knopf, Inc. of New York for selections from *The Collected Poems of Frank O'Hara*, ed. Donald Allen, copyright © 1958, 1960, 1968, 1971 by Maureen Granville-Smith.

In writing on matters that have held my attention over many years, obligations to friends, old teachers, fellow students, scholars, commentators and reviewers, are past reckoning. But certain debts of an immediately practical kind should be recorded—to Joseph Frank, whose invitation to conduct a set of Christian Gauss Seminars at Princeton University was this book's starting point and whose conversation, whenever we meet, is unfailingly clarifying, nonsense-dispersing, and pertinent to all key issues; to Ralph Cohen, who provided space in *New Literary History* (Winter 1974) for an abbreviated trial run of Chapters I-III; to the late Henry Guerlac and the staff of the Society for the Humanities at Cornell University for a year-long opportunity to expand and solidify my arguments, and to James M. Billington, Ann Sheffield, and the staff of the Woodrow Wilson International Center for Scholars for the chance to recast earlier formulations and bring the whole toward completion; to the libraries of Harvard and Cornell Universities, the Library of Congress, and the Concord Public Library for indispensable assistance; to Jonathan Bishop and Alvin Kernan, who at different stages helped rescue the opening sections from an inclination to nit-picking; to Dorrit Cohn and Henry Hatfield, who tolerated and encouraged my foray into Musil; to Mrs. Arthur Sherwood of the Princeton University Press for steadfast support and wise counsel; and most of all to the book's dedicatee, who teaches me daily (as she has for much the best part of four decades) what it is that is most worth trying to understand.

Concord, Massachusetts
September 1985

Literature and the Continuances of Virtue

Five Supervisory Texts:

"When we tire of the saints, Shakespeare is our city of refuge."

—Emerson, journals

". . . the purpose of playing, whose end, both at the first and now, was and is, to hold, as 'twere, the mirror up to nature; to show virtue her feature. . . ."

—*Hamlet*, III, ii

"We are human beings, and in what are we more interested than in human action and human attitudes?"

—T. S. Eliot, "Dialogue on Dramatic Poetry"

"Is it strange to affirm that the ultimate aim of all the arts . . . is to present to man his guiding image? But this guiding image is nothing less or other than the shaping mode of that knowledge which returns as power."

—I. A. Richards, *Design for Escape*

"Everything that man has handled has the fatal tendency to secrete meaning."

—Marcel Duchamp

CHAPTER ONE

Virtue and the Tasks of Criticism

PREMISES

Defending his own philosophical style, William James once remarked that every argument worth making comes out of a "field of consciousness" wider than that mandated by its declared subject and will deviate from what strictly is required because of some contingent anxiety—"the bogey in the background," James cheerfully named it—which for the moment threatens to obstruct understanding. It may temper a little the immodesty of this book's overall design if I say at once that I am not claiming exemption from James's rule. Quite possibly in what follows there are turns of argument betraying a greater preoccupation with short-run speculative misconceptions than I am likely myself, at some later date, to see the need for.

But short-run interferences leave their mark and ought to be acknowledged. As anyone will agree who has tracked the latest disturbances in literary-critical theorizing, literature itself as commonly spoken of—the single work of literature as a locus of value, the act of literary making as a demonstrable good— has for some time been under more than one kind of systematic attack; and the arguments assembled here are offered not incidentally as an affirmation of imaginative literature's concrete value in both respects, as humane resource and as a civil calling to be cherished, among other callings, on its own terms. Where the arts are in question, the first requirement (one should not have to insist) is encouragement, a willing accommodation. Art is one thing, religion another. Yet as regards our initial effort and play of attention I think we owe the enterprise of art something of what, so André Gide argued, we owe scripture— not, first off, metacommentary but acceptance.

Primarily then this is a book of demonstrations, a showing off of certain exemplary acts of literary making and of the central imaginative invitation each projects. I take some such exercise to be the first obligation of literary-critical writing. "Elucidation and the correction of taste," T. S. Eliot once summed it all up; you highlight as best you can the cardinal signature or design while at the same time removing misconceived obstacles to a substantial enjoyment. On this ground what matters most is not the bustle and stir of critical and metacritical system-building but the survival to consciousness of the thing itself, the survival of the very concept of powerful and apposite imaginative invitation; the survival also—as I wrote at the beginning of *Fictions and Events* (1971)—"of the effective community of writers and readers in which literature practically exists and from which its special influence spreads." This is a first reason for writing at length about individual literary works that are of acknowledged importance historically and that first of all have been exemplary to other writers, always the audience of first consequence. It seems evident that any new account of the function of literary statement will be stronger as it answers primarily to works of this class.[1] Their broad familiarity among prospective readers is a complementary reason, my chief aim in this book being simply to return attention to what it is in our reading that decisively kindles and sustains interest, and how to our imagination this whatever-it-is secures its authority.

At the start two working assumptions should be stated which may appear altogether too obvious for comment. But for a number of reasons each has got oddly embarrassing to handle in critical discourse. Each, certainly, is at present overlaid with considerable methodological suspicion.

The first is that so long as we do continue to concern our-

---

[1] This principle can operate, I think, without prejudice to the mass of coexistent writing which in any historical period, besides giving pleasure in its own fashion, serves also to maintain openings for major achievement.

selves with *literature* and with a specifically *literary* history, the phenomenon at the center of inquiry must be the literary work itself, according to its performative character and kind. By this I mean the particular composed unit an identifiable author has understood himself, in his capacity as author, to be producing and his readers understand themselves to be reading—not scripture, not legislation, not business code or mnemonic charm or accidental semiotic inscription (though authors may set about mimicking any or all of these essentially instrumental forms) but another kind of thing with its own expectation-determining name: poem, prayer, complaint, satire, public letter, personal testament, novel, anti-novel, non-fictional novel, novel in verse, "novel in prose" (Pasternak's designation for *Doctor Zhivago*), "comic epic in prose" (Fielding's for *Joseph Andrews*), treatise, fragment, sketch, excursion, meditation, whatever. It is the historically extended coming-into-existence of constructs of this kind, intended as such and—by some identifiable readership—acknowledged and entertained as such, that gives us the type-series we commemorate as "literature."

Literary works will thus be phenomenally different—different in constitution and operation, different in our reception of them—from any comparable sequence of communicative and expressive acts. Whatever signifying properties they share with other discourse, and whatever expressive meanings are exposed or released by this overlap (the domain of the contributing discipline of hermeneutics), will be altered in function and interior relation by the factor of a specifically literary intentionality. This intentionality, wherever it operates, is sooner or later recognized. It is what gives us the classification "literature." Ignoring it, for whatever purpose, means substituting a basically different rule of assessment and understanding. Without it we would have neither "authors" nor "readers" in any distinguishable sense—and in much recent theorizing a runaway apprehensiveness about the predetermining intentionality in all performed actions, all human exchange, seems to me the force that has licensed two very odd

strategies of methodological purification: exclusion of the concept of an *author* from textual analysis, and reduction of the
reader to the effective status of any random and unprepared
signal-receiver.[2]

Imaginative literature will, however, continue to have one
great thing in common with other modes of discourse. Among
the conventions governing the making of particular literary
works will be the steadfast convention—and here is my second
main assumption—that they find their form and reach their
projected end in relation to some definable subject or subjects
already given to consciousness, some matter or condition or
circumstance that can be identified as already having a place in
existing repertories of expression and formulation. Whatever
self-constitutive purpose literary works conform to, they will
be found to address or otherwise attach themselves to one or
another concrete occasion, one or another substantial force
field, of already articulated human experience. Rather more
than one, most probably, in any major case.

This simply means that literature, in the activity of mind
that produces it and that readers are called to in responding to
it, is always about something, an experienceable something
which sooner or later anybody might be required to think

[2] Do we not acknowledge this intentionality in the sturdy convention of the
title, a compositional element we regularly look for in reading and notice as
absent when none appears? Prophets, by contrast, or, equally, producers of
advertising copy—writer-speakers wholly absorbed in the transmission of
coercive messages—simply begin speaking. No one announced "The Ten
Commandments" when the ten commandments were delivered to God's people, nor did Matthew (or Jesus) begin by saying, "Here follows 'The Sermon
on the Mount.' "

To anticipate an objection, something further may be said about continuing
to speak of literary *works*, with whatever implication of singleness or wholeness the word carries, rather than of *texts*. My preference for the common
English usage is unaffected, I think, by questions of coherence and closure or
of closed vs. open form, any more than by the massively observable fact that
authorial conceptions do normally change during composition. Unclosed
forms are still forms, and multiple or seemingly undeterminable meanings
soon enough engender their own appropriate structures of reception.

about and bear witness to.[3] Further, this quantum of imaginable, shareable, discussible experience is never wholly displaced in our awareness by its literary organization. In specifically literary statement (not omitting poems written to the *symboliste* ideal of an utterance wholly discharged to music), we always find some substantial reference to the general interest-system of self-reflecting, self-articulating human life—the same broad interest system, however we choose to define it ideologically, that literary making itself issues from along with all other concerted human activity. This is to say, or risk saying: a work of literature is always (1) a statement *about* human life, and it is always (2) a phenomenon, and exemplification, *of* human life. I might add here that calling it instead a set of statements about other preexisting statements is simply to say the same thing in different words. What *is* life as an object of articulate consciousness if not a continual exchange of statements? To savor Wallace Stevens's lovely truism that "Life consists / Of propositions about life" ("Men Made Out of Words") is in no way to mark out "life" itself as either meaningless or inaccessible.

Should not the central function and service of imaginative literature continue to be understood in these framing terms? It is to bear witness to significant human action, and to the possibility of such action, by recreating concentrated versions of it within some discernible field of occurrence; to bear witness, that is, to what in specific acts of thought and feeling men and

---

[3] "The first word of the *Iliad* directs our minds to anger; something we are acquainted with outside the poem and outside literature altogether": C. S. Lewis, *An Experiment in Criticism* (1961). I would add to this, against the latest primitive skepticism, that it makes no difference whether we think of our participation in experience as occurring through a set of physical and passional events or through a set of coded terms structuring and directing events; whether, that is, we say we know "anger" (come to it, are overtaken by it) as a creatural sensation or as an idea determined by the language system we are circumscribed by. In either case we have to do with a real world of "action and attitude," in Eliot's precise phrase. What psychosomatically we feel and what discursively we say belong alike to our ruling "grammar of motives"—Kenneth Burke's unimprovable title.

women, families and societies, actually do and undergo in life. This includes, of course, what they would do or might dream of doing if life were indeed to yield at last in either personal or collective form to the human imagination's self-figuring grasp. I have always thought Sartre's definition of this service, made just after the Second World War, both accurate and compelling. Above all else, Sartre wrote, literature works "to recover [récupérer] this world by giving it to be seen as it is, but as if it had its source in human freedom"—that behavioral freedom which for Sartre in 1947 would enact itself first as generosity, an unreserved going-out and giving-forth that both lends concreteness to human selfhood and multiplies relations in the actual world (*What Is Literature?* tr. Bernard Frechtman, ch. ii). It is in this way that literature answers to both moral and political expectation, as it will be part of the rest of this book's argument to confirm.

Reasons for current suspicion of these two postulates—that the composed literary work is the determining unit of literary-critical concern, and that every such work addresses something in experience which is already distributed to language—are not far to seek. They are not necessarily the reasons the newest critical theorizing would itself emphasize. They seem to me to have to do less with important new insights into the character of specifically literary statement than with the whole overbearing institutionalization of late twentieth-century life and consciousness.[4] The systematized, globally extended organization of modern social practice and signal-exchange, as it threatens to overwhelm human understanding, necessarily

---

[4] A sense of the problematic character of linguistic specification and reference is hardly to be classed as new insight. Of the basic deconstructionist premise that *no* literary statement can mean anything graspable or possess transportable truth-value, it must be said that the essential finding is so broadly true as to be, in practical use, meaningless. If it applies to all discourse—and this is the core assumption of the discourse philosopher Jacques Derrida—then its being true of literature is of no particular importance to specifically literary analysis. It only reminds us of cognitive limits that since Hume and Kant no philosophically literate reader has lacked awareness of.

puts its warp on the activities identified with literature. Every claim to critical or creative disinterestedness becomes radically suspect, and not without reason; we see them all as enlisted within systems of cultural aggression—political, or patriar-chal, or ethnic, or psyche-centered, or all of these at once—that make freedom itself seem a sorry illusion, an obstinate prolongation of false consciousness. We see literary creation in the same sweeping terms. At whose expense, we learn to ask, did these impressive fabrications, these oddly marketable oc-casions for enjoyment, come into being and acquire authority? What exclusions, what programs of domination and repres-sion, do they covertly support? Necessarily, in both the hier-archy-building that surrounds literary making and in its own deference to one set of societal obligations in place of some other, it becomes an act of "deformation," an abridgment of the full potential growth of human life and human exchange.

The realities of contemporary literary history are a further source of disturbance. Here the pivotal event is a matter of common apprehension, though not often directly acknowl-edged in metacritical debate. It is simply the winding down of the long modernist renaissance in the arts, its subsidence (at times ingeniously negotiated) into parodic afterthoughts and mopping-up operations, and the felt absence—as compared to almost any decade between the 1850s and the 1940s—of any authoritative new company of literary masters and master-works. If much current critical argument seems driven to prove and prove again how scandalously unprovable are all attribu-tions of value and meaning, isn't this in considerable part be-cause its producers have had to come to terms with something unanticipated and indeed unaccountable within their disci-pline of professional preparation: the manifest shrinkage in the very activity that called this discipline into existence? The idea that the proper object of literary-critical inquiry is ulti-mately the freshly accomplished work about something al-ready important to general consciousness becomes measurably harder to sustain when few if any such works are actually forthcoming—but what body of fiction since 1950 is likely to hold attention in the future as the novels of Faulkner, Musil, Proust hold ours? what poetry since Yeats's or Rilke's or Mandelstam's or the young Auden's? What will become of the study of literature when its proper objects are no longer perceived as members of a self-renewing historical order is a question we are having trouble facing up to.

But so long as, with whatever degree of illusion, we do keep at it, I think the following propositions must continue to hold place.

First, to repeat, accomplished works of literature—not perfected, but at some point initiated and at some point concluded, or broken off—will remain what both literary criticism and literary history cannot cease to be about. They are what writers in each instance undertake to produce, and what readers imagine themselves undertaking to read. Second, in order for the individual work of literature to become known as what it is and not another kind of thing, it must exhibit certain identifying characteristics. Whatever its genre, from epigram to mock-encyclopedia, it will register in consciousness as a *form*, and as such will have been produced by an identifiable someone—someone we might as well go on calling an *author*—whose performance in producing it naturally becomes a complementary object of interest.[5] It will have a certain manner of *voicing*, its distinctive matériel being words and statements; and it will thus answer in one way or another to concrete expectations concerning *genre* and *tone*, having been produced for the delectation of a specifiable audience. (Not necessarily a "public": the author-producer himself, or his superego, or God, or some ideal jury of peers—the "English Poets" of

[5] "Speaking for myself, the questions which interest me most when reading a poem are two. The first is technical: 'Here is a verbal contraption. How does it work?' The second is, in the broadest sense, moral: 'What kind of a guy inhabits this poem? What is his notion of the good life or the good place . . . ? What does he conceal from the reader? What does he conceal even from himself?' ": W. H. Auden, "Making, Knowing and Judging," *The Dyer's Hand* (1963).

Keats's poignant self-vision, the "Happy Few" of Stendhal's—is audience enough to start with.) Also it will have a definable and otherwise stateable *subject*. That is, it will be about something graspable in human experience, even if mainly, in modernist fashion, the complex experience of its own making. It will be about something which is already apprehended as discussible or which has become the stuff of intelligent gossip, and which contains within itself—as do both reflective discourse and vernacular gossip—the wherewithal to attract us to think about it and talk about it further.

So far as the inquiry remains literary inquiry, the class of event occasioning it is the individual work of literature, so defined. Here is my warrant for developing an idea of the general office of imaginative literature mainly through descriptions of particular works: descriptions meant to establish (1) how in their main features these works appear to be organized, and (2) what I take them to be centrally about, what is exemplified to consciousness in them.

Within these terms the statements fundamentally required of criticism are likely to be fairly simple. But finding out which simple statements are apposite is a process without shortcuts and without effective completion. Here criticism does converge as a task, and puzzle, with the writing it attaches to. What Melville's narrator in *Moby-Dick* ruefully confesses applies to our effort as well; the best we can produce is but the draft of a draft. Even if we managed to carry through, using variorum editions, an unintermitted scrutiny of the texts before us, we would have to start through again simply to accommodate our own deforming professionalism.

What in any case an acceptable account of literary meaning and value must provide are satisfactory descriptions of the phenomenon whose existence establishes the field of inquiry in question. This, once more, is the literary work itself, the serial artifact we are normally motivated to settle down with and to fix in mind, always imperfectly, as it goes forward, as we go forward with it. And it is in the cumulative transactions of statement and response taking place as such works engage commonly prepared readers that the generic event we are properly concerned with in criticism—literary making and its best uses—seems to me most directly grasped and most profitably considered.

VIRTUE AS LITERARY SUBJECT

The definition of *subject* in Aristotle's *Poetics* still points us in the right direction. It is a sequence of extended action, specifically an action involving passion and change in the existence of some specified personage or community of persons. Subject is thus not identical with theme. A literary work may, for example, bring issues of justice to our attention, so that we can speak of justice as its leading theme; but what it will concretely present is some action of restoring, or failing to restore, certain fundamental life-relationships. Or it will render the action of undergoing the imperatives of justice as a passion and burden. In the greatest work—*Antigone, Hamlet, Michael Kohlhaas*— we follow both these substantial actions at once, and find in the resulting combination of dramatic urgency and reflective penetration the central warrant of literary mastery.

As regards the "most powerful elements of attraction" in literature, Aristotle, speaking to the case of stage drama, listed plot or the particular arrangement of the action as anterior to characterization (with plot and character together anterior to reflective commentary). Plot and character are as interdependent for Aristotle as they are in Henry James's "The Art of Fiction" ("What is character but the determination of incident? What is incident but the illustration of character?"). The opening definition in the *Poetics* of what dramatic poets "imitate" is given in terms of the behavioral capacity of the characters or personages shown in action (*oi prattontes*: those experiencing action), personages substantially greater than ourselves in what they do or suffer, or like ourselves, or lesser—more limited—than ourselves.

The distinctive matter of imaginative literature, I am arguing, is this human agency. As such it has a double existence to our consciousness as readers. In drama and narrative it is chiefly distributed among the *dramatis personae* and the community or communities they compose; in lyric and other soliloquizing forms it is appropriated, more or less restrictively, to a single projected speaker; but in works of any degree of formal complication it will be apprehended in both these ways at once. Page by page, line by line, what we follow is not only a sequence of events predicated as taking place in some community of discourse and exchange. We follow equally a certain manner of apprehending such events and submitting them to reflection. A work of literature thus comes alive to imaginative consciousness by making us sensible of two related things: the predicated existence of identifiable persons absorbed for a time in some nameable condition of being, and—more or less immediately—the outlook and reflective disposition of a predicating author and of some community-in-history his writing necessarily presupposes.[6] Which is to say, literature comes alive to us as in these two ways it makes us sensible of the reality of other persons, identified through an impressionability and power of response which we recognize and anticipate the return of in ourselves. (Because the reality disclosed to us in reading answers to a reality potential to us as well, imaginative literature can also make our own existence more directly palpable to us—which is why at times we ask all too much of it and at other times turn impatiently or fearfully away. This

---

[6] At different times attention fixes on different aspects of literary performance, according to our own changing interests. Re-reading in midlife a novel of Stendhal's, Valéry commented: "I have just re-read a *Lucien Leuwen* which is not at all the one I so loved thirty years ago. I have changed and it has changed. . . . Then, I was reading in a passion the *Life of Henry Brulard* and the *Souvenirs of Egotism*, which I preferred to the famous novels, to *The Red and the Black* and even to the *Charterhouse*. The intrigues, the events were unimportant to me. I was only interested in the living system every event referred back to, the temperament and the reactions of a particular man; in a plot [*intrigue*] after all, but an interior plot": "Stendhal," *Variété II* (1930). The choice, however, is still between different "living systems," made available in each instance within a formed literary work.

seems to me the moral truth in current arguments that the real subject of any work of literature is the mind of the reader.)

Are there any exceptions to this broad rule of referential meaning? Even in extremes of fantasy where gods, trees, cells in the physical body, the dialectic of history, or some pitiless *nouveau roman* inventory of house furnishings assume positive roles, these will be fitted to (as they are apprehended along) a human measure. Quite simply we ask of any work of literature, if we go on with it, what Eugene O'Neill's saloon-keeper keeps asking of the whiskey—is there any "life" in it? (The correct question certainly for whiskey, and the question, too, that Emily Dickinson put to Colonel Higginson, her phrasing of it showing how well she understood his guardian's rigidity: "Are you too deeply occupied to say if my verse is alive?") But the life we respond to as readers is of the type of the intellective, passional life we ourselves bring forward from our own concrete existence as persons—persons-in-history, it is worth tautologically specifying, around whom relationships form and multiply, experience acquires momentum and pathos, and those expectations are engendered which set the terms for further understanding.

In this view any effective work of literature comprises a showing forth, an enactment, a fresh naming, of primary human capacity, under the conditions taken as regulating it—a representation persuasive to us in the degree we are persuaded of its participation in those "forms of life" (Wittgenstein's phrase for what our thought must accept as given) we feelingly know or remember knowing, intuiting, in ourselves. Human capacity and the conditions regulating it, determining its path through experience; or—since consciousness begins in our earliest sensations of displacement and recovery, separation and reactive adjustment—we can simply say, human capacity and the odds against it.[7]

---

[7] Odds: odd or unequal things, matters, conditions, with a notion of opposition or strife; things not conformable, or at variance (*Oxford English Dictionary*: 1, 3).

What then shall we call this "life," this reenactment and showing forth of primary human capacity? "Character" is too limited a term, even if generalized as "human character" or, following Aristotle, "character-in-action." The bias toward individuation in our modern understanding of it (to "create character" commonly meaning to project independently distinguishable personages) and, equally, toward behavioral determinism (character as a disposition permanently incised) leave it too much in hostage to restrictive sociocultural ideologies. But alternatives of the sort I have been using so far—"human agency," "primary human capacity"—are irritatingly unidiomatic. For theoretical statements familiarity in use has positive advantages. Though it can trap the unwary into dogmatic confusions, it also increases chances of genuine discovery: J. L. Austin's point about the value to reflection of ordinary words that embody "all the distinctions men have found worth drawing, and the connexions they have found worth marking, in the lifetime of many generations" ("A Plea for Excuses"). What I therefore propose is that we give this human agency a name, *virtue*, which it has historically borne in the literature whose existence-in-history we are concerned to grasp. As a term directing inquiry, *virtue* has the initial advantage of belonging in one way or another—talisman, shibboleth, expletive, classifier—to the primary vocabulary of western thought and expression since its classical beginnings.

So I arrive at my main proposition. The great subject of imaginative literature is, in a word, *virtue*, broadly understood as the vital presence and force within creaturely being wherever met and consequently, too, within historical experience.[8] Virtue and (to complete the formula) the odds against it, including those inwardly generated, as it acts to maintain itself as a living force. (Does a grand binary classification suggest itself here: the poets/fictions of virtue, and the poets/fictions of

[8] Yeats essentially took this view, though preferring to "virtue" a word denoting the moment of its most intense realization: "The subject of all art is passion," and, "what is passion but the straining of man's being against some obstacle that obstructs its unity" (*Explorations* [1962], 155, 252).

the odds?) Virtue, however, I would emphasize, as distinguished from the four or seven or eight or twelve particular virtues defined in different ethical and religious systems, and especially from anything limited to what Blake jeeringly called "moral virtue." I mean to use the word in an absolute and root sense signifying something anterior to certified behavioral excellence, though at the same time fundamental to any conceivable realization of such excellence.

This usage is, I grant, effectively tautological. "Virtue" is to operate in what follows as a kind of anthropological *quid*; I mean by it that effect-producing property of being and acting specific to its human agents. (These will include collective agents as well, like the chorus of citizen-observers in Attic tragedy or the magnified city-presences of the nineteenth-century imagination: Dickens's—and Wordsworth's—London, Balzac's or Baudelaire's Paris, Gogol's Petersburg, Whitman's idealized Manhattan.) The word itself is one we may never define satisfactorily. Yet it is a word and concept I think we are obliged to go on using, or reconstitute in surrogate forms, if we are to talk consequentially about what it is in experience we are most naturally drawn to talk about.[9]

In the long modern era, with the aggrandizing emergence after c. 1600 of professionalized learning and the capitalist-contractual division of economic labor, "virtue" in its full force of meaning progressively loses authority as a term for what distinguishes the life that human communities value and seek to maintain. The underlying idea of it gets parceled out among competing systems of behavioral explanation, each with its own watchwords. A great deal of modern literary and philosophical history may indeed be described—as will be attempted synoptically in Chapter II—in terms of the deterioration of a unitary apprehension of *virtue* in its root sense and

---

[9] So it may be argued that saving from restrictive definition all that the word "virtue" might comprehend is an ulterior purpose, and reward, of all humane discourse, all imaginative exchange.

the hazardous, history-plagued struggle to recover one. First, though, the word itself needs further investigation.

A clue to the peculiar character and valence of "virtue" as it has survived its antique origins is that, although cognate with that one of the two familiar Latin words for *man* which indicates the human creature acting in full generic strength, its least debatable use has been in association with nonhuman entities: plants, medicines, mineral substances and the like. Here it has meant some vital property or essence of things and, most particularly, a potency within each thing which acts beyond itself to produce vital effects characteristic of itself. The logic of this tenacious usage seems clear. For us the great value of virtue-bearing entities is in their power of effect within us and around us. That is the fixed meaning of the statement, "There is a virtue in it"; the thing in question will "do us good," will substantially delight or nourish or cure us, and it will do this by bringing forth whatever is fertilizing and procreative in our own given being. "Efficacy arising from physical qualities; esp. power to affect the human body in a beneficial manner," is the pertinent *Oxford English Dictionary* definition (*O. E. D.*, 9b). The examples listed there predate Chaucer, whose *Canterbury Tales* provide in the fourth line of the General Prologue a famous use of the word in the explicitly generative sense.

[The argument here would of course have to proceed somewhat differently for non-Latinate languages. But it would not in any case be controlled by the semantic history of the word itself, though the vernacular durability of "virtue" is firm evidence that matters of importance are at stake. *Areté*, the Greek equivalent, though identifying first of all the character of an arms-bearing male leadership, was also regularly used for the nonhuman and inorganic—in Herodotus it is applied to animals, objects, and the land itself—besides serving Homer to name the special excellence of the home-keeping wife Penelope (*Odyssey*, II, 206). *Areté* also appears in a notable passage in Hesiod, poet of stewardship, commerce, and civil peace, to specify that honor which is the fruit of right action, in particular of effective husbandry (*Works and Days*, 289-295). In Germanic and Slavic speech, where classical derivations are more obviously hybridized and imported, the same range of meanings is distributed over a diversity of terms that appear to have undergone comparable transformations. In German it may be *Mut*, in its older and folklorish connotations of *mettle* and mood-determining *feeling* as well as—more restrictively—*courage*, that comes nearest matching the attributive range of *virtus* and *areté*.]

In such ways a physical or physiological component has remained active within the broad concept of virtue; a component which overrides the domain of what is conventionally teachable and cannot be separated from the primal mysteries of birth, blood, sexuality, genius, or creaturely bias. The classical and Renaissance doctrine of the *humors* directly responds to this understanding, as do later pseudo-doctrines like phrenology and physiognomy. It is this irreducible physical presence and consequence, this element of the constitutionally given, that distinguishes virtue from conceptions of moral goodness or from such behavior as properly results from correct training.[10] It appears that every systematic moral calculus must eventually give way to this element or learn how to accommodate its consummating and transforming power. So in narrative and dramatic writing it will be the presence and persistence of virtue in this root sense that transforms our casual acceptance of action and character into a more intense and continuous expectancy. Our deepest imaginative interest in virtue is thus not in what it *is* but in what its life and answering power may be in temporal reality, what effects it is palpably capable of, and most of all whether and how it can, against odds, effect its own further existence and so give itself, and everything it empowers, *continuance*—to reclaim this usefully participial word from its, at present, chiefly legal-juridical use, and to complete my title.

[10] The cognate "virtuoso" provides a necessary lexical bridge in modern usage by isolating, within the domain of the teachable, an extreme degree of performative skill, one beyond ordinary imitation.

What I mean to stress by identifying "the continuances of virtue" as literature's generic subject are the differences between our expectancy with regard to imaginative statement and our reception of scripture or treatise or homiletic discourse. Our interest in literature is not primarily with absolutes like truth or cosmos or salvation. Nor is it with the exhibition of this or that behavioral quality—courage, wisdom, temperateness, rectitude, faith, hope, even *caritas*—although these are what ethical sentiment very properly attaches to. Nor is it with the ideal organization of any particular system of right conduct (nor, except metaphorically, with the "return to Eden" or any other such transcendentalizing scenario: a comment I add not in order to take issue with Northrop Frye's eloquent and humane system of critical description in *Anatomy of Criticism* and elsewhere, but simply to indicate the different angle of consideration I am working from). Rather it is with the drama of the persistence of this fundamental property of creaturely and historical being; its action of generating effects and then abiding through them, and most of all its generating itself in that "behavior" (as R. P. Blackmur once phrased the matter) "that is our life in motion"—its action of carrying itself over into the next decisive moment of life, and the next, and the next.[11]

---

[11] A final test of this approach would be that unique series of works of epic design and scope—*The Divine Comedy, The Faerie Queene, Paradise Lost*—written between 1300 and 1700 within the supervisory framework of an increasingly contested Christian belief. In these undertakings the anthropological substance of virtue is, as it were, dogmatically subsumed within a transcendental hermeneutic. Virtue in its absolute form is overtly defined as lying beyond, or standing over, the field of action of the poem itself. Yet even here one may argue that precisely because perfection or fulfillment belongs to the divine atemporal realm, it can only be approached or adumbrated in a work which is itself temporal in its progressions and sublunary in origin and expressive reference. Though the ultimate fiction of each of these extraordinary poems is the reattachment of the creatural to a higher realm, the particulars each works by come alive to us as they enact events and passions of a kind that common experience might disclose to us in any case.

Certainly Dante and Milton, as well as Spenser, knew they were writing poetry, not scripture. But the organization of what they wrote around a presumptively complete ethical and religious belief system would distractingly

Anthropologically considered, the greatest literature tells us how virtue, in this generative and root sense, declares its presence, gives force and impulse to the life around it, confronts and encompasses obstacles or deterrents, proves and maintains and re-empowers itself and, especially, finds its appropriate motion, voicing, power of predication, within the given world. Literature offers us, that is, a corresponsive figure of how the behavioral composite of human life is constituted and maintained, and what various languages it speaks, in that history which is the distinctive form of our existence as a species. In so doing, literature becomes, conceivably, an agency contributing to that life process, and so (Blackmur's words again) "adds to the stock of available reality," if only by miming the biosocial code of behavior that it, too, competitively derives from and in its own free way—freer than magic, more unaccountable than indoctrination—recapitulates. Though the human mind can reflect upon itself, it cannot get outside itself, no more by way of structuralism or, alternatively, deconstruction than by earlier schemes of self-transcendence. Unique within the phenomenal world, human thought cannot find other reasons why it is allowed to exist as such, or why its existence is permitted to continue. So its distinctive occupation becomes that of inventing such reasons on its own terms—or of bypassing the rule of reasons altogether and making up stories that both reflect and re-enact that continuance of life-as-itself toward which all life's active forms substantially tend.

Thus it is that the elemental literary virtue, the one we respond to with a primitive attraction that undergirds every other legitimating response, is simply inventiveness. But it must be inventiveness, as Blake knew, within the sphere of the

---

complicate any attempt to put them in evidence here. For like reasons I have dropped (with some regret) plans to write a demonstration chapter on two or three of the great Chinese chronicle novels—*The Water-Lair Bandits, Pilgrimage to the West, The Story of the Stone*—in which, too, organized structures of ethical belief and behavioral myth are directly transposed into fiction. I will only say of them that no western writing more abundantly exemplifies a maxim of Robert Musil's, that "fiction is living ethic."

human image.[12] The sense of this human inventiveness, and self-inventiveness, is what binds together in pleasurable awareness the two great poles of attraction in our ordinary experience of literature, the sustained creativity in particular acts of authorship and the sequences of human action predicated in the works resulting; and criticism's best service is in pointing out the real instances of this creativity, with an accurate emphasis and in recognizable proportion. But in so doing we merely direct attention to what as readers we have naturally given our interest to, what indeed has drawn us into the act of reading in the first place—and kept us at it.

LITERATURE, DISCOURSE, AND THE ADVERSARIAL MODEL

Of course imaginative literature does not seek its distinctive ends in isolation from other discourse. *Virtue*, as both agency and concept, is primary for philosophy, too, which is also in devious ways about people (logical or empirical "subjects") and the conditions regulating their existence, and it has an even more central and exclusive place in the sprawling operations of folk consciousness. Accordingly, the actual production of imaginative literature—in historical times, where we can trace it—has always occurred in intimate relation both to systems of philosophic understanding, including the ethical and historical (or typological) content of religious doctrines, and to the repertory of popular beliefs expressed in proverbs, jokes, folk tales and folk rituals, and the formulas of common gossip.

Further, the self-monitoring, self-recuperative character of human consciousness which is assumed throughout these arguments regularly acts within cultural and linguistic sets that

---

[12] Even a work entitled *De Rerum Natura*, a poetic cosmology, will prove to be ethical and psychological at the core, its vision of the material universe powered by a movingly sustained act of human self-apprehension. Consider the account Lucretius gives of sexual excitation (Book IV) as compared, say, to that incorporated into a contemporary cosmology like *Gravity's Rainbow*.

are themselves historically contingent and variable, being subject at each lived moment (as Mikhail Bakhtin has emphasized) to both system-cohering and system-loosening impulsions.[13] Thus the concrete rendering of virtue, the showing forth of its own active "feature"—Hamlet's characteristically exact formulation to the players—regularly pays audible tribute to (1) the approved account of virtue in whatever system of indoctrination currently holds ascendancy and (2) the volatile yet tenacious conceptions that ebb and flow through popular understanding. That is to say, it pays tribute to school philosophy and vernacular myth together, and to the shifting formulas of expression specific to each.

The precise character of this tribute has come to be preoccupying in contemporary criticism. (Something comparable is true of the study of human behavior in general, where nothing is more acridly disputed—by students of language acquisition, by sociobiologists and their critics—than the relationship between individual acts and the matrix of possibility these emerge from.) The whole matter, however, demands the most vigilant speculative attention if theorizing is to avoid all the "sunken reefs"—C. S. Peirce's suitably violent phrase—of conceptual and metaphysical oversight. What in any case needs insisting on is that to move beyond merely notional theories of literature's place within the full commonwealth of discourse, at least four distinct elements must be in place. We will need:

(1) an adequate conception of the literary *work*, which I am reaffirming as, in both its making and its reception, the determining unit of literary-critical speculation;

(2) an adequate conception of *language*, the instrumentality that literature, uniquely among the arts, shares directly with all transcribable communication;

(3) an accurate conception of the actual *literary community*,

---

[13] Bakhtin's terms for this unceasing dialectic in any "live and developing" language are *centripetal* and *centrifugal*. Each instance of language use is seen as a compound of both impulsions. See "Discourse in the Novel," *The Dialogic Imagination*, tr. Caryl Emerson and Michael Holquist (1981), esp. 270-273.

writers and readers together, whose social composition and changing historical status are matters that criticism is too seldom required to define realistically;

(4) an accurate conception—accessory to each of the other three, yet needing independent assessment—of *literary invention* and the manner of its participation in life: what nourishes or enables it, what qualities of mind it reenlivens and extends.

Neglecting any one of these will make for trouble. But not everything can be done at once, and combining this manifold theoretical undertaking with a set of detailed demonstrations, each of them to be independently persuasive, is more than it may be possible to manage both readably and conclusively. I am consoled, though, by the late William Empson's comment that the attempt is likely to backfire in any case. If, Empson wrote, you forcibly bind the theoretical argument and the practical demonstration together,

> you interfere with the normal processes of judgment. The thing becomes disagreeable to read and also likely to excite suspicion, quite rightly I think, because the only way to decide about the examples is by "taste" (granting that taste needs a good supply of examples, and an adequate assurance that contrary ones have not been suppressed), and if you are being badgered by theory at the same time it is hard to keep taste in focus. (*The Structure of Complex Words* [1953], ch. 10)

What I am counting on instead is that a sufficient idea of what is being proposed about literary meaning will come across in the evoked detail of the later chapters. For the moment I want simply to consider this one leading aspect of the matter—the situation of specifically literary statement within the wider commonwealth of discourse and exchange—and to review certain odd prepossessions that have recently gained prominence in critical and metacritical debate.

The shared basis of much recent theorizing about literary meaning—the meaning which as readers we both find and make—has been, I think, puzzlingly reductive on the issue of human capacity in general and the observable character of particular actions and responses. What I find operating is a pinched version of an important concept out of cultural anthropology, the concept of a collective meaning-fund controlling (for authors and readers alike) the specific language acts constituting literary statement. Conceptions of some such primary meaning-fund have become standard for the analysis of all cultural experience—one major source being Saussure's model of a plenary and effectively changeless *langue* subsuming the partial, circumstance-bound *parole* of individual utterances. But how precisely this fund is represented as a phenomenon in history, and how the semiotic repertories in question are described as issuing from it, can make a remarkable difference in the judgments reached of individual authors or speakers.

From the nineteenth-century founders of the modern *sciences humaines* comes the still authoritative notion of a group-defining consensus that is at once behavioral and perceptual, materializing in what Durkheim and Mauss termed *collective representations*. For any one cultural group the over-all system of such representations composes an operative grammar for all thought and all action. It supplies the norms, also the licensed variations, that coordinate everyday life; correspondingly it assigns significance to particular acts and occasions. Within the specialized circumstance of literary making these representations furnish what Northrop Frye describes as the "canons of morality and plausibility" through which particular literary utterances take shape and get understood.[14] In more technical parlance the philosopher Max Black speaks, as regards lin-

---

[14] To Frye the varying evocation of these prevailing canons is what situates for both author and audience each new work's reenactment of archetypal myth. Frye's organizing conception is in fact of two contrasting systems of human understanding. One is changeless in its forms and ruled by an unchanging imagination; the other is in continual flux and answers directly to historical and imaginative contingency. As with the wave theory and pulse theory of light, both conceptions make sense in critical application but are not easily combined.

guistic meaning generally, of the "system of associated *commonplaces*"—a classification valuable to literary study because it identifies the basic compositional material of speech formulas (*topoi*, as an earlier rhetoric systematized them). So the contemporary Austrian writer Peter Handke, taking up a subject—his mother's suicide—made peculiarly difficult by the intimacy of his concern with it, describes himself as starting not from those "facts" he would try as a writer to re-create but from "the already available formulations" covering the whole class of facts in question; starting, that is, from nothing less than the full "linguistic deposit of man's social experience" (*A Sorrow Beyond Dreams*, tr. Ralph Manheim [1974], 29). The point of interest here is that these already available formulations are assumed by Handke to be a surer means of imaginative recovery than his own necessarily compromised recollection. (Yeats was thinking along the same lines when he reaffirmed, in *A Vision*, his conviction that "the creative power of the lyric poet depends upon his accepting some one of a few traditional attitudes, lover, sage, hero, scorner of life": *A Vision*, III, viii.) In Roland Barthes' sketch of how all writing belongs to a discursive "market" or "exchange" system, there is the further, broadly Marxist reminder that the value such formulations have at any given time is substantially determined by the ruling organization of social and economic power. This is so, for Barthes, even where the rituals of literary statement act out the removal of this linguistic wealth, as in a tribal potlatch, to a sphere of "disinterested" or "useless" enjoyment (*Le Plaisir du texte*, "Échange" [1973]).

How precisely does literary making capitalize on this meaning-fund, this linguistic consensus, this behavioral-perceptual exchange system? How, that is, does it position itself in relation to other discourse? In continuing revolt against classical-humanist assumptions of a mutually supportive harmony between literature and reasoned truth (and in transparent reaction against the systematized aggrandizements of modern history), our chief speculative models for this relation have latterly become almost exclusively adversarial in structure.

Literature, in these latest accounts, comes forward only in opposition. Brooking no rivals, it works only to undermine and
explode preexistent ways of speaking. At the same time—especially in the deconstructionist diagnostic, according to
which every delivered utterance can only defer and postpone
true knowledge—literary making by its very nature casts a
blight on the linguistic and cultural space it seeks to enter; and
criticism's whole duty becomes that of protecting readers'
minds from error and disequilibrium. It strikes me that there is
a baleful familiarity about these accounts. Their reliance on a
species of zero-sum thinking resembles nothing so much as the
anxiety-intensive rigors of nineteenth-century economic theory, along with (not unrelated) the equally dismal semen-fund
theory of male sexual potency. For everything newly projected
into the world some equal quantum of vitality and possibility
must be removed, or repressed. Thus every new expressive undertaking is necessarily an act of violence against other undertakings which already exist or might otherwise have come into
existence. The first fact about literary and artistic making is
that something else, actual or potential, has coincidentally to
be unmade. Creation here must be "decreation" somewhere
else, as well as a deceitful "manipulation" of its audience's
consciousness. About all that can be said in favor of the upstart
new construction is that it serves to expose and overturn pre-
vious manipulations.[15]

   In illustration of this adversarial—and, invariably, agonis-
tic—model, we might consider the language of a representative
revisionist essay by Geoffrey H. Hartman, written to promote
truer understanding of literary history's actual dynamic (and
more broadly representative in not being tied to the more drastic deconstructionist position; Professor Hartman writes, in
the main, as a defender rather than accuser of the inventions of
poetry). In this account the "collective representations" sup-

[15] I argued this point at somewhat greater length in reviewing a set of essays
on the express topic of "thinking in the arts, sciences, and literature": "Protocols for Deprivation: The Way We Think Now," *New Literary History*,
Spring 1976.

plying the matériel for poetic thinking are literally synonymous with the "idols of the tribe"—for Hartman as for Bacon something needing to be cleared away—and the poet himself is always radically at odds with them. The poet is thus represented as needing to "confront" and "take up arms against" the beliefs and prejudices of the age, all those "insidious habits of thought" the common culture seeks to bind him up in or weigh him down with. Concurrently what Hartman calls the "*topoi* or fixed ideas of a culture" are characterized as "lurking" and "many-headed," and the poet-hero of this impressive metacritical fiction "best engages them by sending against them their own image, enlarged and purified."[16]

This model, in soberer dress, appears to be supported in various writings of the influential Konstanz theorist, Hans Robert Jauss, though that impression may derive in considerable part from characteristic American distortions and simplifications of a continental original. For Professor Jauss every important new literary work enters the historic commonwealth of discourse as an act of "provocation." (*Literaturgeschichte als Provokation* was Jauss's title for the volume of essays he published at Frankfurt in 1970.) Such provocation can register in a subtle variety of ways; detecting it is not always as easy as Hartman's horror-movie metaphors would suggest. Moreover, to the imaginative writer (as distinct from the destroyer of error) those "already available formulations" supporting

---

[16] "Toward Literary History," *Beyond Formalism: Literary Essays 1958-1970* (1970), 374–375. Is it merely captious to observe that Professor Hartman in his own rush to a purifying confrontation has got hold of the wrong idols? Those of *theater* and *marketplace* are surely nearer his point. In contrast, the idols of the *tribe* are specifically those that according to Bacon are not culture-bound but "have their foundation in human nature itself." Our revisionary theorist also plays a noticeably loose hand with metaphoric allusions. The more you try to picture it, the more improbable it appears that the mirror-shield with which Perseus returned on the Medusa her own dread image—the figure, I would suppose, behind Hartman's closing metaphor—can double effectively as a weapon against "many-headed" Hydra. Or do all these referential crossed wires simply indicate with what unbalancing intensity such arguments have been joined and staged in recent academic criticism?

common habit and prejudice can have, as for Peter Handke, their own corrective appeal; they can help to rescue individual talent from narrowing prepossessions. Certainly Professor Jauss recognizes very well how all literary invention entails a rich complicity with established formulas of statement and the memories and emotions they encode. Also, the composite surprise or even shock the new work delivers may be essentially pleasurable. And it may be chiefly formal or stylistic, a shock only to petrified notions of performative decorum. Much genuinely innovative writing enters literary history by bringing forward modes and styles of discourse not previously admitted to serious use but in themselves collectively formed and stabilized; coincidentally it may find out a new literary audience not previously enfranchised. (For a century and a half after 1700 the new and eventually dominant genre of the prose novel developed largely in this double fashion.) Here the effect of provocation is not in what the new work itself says or shows but in claims that it, too, may belong to the class "literature."

There is, I believe, a crucial distinction to be made here between the activity of literary invention and the circumstances and accidents, in different epochs, of its public reception. The succession of creative events constituting literary history as such is not identical with the entire civil and cultural history that frames it. I am confident that Professor Jauss himself would recognize the force of these various qualifications. Nevertheless it seems to me noteworthy that a sympathetic and knowledgeable commentator finds it possible to summarize the provocation model as follows. The new work of literature "figures a way of knowing which *conflicts* with the ways of knowing of the generation into which it is projected"; it thus *challenges* that generation's modes of perception and valuation and *exposes* its casuistries; consequently "every genuine work of art appears as a *revolutionary* gesture" and is seen as a *threat* by the audience first exposed to it.[17] Jauss himself, it

---

[17] Emphasis added. Professor Jauss's views, set out in his inaugural lecture at Konstanz, are available in English in *New Literary History*, Autumn 1970,

should be said, licenses this reaction by making the public reception of *Madame Bovary* his exemplary instance but describing it in a way that blurs the differences between civil events and specifically literary history. His stress is, first, on *Madame Bovary*'s civil trial on charges of obscenity and, second, its relative failure with the sensation-craving bourgeois public in contrast to the runaway commercial success of Ernest Feydeau's *Fanny* (also 1857), a novel equally scandalous in plot but reassuringly familiar in style and treatment. But clearly these events in the immediate reception of Flaubert's novel tell us nothing decisive about either the dynamic of literary innovation or the subsequent entry of *Madame Bovary* into the continuum of major European literature. More to the point is the prompt elevation of *Madame Bovary* by other novelists to the status of a modern classic, a model for innovations and transformations yet to come. (Among nineteenth-century classics *Adventures of Huckleberry Finn* would offer a more difficult test of the provocation thesis, its tepid reception in polite quarters being splendidly offset by its first—and mass—readership's immediate satisfaction with it.) In all such cases the effect of adversarial provocation belongs to the accident-prone civil fortunes of literature and not to its self-renewing history.

Beyond historical causes already suggested—the widespread discrediting of literary humanism; the absence in recent decades of new work perceived as canonical and transforming by either the core community of authors or the secondary com-

---

"Literary History as a Challenge to Literary Theory"; also in *Towards an Aesthetic of Reception*, tr. Michael Shaw (1982). The summary is Hayden White's, from the same number of *New Literary History*, 179-181. The core of truth in Jauss's position seems to me a premise anticipated by the Russian formalists: that effective writing is a process of defamiliarization (*ostranenie*), a returning of things grown blurringly familiar to their original distinctiveness. Here, incidentally, is one more instance of Romanticist origins for twentieth-century critical discoveries. One of Shelley's arguments in the "Defense of Poetry" is that poetry "makes familiar objects be [to us] as if they were not familiar."

munities of critical opinion; the siege mentality of much contemporary life and the fresh plausibility of scarcity economics
as a principle of explanation—I am more and more persuaded
that the current popularity of adversarial/agonistic models of
literary production directly reflects the withdrawal of serious
criticism into the precincts of the university (a withdrawal, in
the United States, of much of poetry and fiction as well). For
one thing these are models very much better suited to university scholarship itself and its competitive self-forwardings. The
predictable bias of university-based criticism may well be to
confuse the performative categories in question, to merge literary invention with the kinds of discourse appropriate to
propositional truth-seeking. This indeed would tend to reduce
genuine creation (which we hear first of all as a new voice or
new music) to the revision of predecessors' errors. In one way
or another it is to lose touch with the plain sense of Valéry's
cautionary dictum that "the situation of the reader of poems is
not the situation of the reader of pure reasonings."

At any rate the metacritical quarrels of recent times have
had, so it seems to me, the peculiar introversion and also the
peculiar inconsequence of parish or guild quarrels. Arguably
they have had to do less with literature itself than with an aux-
iliary profession's anxiety about holding position within a
massively institutionalized cultural marketplace. Too frequently the newest criticism's eye is on something other than
its proper objects. (The criticism that answers to actual history
is nearly always a criticism responding directly to fresh imaginative power.) Not the least interesting aspect of these disturbances is that they have worked, to date, no real changes in the
canon. In this they differ from the frankly political agitation
for reading-list substitutions by feminists and ethnic populists,
who are concerned (as they should be) with equity and historical justice and with altering their students' social awareness.
Otherwise we see none of the abrupt shifts in reputation and
anthology standing, up or down, characteristic of the turn into
Romanticism or of 1910-1950. Instead there is a homogeni-
zation of accredited examples—every remembered name get-

ting processed in the same way—and a competition to see who is now to supervise the whole inheritance. The picture, in brief, is of a scribe-oriented rather than an invention-oriented literary culture, and its real *hydra* (to return to Hartman's excited metaphor) is a new scholasticism, one that regards all rival approaches with anticipatory suspicion. For where indeed are provocation, confrontation, exposure, reversal, and the accompanying scandals so much the norm—and where, especially, *ressentiment*, that prime mover (Robert Weimann has remarked) for so much contemporary model-building—as in the proprietary world of university learning, beset as it commonly is with "the scholar's melancholy, which is emulation" (*As You Like It*, IV, i)? No doubt academy-centered wars of succession are marginally symptomatic of important transformations in cultural history, but to identify them with the condition of literature itself is, I think, a parochialism singularly disabling.

Adversarial conceptions of both literary making and literary meaning also thrive where psychoanalytic models—mainly Freud's or, latterly, Lacan's—control inquiry. Here, since the inhibiting norm for our imaginative existence is posited as a secret will to surrender selfhood to whatever adversary or control system we most fear, successful invention always requires an act of violently rebellious negation. Further, as it also requires a knockdown argument within the self—an odd literalizing of Yeat's much-quoted formula about the arguments that make for authentic poetry—genuine invention cannot take place without self-violence and self-diminution. As the writer's own hidden negations become the target of exposure in this new style of *ad hominem* critical argument, a "negative hermeneutic" appears inevitable, an *a priori* "hermeneutic of suspicion" (Jürgen Habermas's term).

To cite another essay of Geoffrey Hartman's: every new literary work "is an act . . . of negative creation—a flight from one [interiorized] enchantment to another" (*Beyond Formalism*, 289). Or it is "decreation," a term much in favor at present (one applied, interestingly, in the seventeenth century to souls that stubbornly persist in sin: *O. E. D.*, 1). Or, more aggressively, it is "deformation." Not only do new forms negate the authority of forms already created, the acceptances required by a new voice somehow devaluing every predecessor. The whole language-borne behavior of the writer's mind is itself deformed by the creative effort. But here again—beyond a certain blank disregard for anything enlivening in the actual work of creation, or for the augmentation to any given capacity of mind that normally follows on its being purposefully exercised[18]—there appears a basic confusion between categories of experience. When the idea of "deformation" is advanced by Freud to explain the psychopathology of everyday behavior, or by Piaget to chart the dialectic of thought and speech through which the human infant reaches for an identity both ego-protective and reassuringly socialized, the action of mind being described can be empirically observed and charted. It is not, however, the composing of a work of art, an action that outlasts the circumstance of its occurrence and persuades others of its substantial exchangeability. What Piaget describes as the growing mind's "deforming absorption of reality to the self" may considerably resemble elements in the process of sustained literary creation. Both, Piaget reminds us, are processes of imaginative thinking. But they are not one and the same process. To grow as one must into adolescence is not (yet) to write *The Prelude* or *The Sound and the Fury*—though it *is* of course what you have to do as a reader in order to begin to enjoy them.

THE LITERARY WORK AND COLLECTIVE UNDERSTANDING

My own approach to the matter of literature's relation to other discourse turns (to say it once more) on the principle that while

---

[18] Curiously it is as if the times had surreptitiously canonized the poignant late 1960s flower-child fiction that the human creature is only deformed as it grows into adult capacities and strengths, that there is no feedback of new strength and new delight in the process.

our concern is with literature itself and not behavioral pathology, the composed literary work is the phenomenon wanting explanation. It turns also on the assumption that a rich complicity with popular consciousness is at least as important for literary making as the circumvention of established belief-systems. In this view the new writing we come to value will declare itself and, sooner or later, win recognition through combining in effective relationship a substantial quantity of our commonest ways of speaking; specifically, it will bring together the *mythoi* or "things that are said" in love, gossip, business, work, play (and word-play), superstition, fantasy, vernacular prayer, as well as in school, politics, law, liturgy, philosophy, science, and, self-evidently, literary precedent itself. To sort out these convergent ways of speaking, the good writer will need tact and concentration, a more than usual resourcefulness, and a more than usual resistance to ideological distraction. His labor with words and phrases, none of which he himself entirely invents, may well prove a continual wrestle—as Eliot wrote in "East Coker," after the paradigm of Jacob's midnight struggle. But it will seem natural to him, in writing, to think of these speech-resources as supporting his best effort rather than as antagonistic. What else is there for him to build with? (So Clifford Geertz, coming at the matter from the angle of anthropology: "it is [only] out of participation in the general system of symbolic forms we call culture that participation in the particular we call art, which is in fact but a sector of it, is possible" ["Art as a Cultural System"].)

The effort of mind that concerns us, in any event, is primarily an effort of combination, rather than of deformation or dissolution. So Valéry defined the writer's work in general: "un certain mode de travail combinatoire." Seeing any particular instance of this work as a diminishment of possibility, or as necessarily an assault on the equal standing of any other comparable instance, is likely to mean that critical attention has shifted outside the field of action of the work itself—perhaps to some fear, far from irrational, of an epidemic breakdown of human exchange, or else to fantasies of a logological dreamworld in which every combination of signifiers permitted to the total *langue* is to be realized at once. (It would not be the first time that the imagination of catastrophe and the perfectionist heresy have gone hand in hand.) What new invention does not logically require, I am arguing, is the deconstruction of any existing *parole* or speaker's meaning. "Ce travail," Valéry continued, "consiste en transformations"—and we note at once the crucial change of prefix. To *trans*form preexisting speech-resources is not to warp them punishingly out of recognition—and if "deformation" does not mean that, what does it mean?—but to recover their potential force (or *virtù*) and release it into a fresh cycle of use. It is to revive their residual exchange value (Barthes' highly realistic notion) for the compounding of new figures of meaning.

I can't forbear further comment on this adversarial model, since exploring what is unsatisfactory about it will help to bring into sharper focus the different picture I wish to develop. An essential objection is that it reduces and falsifies not only literary creation but the form of human coexistence generally. In the first place, on every vital issue of action and attitude historical epochs in their fullness are not normally locked into unitary belief systems (which literary works must then either endorse or subvert). What we observe instead will be a prevailing dialectic of encounter and opposition, at times of open conflict, and of accommodation and containment. By this reckoning the collective representations that characterize a culture or an age are themselves, in active use, self-adversarial or contradictory.[19] Within any social ordering, even the most

[19] Wisdom discerns this. "Without Contraries is no progression," Blake memorably asserted, and by "progression" he meant "life." "Without contradictions there would be no world" was Mao Tzedung's version ("The Ten Great Relationships," April 25, 1956). "A thing without oppositions *ipso facto* does not exist," C. S. Peirce strictly concluded (W. B. Gallie, *Peirce and Pragmatism* [1952], 191-193). A complementary form of this, at the hinge of transcendence, may be found in Nicholas of Cusa, *De Visione Dei*: "I give Thee thanks, my God, because . . . Thou hast shown me that Thou canst not be seen elsewhere than where impossibility meets and faces me. Thou hast inspired me . . . to do violence to myself, because impossibility coincides with

"primitive," differing life-interests pull the common sense of these shared formulations in different directions, according to the irreducible differentiae of status, class, age, sex, physical well-being, good or bad fortune, and so forth. The civil contests between differently situated parties and groups are thus, too, contests for meaning and for control of common understandings. In these contests those in power have always the institutional advantage and know very well how to fend off the specter of displacement by interposing a needless censorship. Any questionable new signification can always be set down as the work of provocateurs. But that again seems to me a fact about the specifically political order and not a necessary circumstance of literary making itself.

For those whose first commitment is to political or ideological dominance the real offense of literary creation will be its seeming refusal to commit itself unequivocally to one contending side or the other while nevertheless claiming a right to occupy the whole field of oppositions in question. For it is in the nature of imaginative literature to make its appeal to all sides and specifically to the nucleus of active life within each one (as if instinctively wary of something worse than cultural conflict: the absolute domination of any one party to it). Literature willingly enters into relations with those elements in any proffered vision or faith that seem worth cohabiting with. This can lead to curious, at times regrettable, alliances. But if resolutions to conflict are proposed in major literature, they will be found to be of the kind tending to compromise the privileged self-image of both parties. "A plague o' both your houses" is poetry's response to the false resolution, the human crime, of overt civil war, though characteristically not to its accessory heroism, or folly.

Inevitably then poets do get into civil difficulties, their interest in great disputes being more in the reciprocal flow of ener-

necessity and I have learnt . . . the place where Thou art found unveiled. This place is girt round with the coincidence of contradictories, and this is the Wall of Paradise wherein God abides" (tr. Emma Gurney Salter; quoted in Maria Shrady, *Moments of Insight* [1972], 39-40).

gies, the *virtue* made active by them, than in final solutions. (This authorial bad faith furnishes a common literary theme; see, for example, W. H. Auden's "The Public vs. The Late William Butler Yeats.") The abrasions that follow, however, are events within the specifically political order, taking place along its major fault lines of privilege and exclusion. Attributing the new conflict to literature itself seems to me one more case— normal, to be sure, in bad civil times—of scapegoating, or blaming the messenger.

Imaginative literature, so conceived, is not directly at odds either with philosophic understanding—though it turns away from specifically philosophic resolutions—or with the wanderings of popular consciousness. Its imaginative and expressive pluralism (mongrelism?) appears constitutional to active human thought. I would see this pluralism, moreover, as natural to any tonically extended social and linguistic order. The great contribution of modern structuralism has been to re-familiarize us with two complementary notions: that effective thought and behavior, in or out of literature, (1) cannot be reduced to less than binary or oppositional form, and (2) cannot operate without opening up some margin for unscheduled further invention. (According to Gödel's majestic theorems, as I dimly grasp their significance, this new opening will materialize in any case: see below, 41n). Opposition and antithesis thus enter the activity of literature not because literature is in conflict with the common custom of discursive understanding but because it extends and substantiates that custom.

An example may be useful here. As an instance of the processes in question, the novel *Sister Carrie*, published in 1900, has the advantage of having caused much the same sort of scandal as *Madame Bovary*. Though not brought into police court, it achieved the odd distinction of being effectively suppressed by its own publisher. But the power of offense in *Sister Carrie* was not in the irregular life-histories it unfolded. By 1900 sexual transgression, business crime, Skid Row poverty and suicide were commonplace subjects for the new metropolitan realism—and as regards a house editor's comment to

Dreiser that his "choice of characters ha[d] been unfortunate," it should be noted that in the same publishing season the house of Doubleday, Page was busily marketing Frank Norris's *McTeague*, Zola's *Fécondité*, Bram Stoker's *Dracula*, and a new metropolitan romance by one Una L. Silberrad about the "marred life" of a girl from "the poorer quarter of London."[20] Offense lay rather in the undistracted amplitude and straight-forwardness of Dreiser's treatment, which has the effect of an extraordinary imaginative complicity. But as Ellen Moers could demonstrate in charting key sequences in *Sister Carrie* (*Two Dreisers* [1969]), what filled those sequences out was precisely what had enabled the novelist, despite extended in-terruptions, to complete the whole long project in a few months' time—an assortment of ready-to-hand ideas and fully popularized formulas of expression that gave him, again and again, the detail and emphasis he needed.

More precisely it was the convergence, out of the two or three preceding decades, of several new sources of common lit-erate awareness. There was the everyday metropolitan jour-nalism, with its astonishing advances in mass circulation, that had systematically blocked in both the glamor and the squalor of city life as saleable subjects. On this lucrative ground Dreiser in the 1890s had quickly built a newspaper career in several industrial cities. (He had also built himself a not incon-siderable reputation; a year before he began *Sister Carrie* he was, at twenty-eight, one of a relatively small number of writ-ers and artists listed in *Who's Who in America*.) There was also the booming world of sentimental middle-class entertain-ment—popular theater and, as a source of extravagant publish-ing royalties, the popular song-writing that Dreiser's brother Paul was prospering with—with its recurrent themes of loss, seduction, and family separation. And there was the hardly less popular literature of science and pseudo-science offering, in particular, full descriptions of irregular mental states and

[20] The Doubleday, Page catalogue for 1900-1901 listing these other titles simply omitted *Sister Carrie*.

unusual plant and animal tropisms. In short, in undertaking *Sister Carrie* Dreiser could reasonably feel that there was a sizeable public primed to receive the "picture of conditions" he had in mind, and even to appreciate the unusual seriousness, the combinatory fullness, of his presentation.

How new literary work goes about combining the resources for statement available to it can vary as greatly as the human occasions being registered. In any given instance the *travail combinatoire* may indeed seem pointedly critical or corrective of particular expressive currencies among those it borrows. It can come through to us just as strongly, I am arguing, as affirmative and celebratory, and not the least part of what is affirmed will be fresh possibilities for language itself. In this way good new writing works to reanimate some part of the whole enabling conspiracy of narrative and discursive exchange. Performances with any lasting power to delight and surprise will almost certainly be found to work in both ways at once, simultaneously exploiting and questioning, augmenting and circumscribing, revising but also reaffirming, the "things that are said" at the complementary centers of active experience. My own disposition (appropriate for anyone brevetted to a national literature in which writers like Whitman and Mark Twain, Dreiser and Faulkner, have pride of place) is to think that the greater the new work's investment in broadly popular repertories of statement, the better. "For there is a stronger analogy," Proust declared, his grammar wobbling momentarily under the weight of the insight, "between the instinctive life of the mass of persons and the talent of a great writer . . . than with the superficial verbiage and fluctuating standards of the certified judges" (*Le Temps retrouvé*, iii).

In critical practice the key issue of imaginative literature's tie to other structures of statement seems to me best approached, where possible, through familiar classifications. In relation to other discourse literary statement appears as, literally, parody. It says comparable things but says them in another fashion and to other ends. Because of this divergence literature can indeed be felt as gratuitously competitive, guilty of social offense. So a joke that has its force in addressing basic feelings can be inexcusable if mistimed, and a series of such jokes, tactlessly persisted in, will make for trouble. Popular virtuosos of comic parody like the Marx Brothers or the Monty Python team operate full time, and aggressively, along this porous boundary of bad taste. A Lenny Bruce, striking harder, withers when he cannot keep crossing it—when, that is, he discovers himself servicing an already depraved audience which, alerted to fresh openings, keeps rushing in ahead of him. But it was precisely these unstable issues of competitive decorum that in the Renaissance Philip Sidney was addressing when he defended *poetry* by reasserting its claims to a place alongside, and in vital respects above, the vested interests of *philosophy* and *history*. And modern scholarship has interestingly confirmed the idea of literature's differential coexistence under complex protocols of fitness, as in the epoch-marking theory of the birth of theatrical comedy and tragedy from religious rituals that were themselves still being observed.

In regulating this coexistence every age and society has its guardians who with the preoccupations peculiar to their office are not much interested in imaginative literature as such. In the calmest of seasons their instinct is to be suspicious of it. Everyone knows the cruder forms of this guardians' preference for a literature that endorses the prevailing public indoctrination—among moral majoritarians and gangs of four who want the arts to corroborate right opinions, or nervous commissars whose vision is of a well-policed typographic Park of Rest and Culture. But it should be observed that some such restrictiveness is also implicit in traditional humanism, and remains so down through the latest "great books" or "core curriculum" scheme of instruction. The idea in each case is that literature's proper service is to engrave the great teachable truths of right understanding and acceptable conduct upon the minds of a politically tractable readership. The institutional totalitarianism which, becoming technologically feasible, threatens all civil balance and equity in the late twentieth century appears as the latest and most efficient form of this restrictiveness, which can find provocation in any free act, any unscheduled statement of human feeling.

Up to now, however, such views have played a losing game, though at times dominant for long periods. Something active in the common exchanges of life and speech escapes their scheduling, wanders free of it, and cannot be wholly anticipated or contained within systems of indoctrination. What this further agency is may be hard to specify, or even to distinguish clearly in its insistent re-emergence. But what anyone may discover is that every cogent general theory of human-historical behavior, in order to complete itself, sooner or later proposes the existence of some such heteroclite factor and attempts to give it a valorizing name. ("Original sin" is one such name, dazzlingly pejorative, yet making it inevitable that elaborate teachings would develop to show its hidden advantages to human fortune generally.) Such theories, moreover, situate the free variable in question not only within individual minds but within all the collaborations of human society. They thus usefully confirm a corollary theme of this book: that a literature is major only as it imaginatively re-creates both some essential structure of personal life and some essential structure of social and collective existence. Selfhood and commonwealth: what more than anything will distinguish the examples to be presented in later chapters is their power to render satisfactory accounts of both these spheres of actual life.

If descriptions of this heteroclite factor have a single element in common, it is the imputed presence of the kind of generative and recuperative potency that I am calling *virtue*. Moreover this element is regularly seen not as something superadded to the ordinary operations of mind or society but as something intrinsic that cannot be kept from welling up from within when either system of operations is normally active. It is that structural capacity for producing innovation and surplus which is basic to Veblen's early twentieth-century sociology of institutions and equally to Noam Chomsky's critique in the 1950s of B. F. Skinner's behaviorist theory of mind. It is the "tendency" or "impetus" to change that is implicit in growth itself, and that at moments besets entire species, in Bergson's theories of a creative (autonomic, self-stimulating) evolution. It is the "effervescence" Durkheim found at the living center of the religious cult; the "dépassement" Lucien Goldmann emphasizes ("le caractère actif, transformateur, et pratique de toute action sociale et historique"); the overproduction of "pure signifiers" that in Lévi-Strauss's description of shamanism releases the patient's paralysis of feeling back into the domain of the collectively thinkable and utterable. It is also the overflowing of Blake's mental fountain, by which poems are written and cities rebuilt. It is the primal "excess" which for D. H. Lawrence "accompanies reproduction" and "is the thing itself at its maximum of being" (a formulation Lawrence reclaimed from Nietzsche, who rooted all man's religious and philosophic inventiveness in the "excess," the diseased overgrowth, of defective members of the species: *Beyond Good and Evil*, #62); it is the "fine excess" that for Keats gave poetry its rare power to "surprise" and "delight." To Michel Serres, exploring the structural avatars of Hermes, it masks itself as the intrusive "parasite" that enters the functioning of every life-system and is in fact integral to the system's continuance. To Bakhtin it is simply a "surplus inhering in the human condition" (*The Dialogic Imagination*, 37). It shows up, though as a source of scandal, in linguistic structuralism's conception of the "excess of the signifying over the signified" and in Derrida's post-structuralist fixation on an "opening" in systems of discourse which never can be closed. In every instance I have cited there is the conception of an indwelling capacity for unanticipated further experience which, in the lives of both persons and societies, is realized primarily in an excitement of self-activation and self-extension. Without some such conception the descriptive schema remains incomplete.[21]

[21] If such views are not simply mystagogic but make logical as well as experimental sense, I would conjecture (from a long way short of grasping the mathematics) that support for them can be found in Gödel's theorems about the impossibility of formal systems proving their own premises and thus com-

As finite limits come to be imposed on this power of self-activation and self-extension—which is how systems react against themselves in search of stability, and coincidentally advance in entropy—the self-auditing human intelligence seeks relief among its own increasingly strained recognitions. To make room for what naturally presses from within toward autonomous realization, organized discourse begins to contradict itself (not necessarily with lies direct; a creeping equivocation will do as well). In extremes of civil crisis—as distinct from crises of personal existence, where repression may be all too effective within each life-span—such contradictions are forced into the open, and revolutionary change suddenly becomes conceivable. Or the whole process will already have occurred within one odd sphere of human exchange and now offers itself for confirmation and completion in others.

It was just this kind of civil crisis that historians of political thought have described as overtaking, interestingly, the key word *virtue* itself, or *virtù*, in sixteenth-century Italy, a development that with its extended ideological aftermath has become preoccupying to several schools of contemporary historiography. In Florence around 1500, faith in the fixedness of linguistic meanings was still axiomatic. At the same time disasters in the political order, magnified by the new factor of foreign invasion, were forcing Machiavelli, most notably, to reexamine the basis in experience of the entire traditional vocabulary of political and moral valuation. In such circumstances the totem word itself becomes a key instrument of inquiry and revision. It is projected back into discourse not only to reanimate conventional precepts but to make legitimate the improvisation of new ones; every contending party lays claim to it and is accused by others of deceit and impiety in altering its meanings. Far from being negated, the word continues in major use but in irregular ways—a solecism, in these new contexts, that

---

pleting themselves ontologically, so that a necessary *dépassement* is built into their existence-in-the-world.

nevertheless begins to acquire its own validating constituencies of use and need.[22]

Men of this era, Meinecke wrote, found themselves compelled by political violence and change to acknowledge "the hidden problematic element in all vital forces" and to hammer out new distinctions between right and wrong instances of the circumstance-mastering force called *virtù*. And it is the disputed ground between such instances—the ground of moral and propositional uncertainty where the process of life distills to the human agent's ambiguous power to propose and sustain new premises for action—that the greatest literature, drawn into the field by the fresh energies thus released, thrusts forward, or slides in, or bubbles up to occupy. What becomes sealed or forbidden to scheduled reason provides unforeseen imaginative space, a fresh margin of creative opportunity and freedom. The new *combinatoire*, however, will not necessarily be adversarial or threatening. Imaginative literature, in finding its own footing, does not commonly issue direct forensic challenges to the dominant beliefs and fixed ideas of the age—unless, of course, it is directly forensic literature. In Francis Fergusson's words literature is "both more primitive and more subtle than philosophy." Instinctively on the side of plenary truths and unafraid of vernacular inconsistency, it concentrates its effort on forms of statement outside the scrutiny of system-keepers but already secure in the pleasure and acceptance of some unconscripted audience, high or low, which it finds its own pleasure in getting on good terms with. On good speaking terms, as we say.

[22] Friedrich Meinecke, *Machiavellism: The Doctrine of Raison d'Etat*, tr. Douglas Scott (1957), I, i. See also Federico Chabod, *Machiavelli and the Renaissance* (1958); Felix Gilbert, *Machiavelli and Guicciardini* (1965); J.G.A. Pocock, "Machiavelli, Harrington and English Political Ideologies in the Eighteenth Century," in *Politics, Language and Time* (1971), also *The Machiavellian Moment* (1975); Quentin Skinner, *The Foundations of Modern Political Thought* (1978). The English Civil War brought on a similar lexical and imaginative crisis. Ruth Nevo, *The Dial of Virtue* (1963), describes the ingenuities practised by English poets to absorb the inconceivable phenomenon of Oliver Cromwell and the Protectorate.

For the literature of our long Christian era, is it perhaps the Gospel itself that presents the limit-defining, and justifying, case? "Ye have heard it said . . . but I say unto you": so Jesus directly attacked the old law and proposed a richer, more apposite successor. But that was only the start of his revolutionizing mission. What *charmed* his hearers' imagination into paying attention, what completed their conversion not so much to a new law as to a new collaborative vision of human life (in the world and in history), was something further. It was his perfected mastery of the art of narrative predication, a mastery preserved for us in those homely parable-scenarios that circumvented Scribes and Pharisees by winding a coil of common anthropological truth around their question-and-answer learning. Put to the test of dialectically unresolvable questions, Jesus replied—it is Pasternak's formulation—"in parables taken from daily life, [explaining] the truth in terms of the everyday world" (*Doctor Zhivago*, ii, 10). It was thus that he was perceived on all sides as one speaking with "authority." Moreover, when provoked at point blank with questions of precise legal or philosophical definition—by the Pharisees on the dangerous issue of civil compliance (Matthew 22:15-22), by Pilate on truth itself (John 18:37-38)—he improvised responses which, as it happens, prefigure two of modern literature's most cherished strategies of adaptation and coexistence, drawing in the first instance on the formal authority of a taxonomic riddle (what *are* the things of God that differ from the things that are Caesar's?) and in the second on the indefinable wisdom, or music, of silence.

CHAPTER TWO

Virtue: A Short History

CLASSICAL AND CHRISTIAN VIRTUE

In fixing on the great matter of *virtue*, particular works of literature regularly shadow and exploit what is elsewhere being said in the exchanges that constitute historical culture. That is why criticism needs to know all it can of what at any time these correlative structures of discourse have had to say. What else in practice is the assessment of meaning in literature, and what else the attribution of value, if not a measuring of the one mode of knowing and feeling against these others, in particular against those having the greatest articulated authority? The conscious apprehensions of *virtue* that consequently most concern us derive, in Western civilization, from two primary sources of moral precepting, the classical and the Christian; and much literary history has very properly been written—by good humanists—in terms of the descent and transformation of these moral systems through successive historical periods. Their central content is worth reviewing, however schematically, since major literary statement regularly taps into this content while at the same time pursuing its own expressive ends.[1]

Both Greek *areté* and Roman *virtus* summed up the distinguishing capacities of, first, the good ruler, the man whose excellence was displayed as a prowess in leadership. Etymologi-

[1] I owe several details in what follows to Curtis Brown Watson, *Shakespeare and the Renaissance Concept of Honor* (1963), which lucidly outlines the long descent of Western moral tradition through its major literary and philosophic monuments. Several chapters in Alasdair MacIntyre, *After Virtue* (1981), drawing on another two decades of textual discussion and analysis, rehearse the same history from the perspective of moral philosophy itself and its beleaguered search for universals.

cal linkage of *areté* with the name of the god of war, if allowed, would only underscore the fact that in human affairs this was originally a military prowess, the *aristoi* being those who properly possess it. But already in Homer heroic virtue embraces the more specifically political authority of Agamemnon and the cunning and inventiveness of Odysseus (*polútropos*: he of many devices or turnings); and as Reuben Brower's study of the survival of heroic verse patterns in the epoch of Chapman and Shakespeare reminds us (*Hero and Saint* [1972]), the idea of such virtue leaves plenty of room for those flashes of antithetical feeling—flashes, for example, of counter-heroic submissiveness to misfortune and suffering—which in the *Iliad* distinguish Hector and even Achilles from good-soldier Ajax (and which, in their inconstancy, particularly disturbed Plato's civic moralism). Contemporary French scholarship, following structuralist methods, has pursued these antitheses into the recesses of Greek cultural practice, as in Pierre Vidal-Naquet's account of the reversal of the citizen-soldier ethic in the moratorium of preparation undergone by its *epheboi*—Achilles' withdrawal and transvestism being a classic instance of regression to the antithetical state—or Louis Gernet's of the ambiguity, harboring danger as well as bounty, of the whole class of objects ritually bestowed as gifts, prizes, tribute, and the like (the ambiguity, we may say, of all objects of *virtù*).[2] The same ambiguity invests the adventures as well as the character of Odysseus, who fights his way home bloodily enough through the abysses, traps, suicidal temptations, and evolutionary dead-ends of the natural world and its potencies (the domain of Hades the deadliest of all in its power to seduce imagination). Where immediate impulse is strong, or is strongly called out, *virtue* is most immanent, whatever the immediate consequence.

By the time of Socrates the Greek conception of virtue appears to have undergone an immense irreversible subtilization,

[2] A selection of this scholarship may be found in R. L. Gordon, ed., *Myth, Religion and Society: Structuralist Essays by M. Detienne, L. Gernet, J.-P. Vernant, and P. Vidal-Naquet* (1981).

acquiring the properties of dialectical reason, self-harmony, and something we are taught to call "soul" (*dianoia, enkrateia, psyche*)—though a significant part of what Alcibiades, in *Symposium*, sums up as Socrates' "absolute unlikeness to any other human being who is or ever has been" remains a formidable military valor and coolness under attack. With both Hellenic and Roman thought—the *Nichomachean Ethics*, Cicero's *Offices*—fortitude in battle and right judgment in civil affairs remain prime elements in the pattern of great virtue. But private or domestic capabilities now have an equal place: temperateness, amiability, integrity, modesty, social complaisance. Conversely a hero untrained in these latter qualities, however well-born or high-placed, is in for trouble; so Plutarch (in Shakespeare's hearing, eventually) moralized in the case of the aristocratic bullyboy Coriolanus.

A twofold conception of effective virtue, and so of what constitutes a grand poetic subject, thus descends from classical writings. Spenser reviewed the poetic monuments of this double tradition in the letter to Raleigh accompanying *The Faerie Queene*, citing as precedents Homer's pairing of the "good governor," Agamemnon, and the "vertuous man," Ulysses, and Tasso's return to the same bifurcation with his hero of political virtue, Godfredo, and his hero of personal or ethical virtue, Rinaldo. In Virgil this twofold conception—virtue as martial fortitude and political mastery, virtue as an inward perfection of spirit or soul, as above all *pietas*—combines in the single hero, as Spenser pointed out, but also by extension in the state the hero founds and will rule. That significant virtue is politically collective and yet emanates from the spirit of an individual ruler is of the essence of the classical, and imperial, ideal. We note that it is the prophetic model explicitly renewed in Machiavelli's *Discorsi*, and that it supplies the framing assumption not only in Shakespeare's plays about English dynastic history but in the specifically political action of *Hamlet* and *King Lear*, also of *The Tempest*.[3]

[3] In Professor Pocock's summary: "The only real hope [of mastering *fortuna*] lies in the absolute power of one man of transcendent virtue, who will

Yet Virgil—the European poet, as Frank Kermode's Eliot
lectures (1975) reemphasized, in whom the literary idea of the
classic and the political idea of the imperium most directly
converge—is in some ways a great exception, his hero being
widely perceived as the least independently memorable of epic
heroes. That antithetical element, issuing in some decisive self-
contravention or *dépassement*, appears to be the thing missing. Typically Aeneas's seduction by Dido is felt as an interruption of his and Rome's destiny; his desertion, which is fatal for
her, leaves him effectively unmarked. That destiny, moreover,
is one he exists to serve, rather than an emanation of his own
singular being. Even in the archetypal descent into hell he remains essentially a visitor, though importantly moved by what
he sees and hears; the whole venture, according to the Sybil, is,
literally, "insane" (*Aeneid*, VI, 135), but Aeneas himself
clearly is not.[4]

---

end corruption by restoring virtue in the people" (*The Machiavellian Moment*,
206). In England the ideological contest that developed with the Stuart succession, between the virtue of the monarch and the virtue of the realm, was not
practically settled without a revolution, a regicide, twenty years of civil war
and, a quarter of a century later, the removal of one alien king and the impor-
tation of another, equally alien.

In civil life *power* is transparently the issue. Who, politically, shall have it?
Who, personally, may be trusted with it? How is it to be preserved from either
inanition or cancerous expansion? To the poetic imagination, however, power
as a civil reality tends to be epiphenomenal. What counts is its human, or inhuman, marrow.

[4] These views, or impressions, are certainly arguable. Eric A. Havelock has
shown in the best way, by precise examination of the poetry, that antithetical
moments are not absent from Aeneas's progress, as most beautifully in—at the
beginning of Book II—the late-night speech accepting the burden of Dido's request to hear the grim tale of Troy ("The *Aeneid* and Its Translators," *Hudson
Review*, Autumn 1974). Brooks Otis, in "The Originality of the *Aeneid*" (*Virgil*, ed. Donald R. Dudley [1969]), argues with authority for the presence of an
antithetical dimension throughout the poem but mainly demonstrates, it
seems to me, that one ethically unitary role, the Trojan hero, is systematically
displaced through the opening books by another, the founder of Rome. In
both roles personal agency is radically subordinate to destiny, i.e. to political
myth.

To E. R. Curtius, thoroughly modernist in critical understanding, the decisive "virtue" in the *Aeneid* belongs neither to the story nor to the character of

Elsewhere the rendering of great virtue more regularly embodies that element of the behaviorally inordinate or excessive that I have described as offering to imaginative literature its major openings. This element comes into heroic poetry not only in the intervention of the gods upon human undertakings but in prodigal eruptions of passion and energy within the hero's own being—Achilles' wrath, but also the battle madness that rises in Hector and even in earthbound Ajax, who alone among the great warriors in the *Iliad*, Richmond Lattimore points out, "carries on without supernatural aid." (At the climax of his duel with Turnus, Aeneas, too, reverts to type and is compared in succession to a raging bull, an Umbrian hound, and a siege engine.) The same violent spilling over of human force comes into the medieval *chansons de geste* in the "desmesure" of heroes drunk on courage, or dedication, or self-regard; Roland's long madness is the typifying instance. Behind loom aboriginal legends of Hercules, tormented stepchild of the dethroned mother-goddess, with his drunkenness, seizures, and murderous rages. (There are important equivalents in Old Testament narrative, in the Irish Cuchulain cycle, and in the superb mix of prodigious adventure and knockabout farce characteristic of classic Chinese fiction.) Plato's mythmaking also opens out into these high mysteries. In the *Symposium*, most famously, Socrates completes his inquiry into the supremely virtue-filled passion of love by offering a description of it—as a demonic sorcerer—that for once he does not reason out for himself but takes from the backcountry witch Diotima.

With the Christianization of European thought we might expect this element of morally ambiguous violence to lose force if not disappear, but it really does not. As *virtue* is subsumed

---

the hero, but to the triumph of the poet's art over material alien to his sensibility, which was preeminently contemplative. One consequence for Curtius is that while "the *Odyssey* can be enjoyed in translation, the *Aeneid* cannot" ("Virgil" and "Rudolf Borchardt on Virgil," *Essays in European Literature* [1950], tr. Michael Kowal [1973]). The same essential opposition between the virtue displayed in the story and that of the sensibility behind its telling furnishes the central theme of Hermann Broch's *The Death of Virgil* (1945).

in the covenant of grace, important aspects of the classical ethic are indeed doctrinally undermined, like the correlation of virtue with noble birth, high station, or any fixed distinction of person—the system of courtly love providing, in the chivalric romances, a brilliant adaptive solution to the social confusions resulting. Other aspects are transmuted without losing their distinctive character. Christianity thus gives new force to the dichotomy of public and private virtue, the active and the contemplative life; it celebrates both warfaring pilgrim and self-humbling saint, though officially tilting the balance to the latter. Even for Boethius, in his late antique assimilation of the ethic of senatorial responsibility to that of Christian devotion, it is only at the last that contemplation and a submissive faith gain priority over Roman *virtus* as the right response to temporal disorder (see Pocock, *The Machiavellian Moment*, ch. ii).

Yet at its heart Christian worship reaffirms the apprehension of something in the fulfillment of human capacity that violently overpasses philosophical reason or moral accounting. More substantially than any of the classical virtues except courage (with its physiological name) the devotional virtues of faith, hope, and love are generative forces rather than regulative principles. They take fire within the believer and go out from him into life with the same alchemic or medicinal effectiveness that has been the stablest meaning of "virtue" in common usage.[5] In the Gospels Christ's grace is first made palpable

[5] The era of the Reformation, drawing on both ancient authors and new science, abounds in this apprehension. My too scattered reading in the subject has recently turned up a description, by the English Puritan John Preston, of Christ's love as a "virtue" that "breedes" in believers a "fire" fusing the heart to Christ's; also, in George Fox's journal, a charming vernacular dialogue with himself reasserting the same association of spiritual potency with medicinal and therapeutic functions that obtains in the Florentine debates over *virtù*. God having opened to George Fox "the nature and virtues of things," he considers whether now to "practice physic for the good of mankind" but decides instead on spiritual ministrations. But he will, as he goes about England, reform the malpractices of country physicians. The onetime trouser-maker held strong convictions about the pharmacological properties of food and clothing.

in therapeutic miracles, and we may note that the Authorized Version's description of Jesus as knowing, when the sick woman touches his clothes, that "virtue" had gone out from him (Mark 5:30) reproduces a range of suggestion also present in the Greek original, *dunamis*, the directly physical word for strength or potency. In the Epistles divine grace becomes a more generalized metamorphic force that explodes the soul into a wholly new behavioral kingdom and even, in the phenomenon of glossolalia, into a different linguistic jurisdiction; a break in the order of language is the surest sign that transcendent issues are at stake. There are moments when Paul himself is so transported by the witness he is bearing that he must apologize for talking "like an idiot" (II Corinthians 11:6, 23); and in the first two Gospels there is the crisis of the ninth hour, when the Divine Son surrenders for a moment to creaturely despair and appears to speak, that once, out of character.

These ambiguities of usage are not noticeably cleared up in philosophic discussion. In defining virtue in the *Convivio*—not in its effects, where classical conceptions govern, but in itself— Dante produced the formula that it is "the perfection of its own nature in each thing" (Fourth Book, ch. xvi, tr. Elizabeth Price Sayer; this matches Aristotle's opening statement in the *Nichomachean Ethics* that "the good" must be something "proper to its possessor"). So long as orthodox, anti-Manichean doctrines hold firm, where nothing in nature lacking the creative principle within itself can achieve such perfection, this is satisfactory; Aquinas himself accepted it. Its form and logic, however, apply equally to natures that are framed to wickedness. So in Shakespeare it furnishes both a rational explanation and a species of justification for the perfected villainy of personages like Richard III, Iago, bastard Edmund, and Caliban. All four defend themselves morally in exactly these terms, which carry to alarming excess the familiar *par sibi* topos— right conduct understood as an acting *like* or *from oneself*— that Renaissance poets found authority for in Ovid and Seneca, and that lives on into our century in Freud's disturbing idea that the organism's instincts of self-preservation and self-assertion come to be fulfilled in a hidden wish to "follow its own path to death" (*Beyond the Pleasure Principle*, tr. James Strachey). In the Pythagorean revival of the sixteenth century the aspect of self-definition in these conceptions is elevated into a principle of being. The Pythagorean soul is projected as a number which moves itself without regard to material circumstance, an account much prized by the Elizabethan magus John Dee and thinkers of his kind—though Dr. Dee himself piously declared it was all by God's pleasure. What is decisive, once again, is the factor of self-consummation. An unconditional unit of being is seen as mounted upon itself, engendering its own continuance.[6]

It is worth emphasizing here that the sexual metaphor hang-

---

[6] Is it straining resemblances to imagine the persistence of such thinking one and two centuries later in Leibniz's monad and Kant's transcendental will?

On the *par sibi/sui similis* theme see Brower, *Hero and Saint*, ch. iii and passim; on Dr. Dee, Peter J. French, *John Dee* (1972). A beautifully chaste version of *par sibi* thinking on precisely the point of the ultimate virtue of things climaxes *The Faerie Queene*, in Dame Nature's resolution of the argument between the absolutes of power (Jove) and change (Mutabilitie). All things do change, Nature acknowledges, but what in fact they undergo is self-fulfillment. For,

> . . . being rightly wayd,
> They are not changed from their first estate
> But by their change their being doe dilate:
> And turning to themselves at length againe,
> Do work their own perfection. . . .
> (VII, lviii)

The standard punctuation of this passage, with a semi-colon after "estate," is misleading, and I restore here what seems the clear sense. Only as things act to perfect their own existence do they undergo essential change. Blake, who talked much of "states," would see the point at once.

Most often when Spenser introduces "virtue" as a term in argument, it is simply opposed to "vice." An example is the oddly bitter passage in the prologue to Book V, stanza iv, that speaks directly to the fortunes of "virtue" in current understanding. Perhaps no English poet after Spenser could move back and forth so seamlessly between the great truths of learned and of popular thought.

ing about all such formulations is not mere embellishment. In taking virtue and the ambiguities of its continuance as the central matter of imaginative literature, we are always in reach of the great generative mysteries. Hamlet's postulation of "virtue" as the right focus of the actors' performance offers a case in point. It has Shakespeare's exactness. First, what is to be made active is specified as the very "feature" of virtue: not its ideal form or, in our synonym, its face only but the *fashioning* of it, its intrinsic making. Second, the property in question— masculine as Roman *virtus* and operatively masculine still in Renaissance *virtù*, where it acts to impose mastery on the female principle *fortuna*—Hamlet speaks of as feminine, "show virtue her feature," suggesting or at least not obstructing the notion of a generative matrix whose essential character is creation, and self-creation.

"Virtue" is of course feminine in gender in Latin and the Romance languages (which is not stranger than that *Kraft* should be feminine in German speech or *сила* in Russian). More important it is, like the individual virtues, normally female in allegorical representation—Lady Vertue, ravishing by her beauty, as Sidney describes her in the *Defense*—though among the angelic thrones, dominations, and powers of the heavenly hierarchy the "virtues" are presumably masculine in bearing, whatever their (much argued) sex life. Within history and (mythographers tell us) pre-history, too, contestation can develop concerning the preeminence of masculine or feminine qualities in the composition of *virtue*. An exaggerated emphasis on one set or the other, making now the phallus and now the womb the more or less exclusive symbol of self-engendering being, may well be a sign of cultural disorder and imbalance. It can also, in the arts, summon up extravagant countermeasures. Feminist criticism has not been wrong in exploring bourgeois-era fiction for symptoms of this kind; but in the emphasis on patriarchal prejudice not enough has been made, I think, of odd masculine-feminine fusions within the primary representation of virtue-as-such. A curious instance is the Swedenborgian romance of Balzac's in which fulfilled human nature is

personified in the life-story of the self-marrying woman-man,
Séraphita-Séraphitus. ("Hermaphrodite," the always surprising Emerson once remarked, "is . . . the symbol of the soul.")
The incomparable *Wuthering Heights* works, I think, by a similar logic, the overpowering love of its protagonists having
taken form in the transsexual clairvoyance of a childhood
spent as brother and sister. The aspect of incest in these examples is hardly incidental. In the persistence of incest as a
theme and value in modern writing, we can trace again and
again the same exploratory sexual fusion, particularly where
the work—Shelley's *Epipsychidion*, the "millennial" third
part of Musil's *The Man Without Qualities*, Mann's *The Holy
Sinner*, Nabokov's *Ada*—expressly develops a vision of heroic
self-continuance against the manifold discontents of society
and history. As with the doubling of political and familial conflict in Attic tragedy, overdetermined motives are of the essence in such works.[7]

Virtue Fragmented

The complexities and interweavings in late Renaissance speci-
fications of *virtue* resist programmatic interpretation. The late
Rosamond Tuve's long essay on the "allegory of vices and virtues" (*Allegorical Imagery* [1966], ch. 2) was a valuable reminder that we are not simply to translate back and forth between, say, Aristotle and the moral allegory of *The Faerie
Queene*, notwithstanding its announced organization in

[7] That the potency of virtue encompasses the attributes of both sexes is suggested with extraordinary beauty and poise in Giorgione's *Tempesta* (according to Edgar Wind's persuasive reading of its program). Against catastrophe's
rising storm both the "martial confidence" of the lounging soldier and the
"maternal affection" of the nursing gypsy, as she is traditionally characterized, are going to be required. Both are "characters whose unsettled mode of
life has made them familiars of Fortuna"; that is, they have undergone the best
preparation for the task ahead and will have a better chance of surviving than
the empires and dominions whose ruins stretch away behind them. Their extraordinary repose suggests, too, that their allegorical roles are altogether congenial to them. See Edgar Wind, *Giorgione's Tempesta* (1969).

twelve parts; a reminder also that other classifications of Christian virtue besides St. Paul's—those, for example, deriving from Isaiah's list of Jehovah's gifts to the rod of the stem of Jesse, or that humbler set based on the Beatitudes—were, for romance-epic, equally concordant. Spenser himself, as moral preceptor, may be seen as waging a rear-guard defense of older wisdom (C. S. Lewis's once-controversial arguments for Spenser as the last medieval master seem out of dispute now), trying to hold together a system of multiform understanding that was, in effect, pulling itself apart. What in any case we find multiplying symptoms of all around the beginning of the modern era is that progressive fragmentation and disintegration of a unitary conception of virtue—corresponding to a unitary conception of soul or inner being—which, along with innumerable schemes of recovery and reconstitution, makes up the long modern history of the intuition of virtue-as-such. (So Bakhtin again: after the Renaissance "the wholeness of a triumphant life"—as projected in Rabelais, Boccaccio, Shakespeare—"a whole that embraces death, and laughter, and food and sexual activity, is lost": *The Dialogic Imagination*, 198-199.)

In the remainder of this chapter, which I have risked making both absurdly panoramic and absurdly sketchy, I want to review the main directions this later history has taken. Along the way particular instances will be introduced as symptomatic rather than as historically determining. At every turn, too, a multitude of other equally impressive instances should come to mind and will be counted, I trust, not as oversights but as confirming and substantiating the approach I am taking. If the matter of virtue is indeed central to literature and to human thought, a proper account of its historical transformations would have to be nothing less than an encyclopedia of modern expression.

How, around 1600, an English author of intelligence, wit, and sound humanistic learning could address the tangle of ideas and teachings about *virtue*, and what distinctions he felt obliged to insist on, may be illustrated with a poem of Donne's, the "Letter to the Lady Carey and Her Sister, Mrs. Essex Rich, from Amiens," dated 1611-1612. Here—in the measured tercets that had served Dante supremely well for a philosophic poetry, and would serve Shelley and Wallace Stevens—the following propositions are argued in succession:

(1) there are limited or partial manifestations of virtue which are not the true thing, manifestations informing one or another of the humors or qualities but not the "whole substance" of being;

(2) you may thus have someone who is "a sanguine virtuous man" but is "no better" than that, or one who, leading a "cloisteral" life, has "virtue'n melancholy, and only there"; such a man is "parcel-gilt," not true gold, and moreover is self-deceiving—for, "who knows his virtue's name or place, hath none";

(3) in contrast, there is that one true unitary virtue, coextensive with the complete soul, which is "our soul's complexion";

(4) this unitary and indivisible virtue, though apparently not to be apprehended directly, reveals itself in special signs, above all in a beauty (flatteringly attributed to the two ladies) whose first property is its virtue-engendering influence on others; unlike sensual beauty it never wounds.[8]

Donne's analytical precision speaks for disturbing speculative changes. With the displacement of "humors" psychology

---

[8] For a fuller discussion see Laurence Stapleton, "The Theme of Virtue in Donne's Verse Epistles," *Studies in Philology*, LV (1954), 187-200. Besides pointing out the Platonic origins of these discriminations, Professor Stapleton demonstrates in valuable detail Donne's use of the medicinal identification of "virtue" with "balsam" or "mummy" which Renaissance authors found particularly in Paracelsus.

For Thomas Browne, too, these older meanings remained at least metaphorically active: "But be thou what thou vertuously art, and let not the Ocean wash away thy Tincture" (*Christian Morals*, I, ix). A century later, in Johnson's dictionary—the cohering subject of which, Paul Fussell argues, is "moral virtue"—the first two meanings of "virtue" have to do with moral goodness or excellence. The next five all concern either medicinal efficacy or power and agency in general.

by the compartmented enumeration of "faculties," as most authoritatively in the structure of human understanding erected by Locke in 1690, the very concept of a distinctive indwelling capacity falls into division. "I think therefore I am" is already a radical bifurcation, and diminution. Mind, and self, are perceived in fragments, and the whole is not significantly more than the amalgam of its parts. *Reason* is one thing, *feeling* another, *will* something else again, and *soul*, or *spirit*, little more than a beneficent afterthought in the Creator's mechanic design (though Locke clung rhetorically to the idea of a single superintending "power" of mind, a power peculiarly man's, which can combine and unify what has been separately fashioned: *Human Understanding*, I, xii). Religious consciousness, grown dangerously problematic under the double challenge of schism in the churches and a newly independent natural philosophy, reflects the same fracturing, the same separation of being and spirit. This may be seen even in a poet as little inclined to doctrinal dispute as George Herbert, to whom the property "vertue"—if we take at its word the lovely poem bearing that title—is something allowed to the soul which is radically absent from things as admirable as the sweet light of day, or blossoming flowers, or seasonal regeneration, and ultimately even from the soul's own enjoyment of these phenomena. They "die," it "lives," is the burden of Herbert's verse syllogism.

In the mid-eighteenth century, against a loosening system of common worship, the American theologian Jonathan Edwards labored to recreate a unitary idea of the soul's perfection by describing "true virtue," in his treatise on the subject, as "being's consent to being"—a formulation taken by some intellectual historians as self-defeatingly reactionary and by others as proto-existentialist and modern. But Edwards worked against the current. After 1660 the commoner effect of Anglo-American religious controversy was to divide both mind and being into discrete, even antithetical, functions. Both psychology and metaphysics set themselves to conquering by dividing. Spiritual virtue became the property of a new partial soul which is now called "heart" and stands in opposition to intellect or "head."[9] No Anglo-American theologian, however, pursued this functional separation as rigorously as had Pascal, who condensed his perception of an imbalance in all existence into the bitter theorem that for a genuine Christian the truest virtue must be self-hatred (see Erich Auerbach, "On the Political Theory of Pascal," *Scenes from the Drama of European Literature*, tr. Ralph Manheim [1959], 110). It was through the same intensity of perception, and a comparable gift for maximlike formulation, that Kierkegaard in the nineteenth century undertook to revive Protestant self-scrutiny as a discipline of mind able—in rigorously separating the ethical, the aesthetic, and true faith—to confront the disappearance of an intelligible God from human understanding.

This fragmentation of self-reflective experience, and of any comprehensive understanding of the behavioral good, shows up everywhere. Maren-Sofie Røstvig's study of the "happy man" (1962)—the *beatus vir* descended in humanist tradition from Horace—incidentally provides a rough graph of the fragmenting process in chronicling the steady privatization of images of the life well lived. (Milton's eminently classical praise of a virtue which is not "fugitive and cloistered" speaks for what was rapidly becoming a minority, or sectarian, view.) Correspondingly the figure in poetry of the happy husbandman, a fairly literal embodiment of Horatian pastoralism, expands into a generalized picture of retirement and dissociation as the right goal in life. What carries over from older ideas of virtue-as-such is the premise of inward harmony, now under-

[9] One of the livelier lexical events of recent times was the double reactivation of "soul," among American blacks, and "head," among heads, as unitary terms for the whole self, fully alive and reattached to an ultimate power source (as in Allen Ginsberg's "ancient heavenly connection to the starry dynamo in the machinery of night"). By the same logic of use that operates with "virtue," "soul" is applied collaterally to special sorts of food or music or human bonding ("soul brother") which are considered uniquely reinforcing, while—besides direct sexual meanings—"head" is applied to shops where the means to such reinforcement is kept in supply.

stood as that one condition of earthly existence which is unconditionally worth pursuing. Through the seventeenth century—with its political revolutions, wars of commerce and religion, and deepening economic-institutional division of labor—such harmony of being became harder to safeguard, and the salvaging of personal happiness more and more an end in itself. The ennobling melancholy of the greatly virtuous man— ruler, thinker, artist: the man whose choice of task openly challenges fate—is an idea whose time is fast vanishing. Again the Miltonic instance, the by no means uncitizenly "penseroso," stands near the end of a disintegrating tradition. Around 1700, with the synthesizing ethical optimism of a Shaftesbury, *virtue* subsides into a notion hardly distinguishable from good breeding. For Shaftesbury himself it becomes that "taste of beauty and relish of what is decent, just, and amiable" which gives perfection to "the character of the gentleman and philosopher" (*Miscellaneous Reflections*, iii, ch. 1).

Shaftesbury coolly named this new ethical paragon the "virtuoso." A century before, that transportable word had principally meant someone who explores the secrets of nature and works at refining and transmuting metals.[10] But the last quality Shaftesbury would have attributed to his virtuoso was any alchemical fire of enthusiasm. The preferred qualities are now good humor and natural kindliness, and the man displaying them is held to be both personally agreeable and *ipso facto* a doer of social good. It is a doctrine that conveniently metamorphoses private affluence into collective virtue. The older sumptuary morality of self-denial still kept a hold on common understanding, and so Mandeville's travesty of Shaftesburyan doctrine in *The Fable of the Bees* (1714ff.) could count on an

---

[10] Though it soon was being used disparagingly, identifying a dabbler in curiosa—favorite target for burlesque by critics of the new Royal Society, as in Shadwell's play of 1676—it kept the older connotations well through the seventeenth century. To Joseph Glanvill in 1655 it was the sun-gazers (Pythagoras, Copernicus, Kepler, Galileo, also More and Descartes) who were the "vertuosi of the awakened world," the term carrying here the sense of "illuminati" (*O.E.D.*, 1b).

appreciative audience. Typically the whole matter has become more coffee-house scandal than doctrinal shoot-out. However we interpret Mandeville's *reductio ad absurdum* proof that what really secures public benefit is private selfishness and greed—economic historians take this as a bluff apology for the new speculative capitalism—its affront to morals now seems as bodiless as the ideas it mocks. What by contrast had made Rochester's poetry, a generation earlier, directly shocking to morals was not the ingenuity of its argument for libertinism but its physiological bluntness. The aristocratic Rochester continued to assume that a virtue which did not spill out in "generosity" was not virtue at all but a hypocritical substitute. But in the emergent new social order it seemed harder and harder to display such generosity anywhere except in physical lust; expectably Rochester's poems make the closest association of active "virtue" with sexual "spending." A century later that association kept enough popular force to make the self-dramatizing seducer Lovelace (to his creator's chagrin) as heroically memorable for the first readers of Richardson's *Clarissa* as the angelic heroine herself.

Similar reductions and displacements are the pattern in eighteenth-century France. La Rochefoucauld had acknowledged the reality of virtue but scarcely distinguished it from its antitheses—"the virtues are the frontiers of the vices" is a representative maxim. Virtuousness is a matter of vanity, its operative engine is self-love.[11] In Bayle's *Historical and Critical Dictionary* (1697) the argument narrows to a kind of pragmatic calculus, the article on "virtue" drawing its examples entirely from politics and civil life and measuring everything by the capacity to act properly as historical agent; it thus looks ahead to that independent concern for civil virtue which dominated eighteenth-century political rhetoric and guided Montesquieu's treatment, and subsequently Gibbon's, of the

[11] A lucid account of La Rochefoucauld's position may be found in Jonas Barish, *The Antitheatrical Prejudice* (1981), 210-220.

exemplary "decadence" or "decline" of Rome. In the Diderot-d'Alembert *Encyclopedia* (1751-1752) there is no article on "virtue." There is one, however, on "vice," and "virtue" does find a place on the synoptic chart outlining the grand "Système de l'Homme. Morale. Générale." It is rather under the heading "Bien" that the *Encyclopedia* presents this three-way classification of estimable conduct, with, for each category, a general characterization and a definitive action:

(1) *l'homme de bien*, one who satisfies the precepts of religion—and thus gives alms;

(2) *l'homme d'honneur*, one who rigorously follows the laws and usages of society—and thus keeps promises;

(3) *l'honnête homme*, one who observes in his actions the principles of "natural equity"—and thus deals justly, even with his enemies.

Not much more than a ghostly trace of the full Christian-classical synthesis remains visible here (no more than in the entry on *vertu* in Voltaire's *Dictionnaire Philosophique* (1764), which forthrightly begins: "Can I call virtue anything other than that which does me good?"). The good stemming from the action of virtue is altogether civil and practical. The substance of virtue is now efficiently parceled out for use within the new mercantile-bourgeois discipline of (2) contracts, (3) equitable compensation, and (1) a prudent charity for those incompetent to manage for themselves.[12]

With both French and American *philosophes*, "happiness" as an objective of national policy appears to have a greater place than it was allotted in Hanoverian England. It was never-

---

[12] Diderot for his own part continued, as in the Richardsonian transports of *La Religieuse*, to accept the free workings of passion and sexuality as integral to the moral life: sources of good as well as of wickedness, of the greatest pleasure as well as the greatest suffering. If he had got hold of John Cleland's *Memoirs of a Lady of Pleasure* (1749), he might have added the creator of Fanny Hill, at least privately, to his praise of the creator of Clarissa. Where Johnson's "Vanity of Human Wishes" opens by identifying *all* natural passions—"hope" quite as much as "desire" or "pride"—as equally fatal, Cleland's heroine becomes once again, in the throes of physical passion, "quick-spirited and alive." It is then, uniquely, that the "heart" is touched.

theless a French author who gave universal currency to the antithetical formulation that our best chance for happiness, and
our one unequivocal duty in life, is to cultivate our own garden. Interestingly, in applying a republican purposefulness to
this *faute de mieux* vocation of Candide, the American Jefferson—with his vision of a nucleus of citizen-farmers, each erect
on his own threshold—came as near as any major Enlightenment figure to restoring regenerative force to the concept of
virtue. The breast of Jefferson's small-holding farmer is the
very "focus," or hearth, where God keeps alive the "sacred
fire" of a "substantial and genuine virtue" that otherwise
"might escape from the face of the earth." Yet we can say that
with both Voltaire and Jefferson, once infamy and usurpation
have been dealt with, the actual difficulties of organizing and
controlling power in societies careening toward modern cen-
tralization are not really faced. For them, too, conceptions of
public virtue ultimately contract into a dream vision in which
contemplative happiness and civic responsibility are one and
the same. For Diderot any practical distinction between these
forms of self-realization virtually disappears. In the *Encyclopedia*'s article on "The Encyclopedia"—praising the new *vita
contemplativa* of disinterested (i.e., laissez-faire) accommodation—Diderot offered this homogenizing formula as a whole
and sufficient rule for action in the world: "Whatever does not
have happiness and virtue as its final goal is worth nothing."[13]

Virtue Against Itself

But the era that confidently erected happiness and equability as
supreme ethical and political goals was also the era compelled,
first, to rediscover abnormal psychology in completing its account of human understanding, and, second, to cast doubt on

---

[13] Jefferson's formulations are in *Notes on the State of Virginia*, Query XIX;
his emphatic but rather jumbled metaphors are examined at length in Leo
Marx, *The Machine in the Garden* (1964), ch. III. Diderot's lifelong concern
with "virtue" is efficiently charted in Carol Blum, *Diderot: The Virtue of a
Philosopher* (1974).

whether a word and concept such as "virtue" had any honest meaning at all.

Along with disinterested benevolence, Enlightenment thought yielded up the revolutionary new vice of disinterested perversity, and did so nowhere more ebulliently than in Diderot's prophetic text, *Le Neveu de Rameau* (c. 1770); it was here that Hegel came to the dialectical insight that "self-estrangement" might be essential to "self-preservation" (*Phenomenology of Mind*, VI,B). The trump card for the great composer's scapegrace nephew is simply his claim to normality. Everything unsettling in his conduct, the role-playing, the easy lying, the scorn of honesty and reason in the name of energy and passion, the unrestrained self-indulgence (to the point of self-injury), must be understood by his interlocutor as elements in a behavioral system "exactly framed" to human nature. One thing to notice here is how closely the chameleon-like character that makes Diderot's anti-hero the arch-exemplar of behavioral "bad faith" resembles Keats's account of the poet as someone who has no stable identity, who is "every thing and nothing," who—delighting in all spectacle—relishes the moral dark as fully as its opposite (letter to Richard Woodhouse, October 27, 1818). Keats gives this description, despite its self-deprecating irony, a heroic cast after all, but the suggestion of imposture and trickery is hardly less strong; and since poetry (fiction-making) is in question, the passage stands curiously close to, in the same era, Jeremy Bentham's flat conclusion that any heightened use of language is probably fraudulent and a bar to true understanding. To Bentham the word "virtue" signified the mystification characteristic of any writing not yet purged of pre-scientific associations. It attached to nothing real; it was "a fictitious entity" grounded in the "imperfection . . . of language created long before the phenomena of mind were [properly] studied or understood" (*Deontology* [1834]: a reference I owe to Glenn Kim).

With Rousseau the contradictions projected in Diderot's dialogue-fable, between behavioral obligation and natural constitution, turn Enlightenment self-confidence inside out.

Rousseau's own self-contradictions were self-confessed, but his inability to keep them from taking charge of every argument had the force of philosophic discovery. Confessing behavioral aberrations as if they were normal and exemplary is no longer considered perverse, as it is in Diderot's text and will be with the cynical libertines of Laclos' *Les Liaisons dangereuses* (1782), who confide their views only to each other and none too straightforwardly at that. Rather, it becomes an appeal for public approval, and Rousseau is truly surprised that it is not so received. The recognitions that follow precipitate in what Paul de Man summed up as Rousseau's "ethic of renunciation," an ethic that not only determines the lovers' choices in *La Nouvelle Héloïse* (1761)—where the sacrifice of self to which Richardson's Clarissa was (we are to think) condemned by others is now freely elected as the one way to curb passion—but underprops the social contract as well. Arguably, for Rousseau, it is more a private than a collective expediency which compels subjugation of the individual to the general will.[14]

Rousseau's self-immolating attempt to gain protection from the contradictions of temporal life makes him a proper choice—one who "with the weight/ Of his own words is stag-

---

[14] A comparable ethic of renunciation organizes Goethe's second *Wilhelm Meister* (1821), in which the self's "entrance into real life" leads on to a "pedagogical utopia" where, at no great cost to self-regard, errors of judgment and choice are experimentally corrected by forgiving overseers. Written near the end of Goethe's life the *Wanderjahre* (subtitled *The Renunciants*) appears to represent a certain limit of adjustment on Goethe's part to the convulsions of 1789 and after.

Allowed no such luxury of abdication, the American authors of the *Federalist* letters aimed not to close off the clash of *passion* and *interest* in human affairs but to distribute its self-renewing energies into a correspondingly active civil system. "Ambition," Madison wrote in *Federalist #51*, "must be made to counteract ambition." A system so framed would not only conform to the actuality of human experience—so that the new Constitution could be defended as establishing the least unnatural frame of government—but would dialogically elevate the entire tenor of life: "This policy of supplying, by opposite and rival interests, *the defect of better motives*, might be traced through the whole system of human affairs, *private as well as public*" (emphasis added).

gered"—to mediate Shelley's vision of the grim "triumph of Life" over all happiness and all heroism. (There is a measure of irony in Rousseau's becoming, for an ethical drillmaster like Irving Babbitt, the pied piper of a banefully permissive humanitarianism.) The specter of Life in Shelley's poem asserts with fresh force the myth of some vast power irreversibly at odds with human self-projection. This power runs riot through nineteenth-century mythmaking. It is variously conceptualized—nature, passion, society, race, the nation, the World-Spirit, the world market, the Immanent Will, evolution, necessity, history. Whatever its form, it is, compared with older mythologies of Fortune or Providence, as much more unremitting and humanly unanswering as the coercions of a world-spanning industrial-commercial society were proving to be in comparison to earlier civil systems.

Its imprint is everywhere. In the panorama of Blake's "London" it afflicts every man, woman, and child alive: "on every face . . . / Marks of weakness, marks of woe." For Melville it brings all whose thought runs deepest to the perception of "a wisdom that is woe and a woe that is madness" (*Moby-Dick*, ch. 96). Moreover, figures who must confront this ultimate power commonly brace for the struggle by risking the lives of others, preeminently those they love or are loved by. Or they turn suicidally against themselves, heroic rebellion becoming indistinguishable from self-condemnation. In a literature redefining Hell itself as an agglomerated modern city—"a city much like London," peopled by the undone and unpitied, in Shelley's "Peter Bell the Third"—the re-emergence of Cain as archetypal hero, as in the poetic "mystery" sealing Byron's reputation for infamy, seems exactly appropriate. To another poet-aristocrat, Alfred de Vigny, even the mythic new-world husbandman of Jefferson's republican vision bears this brand and curse. "Caïn le laboureur" he is called in Vigny's American poem, "La Sauvage"—slayer of the red-Indian hunter Abel before settling down as remorseful patriarch of yet one more after-the-fall civilization.

The specter of some power incommensurable with human

virtue (a power that is "speechless" and "placeless" to *Moby-Dick*'s Ahab) is the more paralyzing for appearing random, teleologically indifferent, in operation. Its first attribute—so Hardy instinctively felt—is a mocking disregard for moral deserving. To steal back some of its alien strength, humanity would have to drive itself "beyond good and evil," the formula Nietzsche created to cap a century of transcendentalizing moral argument.[15] The profane but still heroic archetypes of this transmoral titanism are Faust and Prometheus, in the appropriately unplayable *magna opera* of Goethe and Shelley. But in novels of the same era, everyday versions of the figure who makes the turbulence all around him his special assignment regularly turn up as agents of uncomprehending intrusion, like the destructively resourceful Mittler of Goethe's *Elective Affinities* or *Wuthering Heights*' fatuous outsider, Lockwood. In pointedly anti-bourgeois fictions later in the century, such intruders become the catastrophe's initiating engineer, though professing the best liberal ideals: a liberating moral improvement in Ibsen's plays, political revolt in Dostoievsky's *The Devils*, a finer art of behavioral understanding such as modern novelists ought to aspire to in Henry James's *The Sacred Fount*. (Are these meddlers and moral voyeurs what remain of the ambiguous *benefactor* figure defined by folklorists, in a century when bourgeois usages were weakening beyond recovery the older European folk-consciousness?)

---

[15] It makes a difference where such arguments originate. In the seclusion of American village life, where a writer like Emerson, praying to become not "virtuous" but "virtue" itself ("Divinity School Address"), could talk fearlessly of being "the devil's child," his neighbor Thoreau, wishing "to front only the essential facts of life," willingly embraced the chance that he might get back only some "whole and genuine meanness" (*Walden*, ch. 2). The adventure in any case was his own affair; no one else was required to live in the same fashion. By contrast, in Balzac's Paris, where the will to life easily finds other outlets than Lyceum lecturing, the consequences are less easily cordoned off. The "great intellects" composing Balzac's Machiavellian-Napoleonic elite are those who not only "comprehend all things, both good and evil" (*Lost Illusions*, II, ch. 27) but compel others, perhaps all society, along their creative-destructive trajectories.

Both the heroic and the grotesque representatives of the breed in question, both cosmic rebels and self-appointed domestic interferers, act out a human alienation which, to poets and novelists, seems to have grown all-inclusive. For Blake, scenarios of heroic regeneration still made poetic sense. When the just man is driven into exile, hypocritical institutions may still be named as the mediate cause—Blake's membership in the fraternities of artisanship and evangelical enthusiasm had accustomed him to dissidence where vocations are at issue— and poet-prophets may still dream of their overthrow. But to the country intelligence of a Wordsworth, something subtler and deeper than chartered tyranny had intervened. The very principle of attachment by which the human imagination might realize its own active calling within the phenomenal world now seemed in doubt. In Raymond Williams's summary (a comment on Book VII of *The Prelude*, "Residence in London"):

> Wordsworth saw strangeness, a loss of connection, not at first in social but in perceptual ways: a failure of identity in the crowd of others which worked back to loss of identity in the self, and then, in these ways, a loss of society itself, its overcoming and replacement by a procession of images. . . . (*The Country and the City* [1973], ch. 14)

The practical Wordsworthian therapy for such deprivation— therapy indeed for more than one stricken Victorian humanist—is the excursion of withdrawal, undertaken not to embrace absolute solitude but to recover that portion of wholeness which would allow resuming a manageable budget of private duties.

DISPLACEMENTS, SUBSTITUTIONS

Withdrawal symptoms—their sectarian counterpart a redundance of utopias, New Canaans and Fourierite phalanxes, all in some way restrictive—also enter nineteenth-century literature in the form of new limitations on subject matter. The bowdlerization of imaginative writing, the narrowing of its address to the affective life, is a familiar story. Already, during the Augustan ascendancy, the plenary indecorum of *virtue* had been migrating downward into prose comedy and satire and the mongrel structures of the new novel. In the gradual opening up of the novel to major ambition a sexual candor relatively free of metacritical restraint, and a corresponding opportunism of treatment that runs from formal skylarking to an insistent narrative impropriety, are standard features. The exuberance of Fielding's *Tom Jones* (1749) in both respects, and of everything Sterne wrote, stands (for us) in agreeable contrast to the earnest lesson-pointing of *Amelia* and *Sir Charles Grandison*; so too it is *The Beggar's Opera* (1728) rather than *Cato* or *Irene* that remained alive to later audiences. In the 1830s and 1840s a critically unsupervised popular journalism was still the instrument Dickens and Thackeray adapted for a fiction at once vividly panoramic and alive to human quiddity, though each pretended to regret losing the freedom of address enjoyed by his eighteenth-century predecessors.

If we add to this too synoptic account the equally popular genre of the Gothic romance, as exploited by novelists from Jane Austen and Walter Scott to Dostoievsky and Conrad, it becomes reasonable to attribute the whole expanding imperium of nineteenth-century prose fiction to an initial withdrawal into performative modes uncluttered by principles and precedents. One part of the cost, however, was the retreat into private sentiment encyclopedically chronicled in Mario Praz's *The Hero in Eclipse in Victorian Fiction* (1952; tr. 1956). The best novelists may of course be shown to have retained an effective concern for commonwealth and a fully societal virtue. Even with Jane Austen the right attitude toward social dependents is a prime behavioral test—in *Emma*, most consequentially, the treatment of children, wards, and pensioners but also of hypochondriac fathers and of feather-headed protégées and salt-of-the-earth tenant farmers (the authorially approved marrying off of the protégée to the farmer becoming, for us, the questionable element)—while in Scott's romances characters of low rank as well as high are regularly allowed heroic moments, giving force to the myth of reinvigorated national community by which George Lukacs explained the arch-conservative Scott's popularity in liberal-nationalist Europe (*The Historical Novel*, I, ii [1955; tr. 1962]). Apart from historical fiction (and from historiography itself, which flourished), contests for social power now have in the main only private consequences and, even in Mrs. Gaskell's admirable Manchester novels or Dickens's *Hard Times* (1854), change-of-heart solutions.[16] At most, political reality has become a confused rumor from over the horizon—which is precisely how Flaubert, in a matchless segment of *L'Éducation sentimentale* (1869), delivers news of the climactic June Days to his idling lovers at Fontainebleau. The grander formations of life and fortune, the milieux appropriate to heroic virtue, enter the story now only by way of a severe ironic refraction.

In much of this new realism the characters making the sharpest impression play either minor or antagonistic roles. Such were the "originals" of Smollett's labored comedy; such, too, the self-absorbed eccentrics of Dickens and Gogol, and all the rustics, provincial artisans, senexes, profligates, and plain villains whose special animation of speech is a first diagnostic mark, in nineteenth-century fiction, of narrative authenticity. These figures are rarely the protagonists, though moving one such front and center was primary to Mark Twain's breakthrough in *Huckleberry Finn* (1885). But they seem, in each case, to stand nearer the springs of life. The uncouth old man, grotesquely or menacingly unaccommodatable, offers a case of special interest throughout the post-1789 era: a figure always possible to interpret as embodying some dislodged patriarchal virtue that a self-revolutionized Europe felt itself haunted by. In the Lear-like role of purgatorial sufferer he gives his name to Balzac's *Père Goriot* (1835), becoming a signal casualty of the new re-

[16] Who can take seriously Trollope's specifically political vision, or the hint in Meredith's "prelude" to *The Egoist* (1879) that he is anatomizing British imperialism?

ligion of success preached by the shape-changer Vautrin. As Wordsworth's leech-gatherer and in roles like that of the artisan/paterfamilias Caleb Garth in *Middlemarch* (1871-1872) or the city-pent countryman Job Legh of Mrs. Gaskell's *Mary Barton* (1848) he supplies a pastoral corrective to the disintegrations of selfhood and social balance elsewhere displayed. He has a wonderfully varied place in Dickens's portrait galleries, from *Bleak House*'s Turveydrop ("Wooman, lovely wooman, what a sex you are!") to the looming Magwitch of *Great Expectations* (1860-1861). As Tolstoy's dying Ivan Ilyich (1884) he pays the price of a whole society's degeneracy. And he is shadowed all along by an antitype representing not squandered parental authority but something primordially hostile or indifferent to nurture of any kind, as with the "ancient men" of Blake's mythmaking or certain baleful hangers-about in midcentury novels like Hawthorne's *The Blithedale Romance* (Old Moodie) or *Wuthering Heights* (the servant Joseph). Is the wild old wicked man of Yeats's final poems a creation of the same kind—reassimilated, by way of Irish myth, into a great poet's primary mythology?

Where these eccentric type-figures of discarded or foresworn virtue regularly occupy major roles is in the mass of shorter fiction produced in the nineteenth century—a body of work insufficiently accounted for in descriptions of the literary character of the age, yet as rich in invention as the full-scale novel. It is in compressed forms like the novella and the tale (preeminent in the prose literature of Austria and Germany) that literary pastoral most flourishes as an imaginative counterforce. If the multi-volume novel spoke increasingly to the experience of a social class and readership brought to power by the capitalist-industrial revolution—a class easily flattered by detailed representations of its unprecedented ascendancy, yet already in terror of violent overthrow—the novella or tale with an out-of-the-way setting as practiced by contemporaries of Balzac and Dickens like the Austrian Stifter or the Russian Lermontov served as a kind of escape hatch, a way of getting through and beyond the unpitying bourgeois looking-glass.

(So, coincidentally, did the odd new fashion of nonsense literature, most of all in imperial-industrial England, as with Lewis
Carroll and Edward Lear.) The simplifications of life which
these modes and genres make formally legitimate answer expertly to the longing of middle-class readers for a less vulnerable existence, one in which actual historical alternatives, past
or future, stay well out of sight.[17]

A more circumstantial version of anti-modern pastoral and
its defense of lost or imperiled virtue develops in the vogue for
stories celebrating provincial life and manners, a vogue continuous from the beginnings of the industrial revolution. The remarkable appeal of Goldsmith's *The Vicar of Wakefield*
(1766), published at the moment James Watt was reinventing
the steam engine and popular across Europe for nearly a century, was a conspicuous portent. Throughout this era revolutionary shifts in the balance of population and wealth from vil-
lage-centered countryside to the industrial and bureaucratic
city are steadily matched by a reverse migration of property-
class sentiment and taste. Examples will flock to mind for any
confirmed explorer of what came to be called local-color writing, from *Our Village* (1819) to *Our Town* (1938). Early and

---

[17] Walter Benjamin, writing on Leskov, describes the genre of story-telling
as "an artisan form of communication" expressing the pre-industrial ethos of
craftsmanship and patient, individualized work. It particularly incorporates
our human instinct to imitate "the patient processes of Nature" and to produce—Benjamin quotes Valéry on this point—"miniatures, ivory carvings . . .
stones that are perfect in polish and engraving, lacquer works or paintings in
which a series of thin, transparent layers are placed one on top of the other":
i.e., objects of *virtù*. Under modern conditions these, of course, are the work
processes that no longer pay their way.

At the further remove of the fairy tale, resuming in the nineteenth century
its old power to beguile cultivated minds, these simplifications are refined to
the point of laying bare the structure of human virtue's elemental self-audit.
To cite Benjamin again: "the fairy tale polarizes *Mut*, courage"—humanity's
means of opposing mythic force—"dividing it dialectically into *Untermut*,
that is, cunning, and *Übermut*, high spirits" ("The Storyteller: Reflections on
the Works of Nikolai Leskov," *Illuminations*, tr. Harry Zohn [1968], 102).
Victorian literary fantasies for children performed, or attempted, comparable
functions.

late, realism of incident only marginally disturbs an essential idealization of country, or country-house, life. Yet in all such writing the impulse to recover a lost singleness and harmony of being, in our terms a lost *virtue*, never quite dissipates the air of powerlessness and inanition overspreading the life and the lives displayed—a combination of themes and tones that Chekhov would bring to perfection.

The judgments symbolized in modern pastoral are not simple. But from the beginning they bear a clear if not always direct reference to the systems of domination centered in the new industrial and administrative capitals, modern power's self-fortifying strongholds. From the post-colonialist perspective of c. 1960, such judgments may strike us as anticipating the revolutionary pastoralism of much of the underdeveloped or "third" world—a resistance foreshadowed in Melville's formal opposition of Polynesian society to an imperializing Christendom and made systematic in Conrad's and Forster's exposures of colonial rule and in the programmed vision of Lawrence's *The Plumed Serpent*.[18] A corresponding resistance may be seen in the convention of placing the story's action at some safe temporal distance, commonly a generation earlier than the moment of writing. This convention took firm hold with the great popular masters of the novel whose practice Kathleen Tillotson surveyed in *Novels of the Eighteen-Forties* (1954); the eighteenth-century novel, by contrast, is conventionally set in the immediate present. What was wanted was a temporal preserve as insulated as the enclosures of regionalist fiction, a sphere of action and relation undisturbed by

[18] The suggestion that Lawrence's Mexican novel looks ahead to the cultural politics of third-world resistance I owe to a valuable dissertation by Nack-chung Paik, "A Study of . . . D. H. Lawrence's Thinking on Modern Civilization" (1973: Harvard University). The same ideological conflict, each party asserting *cultural* superiority, reemerges on the revolutionary left. Raymond Williams's survey of "the country and the city" in English writing ends with a coda on the opposition between the classic Marx-Lenin disparagement of "rural idiocy" and the Maoist ideology of regeneration from the countryside.

current alarms though still warm in the memory of the writer's principal audience. Dickens, Thackeray, and George Eliot all made regular use of this convention, so that in novels of high moral and social purposefulness written as late as the 1860s a world could be evoked in which the steam railway has only just appeared as a demon of change and the emphasis falls instead on the virtue of defying or else ignoring everything it represents.

Characteristically, it was George Eliot who openly defended this distancing of the anxieties likely to be active for her own readership, at the same time attacking in the name of ethical truth that worship of a wholly idealized beauty by which the same readership, buying its way into the arts in general, was disguising its ruthless acquisitiveness. In *Adam Bede*, ch. xvii (1859), George Eliot discusses at length the delight she herself has found, and means others to find, in "faithful pictures of a monotonously homely existence" (a definition of preferred subject matter only slightly less dispiriting than that of "the ignobly decent" proposed a generation later by one of the scribblers in Gissing's *New Grub Street*). Her point of reference is the Netherlands genre painting whose moral charm the historian Taine would shortly urge on his Second Empire audience as an alternative to grandiosity. Here (George Eliot writes), looking at "those old women scraping carrots with their workworn hands, those heavy clowns taking holiday in a dingy pothouse, those rounded backs and stupid weather-beaten faces that have bent over the spade and done the rough work of the world—those homes with their tin pans, their brown pitchers, their tough curs, and their clusters of onions," we are brought back to that other beauty of "deep human sympathy" from which "world-stirring actions" conspire to detach us.[19]

---

[19] The *Adam Bede* passage is duly highlighted in Praz's *The Hero in Eclipse*. A passage in Thackeray's *Pendennis*, also cited, characterizes the "virtue" of any well-bred English lady as at once "angelical" and "awful," epithets bracketing the modern disintegration of the old word and concept with a terminal precision. Praz's book is a storehouse of evidence about the new society's wariness of virtue-as-such.

The implications of this homily on the restorative virtue of the lowly and unimportant are not, I think, fully worked through—*Middlemarch*'s closing affirmation, twelve years later, that "the growing good" of the world may depend on "unhistoric acts" will develop them further—but the judgments and conclusions pointed to might be diagrammed as follows:

(1) Given the dissevering impact of modern reality, we more and more need the leaven of an outreaching sympathy if a life tolerable to feeling and conscious selfhood is to continue at all;

(2) such sympathy, however, is the virtue least to be expected from the officers and overlords of the age, including even the right-thinking people who buy my novels and thus support me in my own (not unambitious) career;

(3) therefore we must cherish those sectors of life, increasingly fugitive, that have not yet got split apart or submerged in the system—just as we prize the recollection of those plainer times when actions of virtue were commonly and directly produced. Yet we must confess the inability of men and women from these bypassed sectors to change life in general, or even to survive the encounter with it. The world we have constructed is indeed too much for us.[20]

[20] For writers this world is increasingly that of the modern metropolis. So the organism of London—"enormous . . . monstrous . . . cruel devourer of the world's light"—controls Conrad's prevision of the century ahead in *The Secret Agent* (1907: see Conrad's 1920 preface). Henry James, on the other hand, born directly into the world's fair of modern city life, could see well enough its systematized violence to persons but could also feel that a writer of fiction could only post watch accordingly and make the best of what he found. Any number of passages in the superb New York chapters of James's *The American Scene* (also 1907) would serve us here, but this earlier one from *Essays in London* (1893) catches the city's compelling attraction for a writer preoccupied with the transformations of human selfhood. Of the "mighty ogress" of contemporary London, shifting capriciously "from one sort of prey to another," James wrote: "the heart tends to grow hard in her company; but she is a capital antidote to the morbid. . . . She may take away reputations, but she forms character. She teaches her victims not to 'mind,' and the great danger for them is perhaps that they shall learn the lesson too well."

VIRTUE BUREAUCRATIZED

Oppressively in nineteenth-century writing, virtue in the human person is perceived as warping into strangeness and limitation. Occupational and professional deformation is its characteristic new form. (Classic Darwinism, the new dismal science, saw in this process of adaptive deformation the principle of life behind every new ascendancy.) As the century advances, imaginative writing—much of graphic art, too—becomes preoccupied with the functionally determined virtue, or lack of it, of the professionalized classes, the "new men" of the new age. In acquiring unprecedented historical power, such men have presumably taken on a corresponding responsibility. But neither the power nor the responsibility is felt to belong to them naturally, in sharp contrast to the patriciate they have displaced.

These new middle and professional classes first enter modern literature by renewing the stereotypes of Roman comedy; in the seventeenth century, Erich Auerbach reminds us, "[w]hen a judge, or a lawyer, or a physician appears on the stage, it is always in a comic and repugnant role" ("La Cour et la Ville," *Scenes from the Drama of European Literature*). Art in the high bourgeois age continues to exploit professionalized self-importance for satire and farce, as in Daumier's biting caricatures or (minor instance) the double-edged comedy of Dickens's medical apprentices in *Pickwick* (1836). With such failed professionals as the scholar (Casaubon) and doctor (Lydgate) of *Middlemarch* it learns to add a measure of pathos, even of forgiveness. But it also clothes men of this type with an appearance of mastery over the lives of others that is menacingly amoral. Their power (or *virtue*) inheres in the mysteries they serve, and it is the more absolute for the impersonality of their dedication to it. It too now serves invisible hands, the suprapersonal forces controlling all existence. The manipulative potency of Dickens's ultimately benign, and fallible, Jaggers in *Great Expectations* as well as of the sinister Tulkinghorn of *Bleak House*; the overbearing central figure in Eakins's great painting of Dr. Gross in his surgical clinic, with the figure of maternal charity turning away in horror; Ivan Karamazov's God-displacing Grand Inquisitor—with none of these (limiting examples to Auerbach's lawyer, physician and judge) is there any question of neo-classical ridicule or condescension. The ambivalent respect once paid to the aristocrat's irresistible assumption of privilege is now transferred to the case-hardened professional man.[21]

One important subtype of professionalized virtue appears not among the masters of these new-model power systems but in the self-sacrificing personnel recruited to protect them. Military and paramilitary officers are standard in such roles, from the self-denying patriots of Vigny's *Servitude et grandeur militaires* (1835) to Tolstoy's battle-hardened aristocrats and Conrad's disciplined sea captains. Officers who abuse these commissions, like surgeons who contrive to kill their patients, are frequent enough in nineteenth-century fiction, not usually as protagonists. But subtler cases now come forward: Hardy's parvenu Mayor of Casterbridge (1886), or Fontane's husband in the Prussian tragedy of *Effi Briest* (1895), caught between protocols of aristocratic honor and administrative career-making. The careworn captain of Melville's *Billy Budd* (1888-1891) is a case of special interest, being forced to assume that one particular office, of hangman, which on the collapse of Enlightenment political optimism the reactionary ideologue De Maistre had identified as the fulcrum of all social order. In one way or another all these figures absorb into themselves a sacrifice of natural feeling, and thus of creaturely virtue, that is seemingly demanded of them by modern civilization itself. Their vocations approach the priestly, but the power they ex-

---

[21] Russian fiction in particular adds the feared profession of government investigator, as in *Crime and Punishment* (1866) or, parodically, Gogol's *Inspector General* (1836). In *Anna Karenina* (1875-1877) the bureaucrat Karenin is by no means overmatched by the titled army careerist Vronsky, and the conflict between the disciplines they represent, as it destroys Anna, is not displaced as the story advances by the alternative presented in the pastoral hero, Levin.

ercise blights rather than nourishes the essential human succession.[22]

There are also, expectably, the anti-professions, where a human vitality disinclined to self-sacrifice clears space for itself along the margins of the new era's partitioning of required functions. This is mainly done by inventing problematic new functions (a solution somehow unavailable to Turgenev's "superfluous man"). The *private detective* formalized by Poe is a threshold case. Self-appointed to work that is still nominally in the public interest, he goes about it with a disturbing independence and self-satisfaction. The *secret agent* is another such, though commonly at odds with himself as well as with ordinary loyalties. The purest of these new anti-professionals is perhaps Baudelaire's *dandy*, who takes all the business of metropolitan Paris, day and night, as his voyeur's domain— unless it is Goncharov's eponymous hero (1858), who invented the profession of doing nothing at all and so gave a

---

[22] The priest himself, or minister, or—shrewd shift—minister's son, keeps a place in major fiction, chiefly as an exemplar of broken faith: Hawthorne's Dimmesdale, Charlotte Brontë's St. John Rivers, Hardy's Angel Clare. In contrast one of Chekhov's finest stories, "The Bishop," recovers by indirection the sacrificial theme, and in our century Gide (*La Symphonie pastorale*), Bernanos (*Journal d'un curé de campagne*), Silone (*Bread and Wine*) all return to it.

The new man of science also makes a rallying point for older myth, notably the Faust-Prometheus myth of a breaching of sacred limits. Hawthorne was fascinated with the type and to good advantage, as Taylor Stoehr has painstakingly shown in *Hawthorne's Mad Scientists* (1978). So, too, Bazarov in Turgenev's disturbing *Fathers and Sons* is a scientific inquirer and, in a not quite random accident, is self-destroyed. The same myth organizes Mary Shelley's precocious tale of a "modern Prometheus," Dr. Frankenstein, and returns in the new-model science fiction of Jules Verne. The comic underside of the Faust tradition also persists. William Empson pleasantly speculated that Lewis Carroll's White Knight represents the Victorian research scientist, "who was felt to have invented a new kind of Roman virtue; earnestly, patiently, carefully . . . without sensuality, without self-seeking, without claiming any but a fragment of knowledge, he goes on labouring at his absurd but fruitful conceptions" (*Some Versions of Pastoral* [1935], ch. 7). The whole reflexive latter-day phenomenon of professional-class self-pity has made much of the lonely, burden-bearing research scientist, as with Sinclair Lewis, A. J. Cronin, C. P. Snow, and the not quite masterly Fitzgerald of *Tender is the Night*.

name, Oblomovitis, to the behavioral disorder most feared by society's new personnel managers.

In their several ways these liminal figures are also a depersonalizing society's purest victims. It is they who have most fully internalized its amputations of human capacity. (Alongside may be placed their occupationless female counterparts, the Beckys, Emmas, Zenobias, Annas, Lily Barts, and Edna Pontelliers whose resistance to subjugation has a private legitimacy that only makes more certain, in each story, their eventual punishment.) Most frequently such figures act out illicit versions of the system itself—thus the *gambler*, who voluntarily exposes himself to the condition of randomness and serial instability that all life approaches in a credit-risk society; or the *grand criminel*, making a defiant show of actions that others connive in from behind legalized screens. Such men must be admired (it is Rameau's nephew's point) for maintaining a "unity of character" necessarily forfeited by the respectable and right-thinking. At least they are not hypocrites, and they are palpably nearer the fortune-mastering creativity attributed, traditionally, to virtue itself; they have more nearly engendered their own lives. But only a step further are the clinically deranged, or worse, who maintain unity of being only by surrendering unconditionally to the machinery of dehumanization. With these, human agency survives only in appalling mutations: in the operations of madness—an acknowledged Victorian calling; in the self-alienation of the *doppelgänger* (Poe's "William Wilson"); or through the limiting-case anthropophagy of the vampire, most literal of character types reaching back to the older physiological understanding of regenerative virtue.[23]

All these variants—the isolation of the professionally dedicated, the alarming self-indulgence of their antitypes—come together in nineteenth-century literature's full-dress mythol-

---

[23] Theodore Ziolkowski, *Dimensions of the Modern Novel* (1969), devotes separate chapters to the newer fictional typologies of criminal and madman.

ogy of the virtue of poets and artists. Other selves, acting on fixed commissions, are absorbed into the machinery of their assignments. Poets alone, serving instead a power enthroned within, "measure the circumference and sound the depths of human nature with a comprehensive and all-penetrating spirit": Shelley's account, in "A Defense of Poetry." But even for Shelley the power through which poetry intervenes to "transmute all that it touches" resembles in operation nothing so much as the hidden hand of the new economics. In both doctrines "unacknowledged legislators" act irresistibly to produce the significant results. So according to Goethe the permanent impression art makes on us is always communicated as "a hidden force," and there is no telling how far or how deep its influence ultimately reaches (*Wilhelm Meister's Apprenticeship*, Book V, ch. x).

There are innumerable definitions of the poet's or artist's great service, which is coincidentally private and public, spiritual and civil. There is also no doubt of its terrific cost. Emerson's set-piece description in "The Poet" is untypically optimistic: the poet "stands among partial men for the complete man, and apprises us not of his wealth, but of the commonwealth." Rather nearer the central myth is the fate of Emerson's own poet-prophet Uriel, whose cosmos-shaking pronouncement of the parity of force between good and evil proves "withering" when transposed into self-knowledge. To Shelley, making the poetic vocation itself his core subject, its consequence is invariably catastrophic. The poet-hero rushes into a "self-centered seclusion" which is avenged by its own inward fury ("Alastor"); he must bear the brand of Cain—or a crown of thorns ("Adonais"); although the "unseen power" he clasps to himself can teach him to "love all mankind," it first makes him "fear himself," as if forever cut off from such love ("Hymn to Intellectual Beauty"). He pursues, that is, a course already marked out in biographic reality by Rousseau and Christopher Smart, Hölderlin and De Sade, and retraced in the century following by Clare, Poe, Nerval, Gogol, Baudelaire, Ruskin, Lautréamont, Nietzsche—madmen, isolatoes, monsters of misapplied sensibility, effective suicides, all willing to be annihilated for the sake of their art's alchemic energy. Even Whitman's great fiction of a poetic self made procreative by union with its own physical body ends ("Song of Myself," #52) by accepting a dissolution the poet has arguably been in search of—D. H. Lawrence was convinced of this—all along.

Literary romanticism in general dramatizes itself as willing to pay any price to repair the numbing opposition of spirit and energy, ultimate cause of that division between a "literature of knowledge" and a "literature of power" which De Quincey would affirm as an absolute of critical experience even while awarding higher honors to the second kind, the writing which did not "teach" its readers but affectively "moved" them. The recovery of natural human power, its generative release from the hiding places it had withdrawn to, is universally preoccupying and shapes argument and vocabulary together. Shelley, returning to Greek originals, felt obliged to translate *areté* as "virtue-and-power" in order to reestablish virtue's capacity not only to oppose its great antagonists (circumstance, the Veil) but to penetrate them and to sustain that penetration. So for Wordsworth the "renovating virtue" within certain spots of time—a "vivifying virtue" in the 1805-1806 text of "The Prelude"—is first of all a virtue that "penetrates, enables us to mount/ When high, more high, and lifts us up when fallen." (How have psycho-sexual deconstructionists missed *that* sequence of X-rated verbs?)

And despite poetry's fear of new science and its profanations, the effort to rejoin virtue and potency goes forward in literature, too, on a putatively scientific basis. We find the appeal to an experimental science of natural force in the writing of Goethe and Shelley; in Stendhal, Balzac and Victor Hugo— the contemporaries in fiction of Fourier and Auguste Comte; in Tolstoy, Zola, Strindberg, Proust, Musil (but less commonly among the major British and American novelists; Dreiser and Lawrence are the self-taught exceptions, along with self-invented polymaths like H. G. Wells and Jack London).[24] In the

---

[24] A proper account of the impact of the new science on the virtue-attentive

new poetics of continental *symbolisme* where the sickness
unto death of everything customary or institutionalized is an
article of faith, this trust in new experiment is transposed into
a relentlessly impersonal science of language. Insofar as the
writer himself remains present in his work, it is as the self-sacrificing practitioner of an "alchimie du verbe" through which
selfhood itself dissolves into otherness, its *je* becoming *un
autre*—Rimbaud's revolutionary maxim. But insofar as the
purification being sought is always unattainable, one uncom-
promising subgroup within the poetic community begins its
countermarch towards the purgative suicide of silence and
blankness. Mallarmé is definitive here, the inventor (it is Robert Lowell's comment) of a style which would make writing itself essentially impossible.

Virtue (Heroic) in Default

What also remain divided throughout the modern era are the
political or civil and the ethical or spiritual intuitions of *virtue*.
Kleist's extraordinary novella *Michael Kohlhaas* (1808) gains
much of its prophetic force from an undistracted rendering of
the consequences of this division. An honorable man's passion
for justice is satisfied only as it grows into a self-feeding mania
and totally disrupts the system of order it initially appeals to,
and it completes its work only by accepting self-obliteration;
yet it registers at every point an inexorable self-fulfillment.
Writers, historians, and philosophers as well as novelists and
poets seem able to imagine either great personal virtue or great
collective virtue (in our sense of generative efficacy) but not
both at once. In the real historical world, power increases by

---

literary imagination would have to begin by separating out the cruder sorts of
nineteenth-century positivism and determinism, which proposed to do away
altogether with a distinctively moral calculation. It is worth recalling how
threatening this science-based materialism could seem. Thus William James:
when a writer such as Taine tells us that "vice and virtue are products like vi-
triol and sugar" and implies that our search for the rules of behavior should
be entrusted to the chemical laboratory, "we feel . . . menaced and negated in
the springs of our innermost life"; "our soul's vital secrets" seem threatened
(*The Varieties of Religious Experience*, Lecture I [1901-1902]).

leaps and bounds. But it no longer wears a human face. The French Revolution as Carlyle celebrated its prodigious advance is the material expression of some vast prepotent world tendency that nevertheless, in its day-to-day unfolding, appears officered by mountebanks and scoundrels. When history does deliver up a statesman Carlyle can admire, like Cromwell, it does so in a famously "good" but losing cause, and the hero himself is prophetically dishonored in the aftermath.

Among actual heroes it was the self-crowned emperor Napoleon who decisively challenged nineteenth-century judgments. In any calculation of human greatness there was no honest way of denying him a place in the first rank. But except for a Stendhal, incidentally celebrating Napoleon's double regeneration of French law and French prose style, it was fairly impossible, looking back, to see Napoleonic power as nobly revivifying. Emerson—making as usual the best of a difficult case, and assimilating it into his own equivocal dream of greatness—contrived in the end to discover in Napoleon a distillation of all commonness, a consummate example of "how much may be accomplished by the mere force of such virtues as all men possess" (*Representative Men*, ch. VI). Here was "no hero, in the high sense," despite his quarter century of continuous conquest, but a supremely efficient impersonator in whom "the man in the street finds . . . the qualities and powers of other men in the street"—and therefore also an embodiment of the grossest vices. To Nietzsche the career of Napoleon was most remarkable for what it revealed about humankind in the mass: the slavish desire of modern "herd-men" to entrust their infinite self-contempt to the will of a super-immoralist who would deliver them from uncertainty (*Beyond Good and Evil*, #199). Tolstoy, too, confronted Napoleon as a kind of presumptuous rival. In the vast perspectives of *War and Peace* the French emperor is cut down to moral size—to be replaced, for world-historical admiration, by a native antihero whose portrayal only confirms the impersonality of nineteenth-century conceptions of supreme human effectiveness, for the rendering of Kutuzov is surely that great novel's most dreamlike charac-

terization. It is as idealized as the treatment of eminent statesmen in Victorian political biographies. It is also a singularly
pure demonstration of modern historicism, the displacement
of *virtue* into an image of the historical process itself. In Hardy's epic pageant, *The Dynasts*, there is a further displacement, or distancing. Not only Napoleon—seen, not unsym-
pathetically, as a theatrical puppet soldiering on despite a
shrewd sense of his own factitiousness—but all of human history appear gripped by forces beyond human reckoning.

Correspondingly in the novels of Dickens, Balzac, Zola, *virtue* in anything like its original sense—the incremental advance of human capacity in the face of contrary fortune—exists only as a function of the general life of society. The
fictional worlds of each of these profligate inventors are worlds
without heroes (except sentimental heroes of submission and
absurd heroes, or villains, destructively self-polarized). For
Baudelaire the "heroism of modern life" resides in the collective and anonymous jostle of the metropolitan crowd and is
best represented in the disposable boulevard caricatures of a
Constantin Guys. (Courbet presented a provincial counterpart
in the packed mourners—individually grotesque, collectively
massive and unyielding—of the panoramic "Burial at Or-
nans.") What remains of human greatness is divided up, for
Baudelaire, among the sacrificial trinity of poet, priest, and soldier, no one of them having it complete (*Mon Coeur mis à nu*,
#48). So with chroniclers like Hardy and Faulkner, who lean
toward the generic human case as opposed to the fine individual consciences idealized by Henry James, the determining
story is nearly always multiple or collective, notwithstanding
the brokenness of the collectivity in question. A graduated yet
essentially fixed and determined field of behavioral possibility
is established whose full potency no character or relationship
can ever come near assimilating.[25]

[25] With Hardy and Faulkner the essential story runs what seems a preestab-
lished course, the quality of its human agents becoming manifest in their different ways of suffering what overtakes them. These two strong, artful
minds—wisdom-grasping but speculatively incurious, and at their flattest in

When in modern writing we come upon a projection of individual virtue that is not sentimentally inflated, it is likely to have the disarming exiguousness of Forster's powerless triumvirate, "the sensitive, the considerate, and the plucky." Here, seventy-five years later, is what Baudelaire's moral avatars of poet, priest, and soldier have come down to. Even on this limited ground, where virtue-as-such materializes in at best a personal decency and balance that must be their own reward, a fully reasoned concern for human recovery and continuance has commonly seemed, since 1900, to have been relinquished to psychoanalysis, that self-bureaucratized *scienza nuova* whose laissez-faire attitude to the coercions of civil life may be taken as one of our century's most characteristic, and perplexing, ideological scandals.

In Anglo-American writing (to round out our survey of representative tendencies with a single twentieth-century case) it is perhaps Yeats who clung most tenaciously to the dream of reversing this historical declension. Yeats's authority as a writer has lately come under widespread attack. But his achievement, for all its undeniable singularity, still seems to me the one by which ranking-order claims for other twentieth-century poets (in English) are to be measured. A poet unfashionably set on personal glory, Yeats turned to advantage his historical situation in an anachronistic cultural order. Building an imaginative province for himself as a privileged insider-outsider in backwater Ireland, he could the more naturally keep modern mass society from constraining his consciousness of life while at the same time searching out a confirming science where (as

---

delivering general pronouncements—seem to me supremely, in modern Anglo-American literature, the "poets of the odds" (see above, pp. 15-16). Their writing gains the strong effects it seeks, but it is the indistractibility of their grasp that compels assent, not the "thought-adventure" (D. H. Lawrence's term for what centrally matters in imaginative writing). By comparison Lawrence's narratives and characterizations may strike us as improvised and unfinished. But it is possible to read them as answering more directly to the sequences of life we ourselves are conscious of living through—and know ourselves, so far as we do, *by* living through.

he saw it) the Elizabethan poets had found theirs, in the self-contained universe of magic, alchemy, Pythagoras, Rosicrucianism, and the rest.

Yeats, though, looks less eccentric if we see his life's effort as emerging in response to the same fragmentation and compartmentalization of experience that provides the interpretive focus for every serious modern scheme of analytic understanding. Even *A Vision* yields to this approach. What stands, literally, at the center of the book—making up its longest section (Book I, Part III)—is a descriptive table of the historically documented properties of realized virtue. Of the twenty-eight divisions in Yeats's grand scheme only two have transcendent standing, the phases of a totalized fullness of self-being and of a total emptying out. The rest find confirmation in the heterogeneous life-records, real and imagined, Yeats adduces from western society's long, always turbulent history. And though all twenty-eight have their place within a unified behavioral theory and myth, each subtype is perceived as separate and self-contained. Each casts its own historical shadow and is shadowed in turn by everything it excludes or opposes.

The exact bearing upon individual poems of this descriptive-analytic system is never an affair of simple correlation. Each major poem became for Yeats, as he built it up, the kind of thought-adventure or trial of first principles that Lawrence proposed for the writing of novels. (Yeats came late to Lawrence but read him, Richard Ellmann tells us, with active pleasure: *Yeats, The Man and the Masks* [1948], 276.) Underlying judgments of the prospect of life are thus continually at risk with Yeats and continually shift and change. Has any other modern poet more rigorously disciplined his own eloquence, throwing away, as Yeats's drafts and revisions show us, not only lines but whole stanzas that would have been the making of lesser reputations? In the moving elegy to Major Robert Gregory, written when the inquiries leading to *A Vision* had barely begun, Yeats had imagined "soldier, scholar, and horseman"—military virtue, contemplative virtue, and a characteristically strenuous form of rural retirement—as reunited in a single man (who was also, in the poet's elegiac dream, a "great painter," a parochialism of judgment that only a little un-steadies the poem's commemorative authority). But in the late ballad, "Long-Legged Fly," a briefer statement yet apoca-lyptically universal, virtue again divides into antithetical con-figurations. There is the potent self-concentration that in a Caesar constructs and sustains great civilizations or in a Mi-chelangelo creates equally prodigious works of art, but there is also the virtue—sensuous, unreflecting, immaculately ambi-tionless—which is any human child's birthright. Yeats sings, of course, the complementarity of these archetypes of virtue (and in the process explictly restores sexual energy to the amalgam). Yet if this second, instinctive virtue substantially enters the im-perial world at all, so the poem declares, the result will not fail to be a subversion and displacement, as great Troy was over-thrown by the working of one young woman's bodily grace.

Virtue in the Eye of Criticism

Yeats was his own best ethical and imaginative subject, all the more so after systematically undertaking in midlife to move beyond the art-studio paradigms and Irish-nationalist fervors he was bred to and extend his visionary grasp to a full-scale myth of European history. His example brings us back to the privileged sanctuary, for high-modernist understanding, of virtue-as-such: the idea of the artistic vocation itself. (Inevita-bly, during our post-modernist moment, this idea is under heavy attack.) That it is ultimately the power and reactive sub-tlety of the writer's own speaking which establishes interest and makes itself the meaning of meanings in the delivered work—the idea is too familiar to need a new volley of illustra-tion. ("One is not a writer," Sartre put it, "for having chosen to say certain things, but for having chosen to say them in a certain way": *What Is Literature?* ch. I.) We still tend to think of it as a modern idea. We observe it holding ground in critical notions like that of the "performative self," developed to take account of irritatingly consequential performers like Norman Mailer or Robert Lowell. But of course it traces back at least to the beginnings of Romanticism; certainly it is in Blake's un-yielding vision of the Just City as one ruled by artists and true scientists, as it is in Novalis's of poetry itself as that which alone in living experience is "truly and absolutely actual" and of the actualizing poet as a "free nomadic visitor" bringing liberation and peace to the created world—Hercules and Orpheus together.[26] Yeats's completed version of this model of poetic value both affirms its self-reflective heroics and acknowledges to the full its equivocality to common judgment. His description of "active virtue" as "theatrical, consciously dramatic, the wearing of a mask" (*Memoirs*, ed. Denis Donoghue [1973], 150) subsumes not only his own self-referential account of the proper character of the poet. It embraces as well the all-inclusive principle of self-continuance through the live circuits of an irresistible bad faith which had made the life exemplified by Rameau's nephew so alarming—and persuasive—a portent.

What finally we can observe in all the instances so far cited is the redistribution of moral understanding in ways that are always in some measure problematic. (But once more, *redistribution*, or *recombination*, rather than *deformation, deconstruction, decreation*, and the like; to insist on adversarial and

---

[26] *Heinrich von Ofterdingen*, II; quoted in Karl Barth, *Protestant Thought from Rousseau to Ritschl*, tr. Brian Cozens (1959), 235.

A recurrent intuition that the greatest art is, first, self-validating and, second, inseparable from the virtue of great individual performance, long antedates its consolidation as a Romantic/modernist article of faith. There is no necessary conflict between this intuition and classicist conceptions of art's or poetry's utilitarian service. The attribution to Shakespeare of an all-infusing "sweetness" and "gentleness" may have had a touch of condescension, coming from scholar-poets like Jonson and Milton, but it acknowledged a quality within the poet's effort transcending schooled correctness. Art history, from the Renaissance forward, furnishes an abundance of such cases. Certainly it was not some surpassing orthodoxy in Michelangelo's conceptions of sacred history, nor the purity of his personal faith, that earned him the epithet *divino*. With Dürer (Erwin Panofsky explains) the characterizing word for extraordinary mastery is *power* (*Gewalt*). It refers to a quality artists themselves are the first to identify: "true artists recognize at once whether or not a work is powerful [*gewaltsam*], and a great love will grow in those who understand" (quoted in *The Life and Art of Albrecht Dürer*, 4th edition [1955], 164).

negative terms is, first of all, to attribute a greater immediate
consequence to particular literary-historical actions than will
survive realistic examination. It is textual positivism's standard error.) Though the primary force I am calling *virtue* is accepted as the very principle of active life and is correspondingly attractive to active imaginations, it is also understood as
a force which, in any institutionalized perspective, can isolate
and substantially unsettle those in whom it most energetically
flourishes. But this says nothing more than that it answers, entering consciousness, to an ambiguity that is the profoundest
manifestation of life itself at the flashpoints of growth and
change.

Our pleasure and active interest in major literature, I am
proposing, is in direct proportion to the intensity and to the enacted persistence, or continuance, of the figurative, narrational, stylistic rendering of virtue, so understood. This interest naturally divides between what it is that happens and how
it is made to happen; between the concrete textual sequences
of the works in question and those acts of mind (and thus of
historical culture) which we imagine producing them. On
either ground, in any case, the first task of critical elucidation
is to uncover the terms of that intensity and trace out the imaginative logic of that persistence.

～

The great and decisive test of genius is, that it calls forth
power in the souls of others. It not merely gives knowledge,
but breathes energy. There are authors, and among these
Milton holds the highest rank, in approaching whom we are
conscious of an access of intellectual strength. A "virtue
goes out" from them. ... The works which we should
chiefly study, are not those which contain the greatest fund
of knowledge, but which raise us into sympathy with the intellectual energy of the author, and through which a great
mind multiplies itself, as it were, in the reader. (William El-
lery Channing, "Milton" [*Works*, I, 30-31])

CHAPTER THREE

"Our Means Will Make Us Means":
Hamlet and *All's Well That Ends Well*

> ". . . for if our virtues
> Did not go forth of us, 'twere all alike
> As if we had them not."
> —*Measure for Measure*, I, i, 33-35

As a first test of the argument about literary meaning proposed in my title, the play *Hamlet* offers several practical advantages. In the first place everyone knows it, and knows also various controversies about it—controversies apparently dating from its opening performances in Shakespeare's revised version (so it has been deduced from hints that survive concerning reactions among its first London audiences). There is also the timing of its composition, which occurred at the historical moment, just after 1600, when the idea and image of *virtue* were richly alive in general consciousness but on the point of that progressive fragmentation and semantic-philosophic disintegration constituting their prolonged modern history. As to the play itself, its energy and quickening power, as a text and in production, are a byword; consider for a starter the role it plays in the design of *Wilhelm Meister, Ulysses, Bend Sinister, Doctor Zhivago*, or Iris Murdoch's *The Black Prince*. Think also how problematic it remains, unique perhaps among masterpieces in regularly tempting admirers to fresh reconstructions of its essential action. In recent times we have had a play, by Tom Stoppard, retelling the basic story from the point of view of poor Rosencrantz and Guildenstern; given the popular success of that, it seems surprising we haven't been shown Claudius's version—or Gertrude's, an interesting project for

the new feminism. There *is* a nicely cynical, and topical, re-
writing of the play's curtain speech, given to the character who
succeeds to power at the action's end, by the Polish poet Zbigniew Herbert, the terse "Elegy of Fortinbras."

A more personal reason is simply that it was at a performance of *Hamlet* in 1963, the one uncut Q2-F1 performance I
happen to have seen, that my framing proposition leaped out
and demanded recognition; most electrically in the closet scene
when Hamlet breaks off a tirade against the corruption his
mother is now party to with the half-line (spoken in this performance with a sharply punctuating shift of tone), "Forgive
my this my virtue" (III. iv. 152).[1] The word makes sense there

---

[1] Text: *The Riverside Shakespeare*, ed. G. Blakemore Evans (1974). The
performance I am recalling took place in Roberts Hall, Haverford College, on
November 21, 1963, and was directed by Robert Butman, who with the same
fidelity to Shakespeare's text had also directed *All's Well That Ends Well* at
Bryn Mawr College in March of the same year.

In writing on Shakespeare the points at which earlier commentary has
shaped or anticipated one's judgments and conclusions are beyond identifying. I am consoled by the resignation expressed by most Shakespeareans on
this score. Besides authors and titles cited below in the text and footnotes I
have found the following especially valuable. On *Hamlet*: Francis Fergusson
on the play's dramatic coherence (*The Idea of a Theater* [1949]); William
Empson, invariably rewarding, on the logic of Shakespeare's manipulation of
the revenge structure ("*Hamlet* When New," *Sewanee Review* 61 [Winter,
Spring 1953]; D. G. James (*The Dream of Learning* [1951]), for—characteristically—a sense of issues and themes that is hard to summarize but much
harder to avoid absorbing; Harry Levin on the play's distinctive language (*The
Question of Hamlet* [1958]); Owen Barfield on form in "The Form of *Hamlet*" (*Romanticism Comes of Age*, new ed. [1966]); Reuben Brower on the
play's involvement with the "heroic" tradition of action and verse rhetoric
(*Hero and Saint* [1972]; several essays in the Shakespeare Institute Studies volume on *Hamlet* (1963), in particular those by David William, G. K. Hunter,
and Patrick Cruttwell—but the whole collection is excellent. On *All's Well
That Ends Well*: general essays by W. W. Lawrence (*Shakespeare's Problem
Comedies* [1931]) and Muriel Bradbrook (*Shakespeare: The Comedies*, ed.
Kenneth Muir [1965], and text Introductions by G. K. Hunter (Arden, 1959)
and Barbara Everett (Penguin, 1970). A debt of a different kind is to F. O.
Matthiessen, whose lectures at Harvard in 1948-1949 first formed my critical
understanding of what Shakespearean commentary might most profitably un-
dertake.

simply in opposition to "vice," and it is paired with "vice" two lines later; in another six lines it appears yet again with the same restricted bearing—"Assume a virtue, if you have it not"—immediately after Hamlet's plea to Gertrude to "go not to my uncle's bed." The whole scene, however, is crammed with the play's much-remarked imagery of sickness, physical blight, poisonous corruption, so that the medicinal and therapeutic significances of "virtue" are made active by contrast. This richer sense is also directly underscored; virtue, in the same speech of Hamlet's, must plead with vice to be allowed to "do him good" (III. iv. 154-55). Further, the shift of tone and address in that half-line, so characteristic of the stylistic rush and tumble of the whole play, directly follows the crisis of the Ghost's reappearance and Hamlet's fit of "ecstasy"—Gertrude's word, repeated as a shocked expletive as Hamlet begins his speech—and we come to this run on the word "virtue" through three quick repetitions of the associated word "madness" (III. iv. 141-46).

~

As it happens, "virtue" appears in *Hamlet* more frequently, with one exception, than in any other play of Shakespeare's, the exception being *All's Well That Ends Well*.[2] The word-count approach to theme and meaning is not at all foolproof and requires caution in use; the play, for instance, making the greatest use of "virtuous" (the moralistic adjective that does not appear in any text of *Hamlet*) is *Richard III*, a play not famous for argumentative subtleties. But the notion of a particular absorption by Shakespeare, at this stage of his career, in the phenomenon of virtue-as-such is not hindered by the fact

---

[2] It deserves pointing out at the start that although *Hamlet* builds on the conventional assumption that high virtue is to be found among princes, warriors, and kings, *All's Well* slants provocatively away from that premise. In both plays, however, the reciprocal process by which integrity and health in the ruler and integrity and health in the kingdom activate and reinforce each other is taken for granted. It forms, so to speak, the ideological bottom line.

that the word's most concentrated use occurs in that 1601-1604 run of morally unsettled, intermittently cynical plays which *Hamlet* introduces: sixteen times in *All's Well*, fifteen in *Hamlet*, fourteen in *Measure for Measure*, eleven in *Troilus and Cressida*. (There are arguments about these datings but almost none about the resemblances within the group.)

In *Hamlet* the word's use covers the common range of meanings, omitting only a direct association with the Machiavellian theme of political virtuosity. When Laertes cautions Ophelia against Hamlet, the first sense is chastity; as such, virtue is liable to violation or sickness ("canker," "contagious blastments": I. iii. 38-42; the full trope precisely anticipates, we note, Blake's program in "The Sick Rose"). Elsewhere virtue is an undifferentiated goodness or integrity of being within a larger system of antithetical force, which it will either repulse or "take corruption" from (I. iii. 16; I. iv. 33; I. v. 53; III. iv. 42). In one violent metaphor of Hamlet's, "virtue," turned mutinous, can "be as wax/ And melt in her own fire" (III. iv. 83-85). In another given to Laertes, "virtue" is the vital power of seeing, behind the merely receptive "sense," that Laertes' tears may "burn out" (IV. v. 156). In two striking instances besides the one already cited, medicinal and regenerative properties are emphasized: when Laertes speaks of the rare poison he will use against Hamlet (IV. vii. 144) and when Hamlet denies to Ophelia that "virtue" ever breeds the old Adam out of us (III. i. 116-118) and thus contradicts the Court's cagey hope that Ophelia's sum of "virtues" will homeopathically tranquillize that "wildness" in him which her beauty has supposedly aroused (III. i. 39-41).

It is to just this kind of verbal and figurative detail, perhaps also to some supporting frame of Renaissance philosophy, that appeal is usually made to resolve those famous problems of motivation and characterization the play has been thought to impose on its readers—Hamlet's alleged delay; the fits of brutality in his behavior and moral reasoning, and the proportion there of assumed or real madness, also of envy and ambition; the "honesty" of the Ghost; the condition of mind at any given moment and the degree of conspiratorial awareness in Claudius or in Gertrude, and so on. These arguments, seeking to rationalize Hamlet's behavior or else to bring the play as a whole into scene-by-scene coherence, are certainly worth attempting, even if in most cases (including T. S. Eliot's notorious tut-tutting of the play's defective artistry) they give an impression of being based on some severely abridged or else slanted and overcluttered stage performance. Invariably, too, the argument runs into casuistry, for by ideal standards of form inconsistencies are really there, and the textual situation is peculiarly unsettled (there appears to be no way of resolving conclusively the claims of the First Folio against those of the "good" quarto or determining what light the "bad" first quarto may shed on the building up of the play as we now have it).[3] But one's real hesitation with such arguments is that they tend to distract from the primary impression the play makes—the exceptional urgency and momentum of its developing action, and a charged expansion of thought and articulated feeling that animates passage after passage in the most rapid succession.

For what one wants to say first about *Hamlet*—without brushing aside real difficulties—is that its extraordinary vivacity and tension are embodied in a continuous activity of realized poetic statement, of concretely enacted argument and strenuous analytic figure-making ("strong" lines and multiple tropes) applied over a very wide range of civil, natural, and supernatural systems and processes. Indeed, this activity of poetic making, and disclosing, is so much the instrument of the

---

[3] My own theatergoer's experience of *Hamlet* has been that if, besides actors who can speak verse, you have the full text yet have it played at top speed and without interruption for scenery-moving, doomy pauses between lines, and the showing off, Wopsle fashion, of stockings; and if you have a properly energetic and dangerous Claudius, insolent, forehanded, unmistakably in command, as well as the kind of Ghost Wilhelm Meister's theatrical company presented who from his first redundant two-word speech ("Mark me") acts out a passionate anger that is nevertheless "spiritual, slow, and inexhaustible," though Hamlet's paralyzed reaction to him, in the *Wilhelm Meister* production, seems badly misconceived—anyway, if you have these things, the play can seem stunningly coherent.

play's immediate effect on us as to compose its primary meaning—or at least to explain its extraordinary afterlife in general European consciousness: an instrument of self-definition, as noted, for poet-novelists of the stature of Goethe, Melville, Joyce, and Pasternak.

The fact that much of this poetic activity is concentrated in the role and discourse of Hamlet himself (the longest role in Shakespeare) has authorized an unusual degree of biographical speculation. I think this is legitimate enough, though of no special help in staging the play or even in "interpreting" it. There *is* a special authorial presence in the play, one that may be objectively characterized. It seems to me one of those works (*Moby-Dick, The Tale of a Tub, Wuthering Heights* are others) in which we feel the substantial presence, the coming together in immediate combination, of three biographical factors: (1) a still advancing consciousness of personal authority and mastery, of the kind Pasternak in his brief essay on *Henry IV* wittily evokes in imagining the young Shakespeare coming up to London; (2) a rapidly widening, deepening, overflowing recognition of the totality of the given world's convergent systems of conduct and causation; and (3) a first full personal apprehension of some inevitable pull downward of time and casualty: the checking of enterprise, the cost of high accomplishment, the expense of action—all major themes in the sonnets, too, where we are customarily less hesitant about finding biographical clues within Shakespeare's handling of poetic convention.

The text of *Hamlet* overflows with concrete descriptions of the composition and operation of things-in-the-world, the whole supporting and constraining matrix of both human and natural life; descriptions, that is, of the actual "form and pressure" of the process by which things-in-experience come full term and are delivered of their quantum of virtue. We hear much about psychic and moral states, facts of common experience frequently defined with clinical precision by the device of hendiadys (see George T. Wright, "Hendiadys and Hamlet," PMLA, March 1981). The first fully voiced tonal clue is

Francisco's "I am sick at heart" (I. i. 9), and we hear throughout the play of men and women who are "hot and full,"
"puff'd and reckless," "desperate with imagination" or else
"dull and muddy-mettl'd," who have "thorns" in their bosom,
whose "sense is apoplex'd," whose very breath must be drawn
"in pain," whose "compulsive ardour" makes "reason pander
will," whose thoughts will turn "bloody," who are or are not
"fit and season'd" for what is still to come. These figures,
moreover, are insistently physiological, sometimes by synec-
doche, more regularly by a direct naming of organs and processes. Hamlet characteristically advances from the one to the
other when he imagines the First Player cleaving "the general
ear with horrid speech" but then amazing "the very faculties
of eyes and ears (II. ii. 563-566). Eyes, also eyelids; ears—all of
Denmark is a poisoned ear, the Ghost announces (I. v. 36-38);
breath and smell; heart and blood, or "coagulate gore";
brows, tongues, knees, sinews, moles and spots, complexions,
private parts, lungs, liver, pulse, cock and semen (in one of
Ophelia's songs);[4] and also some unnamed thing within
"which passes show" (I. ii. 85) but which, as it grows larger,
the black gall of melancholy may soon hatch (III. i. 164-166).

And brains: a word used more frequently in *Hamlet* than in
any other play and given peculiarly physical emphasis, from
Guildenstern's "much throwing about of brains" on the matter of the actors' controversy (II. ii. 358-359) and the Saturnian gravedigger's "cudgel thy brains no more" (V. i. 56) to the
major context of Hamlet's agony—"About, my brains!" when
the Player's passion shames him (II. ii. 588); the "brains still
beating" which have put him "from fashion of himself" (III. i.
174-175); the "brainish apprehension" and "very coinage of
your brain" that Gertrude identifies in him (IV. i. 11; III. iv.

---

[4] "By Gis, and by Saint Charity. . ./ By Cock, they are to blame" (IV. v. 58-
61). The O.E.D. defines "gis" as "a mincing form of Jesu," and textual notes
commonly agree; but one may also reasonably guess that it is a forerunner of
our colloquial "jism," having perhaps—along with "gist"—the same Latin
root as "ejaculate." "Juice" is a dialect variant. Jamieson's Scottish Dictionary
gives "jizzen-bed" as a synonym for childbed.

137). Laertes, too, in agony at his sister's madness, cries out, "O heat, dry up my brains!" (IV. v. 155). Even as Hamlet talks at leisure with Horatio, the word pushes forward to catch the sharpness of his sense of being "benetted with villainies": "Or I could make a prologue to my brains" (V. ii. 30). After hearing the Ghost, he had vowed to purge "the book and volume of my brain" from every commandment but the one—to unfailing re-membrance—he has just received (I. v. 102-103).

A series of speeches through the play alludes to the general system whereby blood, breath, or heart presses through the tongue into speech—or the heart will break—in such a way that words or thoughts either do or do not take proper effect (I. iii. 59, 116-117; III. iii. 97-98). The full composition or piece of workmanship which, taken for all in all, "give[s] the world assurance of a man" (III. iv. 60-62) is evoked several times, either as it recreates itself (Hamlet summoning a new physical being after his charge from the Ghost: I. v. 93-95), or as it is lacking (in actors seemingly assembled by incompetent journeymen: III. ii. 28-35) or is described as falling apart, los-ing interior connection (the burden of Hamlet's inquisition of Gertrude in front of the portraits: III. iv. 53-67), or as it is ap-pealed to, when action falters, in relation to its sanctifying or-igin ("Sure he that made us with such large discourse . . .": IV. iv. 36-39). A comparable run of phrases for things decom-posed or disjointed and out of frame, for thoughts unpropor-tioned, music out of time and harsh, hearts cleft in twain, souls full of discord or self-divided and fighting, is more or less con-tinuous through the play and near the end underlies the pecul-iar power and excitement of Hamlet's narrative to Horatio about the inward change that has readied him for the closing struggle: "Sir, in my heart there was a kind of fighting/ That would not let me sleep" (V. ii. 4-5).

The right composition of various public acts and procedures is also repeatedly discussed; here, too, the effect is to thicken the material context in which dramatic character acquires di-rection and force. Polonius fusses over correct and incorrect forms of public speech, in council and in the theater (II. ii. 86-

92, 498, 504), besides expounding to Laertes his cautionary discipline of practical prudence (I. iii. 59-81). Hamlet twice speaks feelingly about "honest" and "well-digested" plays and about properly contrived performances of them (II. ii. 434-445; III. ii. 1-45); and despite his own dejection he delivers his double encomium on the beauties of macrocosm and microcosm with memorable eloquence (II. ii. 295-308). That speech ("I have of late . . . lost all my mirth . . .") is representative of a further set of more extended poetic figures vital to the play's imaginative grasp. These figures describe whole systems of action and experience—the psychosomatic systems by which strong grief or fear or love or guilt can flush through a man's creaturely being, or some one defect corrupt all his virtues (I. iv. 23-36), or a careful exercise of abstinence (as Hamlet tells his mother) gradually change the very "stamp of nature" (III. iv. 165-170); the calculated system of worldly usage whereby virtue is galled (I. iii. 36-44) and slander may be spread (enough slander, as Polonius elaborately instructs Reynaldo, to keep the reins on a young fellow but not so much as might dishonor him: II. i. 17-35); or, metaphorically, the system of fingering that is right for getting music from a recorder yet grievously wrong for dealing with a proven friend (III. ii. 350-372).

Of particular importance is the great ambiguous system of court rule, a dramatic (and hermeneutic) matrix for the play as a whole. Claudius, before his villainy is known to us, casually apostrophizes this version of political order as a system of bodily health (I. ii. 47-49). Polonius savors it as a "trail of policy" (II. ii. 46-48). Hamlet derides it as cynical flattery and abasement (III. ii. 56-62), and in an extraordinary figurative homily Rosencrantz (the "administration spokesman" of the play) defends it on high, pure, reason-of-state grounds by way of endorsing the preventive strike against Hamlet shortly to be launched by the ruler whose real character and intention he still fatally misunderstands (III. iii. 11-23).[5]

---

[5] Rosencrantz's speech assimilates the Machiavellian antagonists of *virtù*

There are also structural descriptions, as the drama intensifies, of heaven's system of governance and retribution—Hamlet with due contrition accepts being appointed its instrument (III. iv. 173-175), Claudius in perfect bad faith snaps out his own one-line allusion to it (IV. v. 219); of nature's system for generating from love itself both the thing that seals love to its object (IV. v. 162-164) and the antithetical thing that snuffs love out like a candle wick (IV. vii. 114-115); of nature's system, in conjunction with time, for decomposing corpses (V. i. 163-172) and converting dead emperors into dirt-common plugs and bungs (V. i. 202-216). Finally there is that overarching supernatural system from which, with the Ghost, the central action first emerged and which is invoked again and again at critical moments—as divine judgment in Laertes' rebuke to the priest who buries Ophelia with "maimed rites" (V. i. 240-242) or in the ironically paired speeches of Claudius and Hamlet in III. iii, when the one attempts to pray and the other argues himself out of dispatching his adversary with a stab in the back; as a violent legislative disciplining of the strumpet Fortune (Player's speech: II. ii. 493-497); as a kind of Valhalla when Fortinbras queries the summoning of so many dead princes at a shot (V. ii. 364-367); but most memorably, perhaps, as a force of providence adapting human undertakings to its hidden purpose as Hamlet, in two extraordinary speeches in the long last scene, settles his mind for what remains to be done (V. ii. 7-11, 219-224).[6]

---

and *fortuna*. The King's power is itself seen as "a massy wheel" which, when it goes down, drags everything else to ruin. In general *Hamlet* offers no provocations to mainstream political theory. That a usurped power is likely to collapse statecraft into blustering watchfulness is common wisdom.

[6] The major soliloquies build on the same kind of analytic figure-making. The most famous (III. i. 55-87: "To be or not to be . . .") recovers organization, after the broken syntax and mixed metaphors it notoriously begins with, by making a survey of that tripartite structure of systems which in massed combination can turn the most resolute enterprises out of their course—(1) ordinary life and its tormenting institutions, (2) mortality and the mysteries and risks of what comes after death, (3) the harrowing psychological mechanism that condemns us to irresolution in the double bind of these two outward systems.

All this exposition of activating systems and structures, each generating its portion of energy or *virtue*, admirably substantiates the play's sinuous but close-woven plot. From the charged opening moments—with the soldiers on watch bringing scholarly Horatio to see with his own eyes the terrifying Ghost, and with Claudius's inadequately explained refusal to let Hamlet return to Wittenberg—it is all plot and counterplot; Hamlet carrying the attack for a while, the King soon counterattacking with great promptness and resourcefulness, especially after the crisis of the play scene. Any production that allows these next eight or ten scenes (however counted) to run forward as fast as the text warrants, from the summons issued to Hamlet before he can absorb the success of his "mousetrap" to his being put under guard and shipped away to England and execution, should, I think, put an end to questions about inactivity and delay. Except of course as such questions are raised by Hamlet himself, whose high qualities are always spilling over into exaggerated self-reproach: a mark of the special characterological virtue of the protagonists in both these plays.

These plots and counterplots end in the play as they began, with schemes of poison—applying drastic agencies of change to the vital being of others. But systemic transformations of this kind and degree are in fact continuous through the play and constitute its chief dramaturgic reversals. Hamlet's grief and disgust at the start and then, coming with nearly unbearable impact, the Ghost's disclosures combine to work that "transformation" in him for which Claudius instructs Rosencrantz and Guildenstern to search out the hidden reasons (II. ii. 4-18). His "mousetrap" scheme works like a trace drug shot into the King's system, and though Claudius waits out the dumbshow and the provocative dialogue in the main play, he rises on cue at the clinching word "usurps" with which the poisoner Lucianus describes the working of his concoction on *his* uncle the play-King (III. i. 255-265); the word clearly is meant to have full force. A moment later Hamlet tells Guildenstern that more purgation of this kind will plunge Claudius deeper into distemper (III. ii. 304-307); with his mother, next, his virtue is heart-cleaving (III. iv. 156); soon we hear that his passion and wildness, causing the death of Polonius, have divided Ophelia from herself and poisoned her with grief (IV. v. 75-76). A like force of effect is now being imputed simply to Hamlet's speech—it is one with the whirl of events all around him—that would strike even judicious Horatio dumb (IV. vi. 24-25), just as the great love the Danish populace is reported to have for Hamlet would, if let loose, work alchemical transformations upon the whole body politic (IV. vii. 18-21).

This working of drastic effects by agencies of penetration and transformation (of which Hamlet himself becomes the foremost exemplar)—this effective litany of how *virtue* actually operates in life—repeatedly materializes in the play with explosive suddenness, and never more conspicuously than at the end, when the right resolving action flares up in a few quick lines; Hamlet strikes down the King within fifteen stage seconds of catching him in his final villainy and with barely twenty clipped-out words of his own. Correspondingly it materializes in the play's language, in a continuous vocabulary of explosions, bursts, crackings, hatchings, and violent births. News of the Ghost makes Horatio prophesy "eruption" in the state (I. i. 69); Hamlet at the same news imagines foul deeds breaking into view from where they have lain hidden (I. ii. 256-257); in one concentrated double instance he cries to the Ghost, "Let me not burst in ignorance, but tell/ Why thy canoniz'd bones . . ./ Have burst their cerements" (I. iv. 46-48); to Ophelia his anguish seems to "shatter all his bulk" (II. i. 91-93); his talk to Guildenstern "starts wildly"—i.e., breaks free of the apparent subject (III. ii. 308-309)—and to his mother his spirits "wildly" start from his eyes toward an unreal object (a very literal description of "ecstasy": III. iv. 119); Claudius fears the abrupt "hatch" of his melancholy (III. i. 164-167), and with good reason, for Hamlet shortly responds to the plots tightening around him by threatening to hoist them with their own petar, blow them to the moon (III. iv. 206-209). In the end he himself bursts with "strange" and "sudden" haste back into Denmark, the personification of self-crystallizing energy

(IV. vii. 46-47), to set in motion the point-to-point clash of "mighty opposites" (V. ii. 61-62) with which in fact, but not as either of them planned it, the drama ends.

The two lines of figurative argument I have been tracing— the strong working of either poisonous or virtuous effects; the explosion of self-released force from within tormented bodies or tightdrawn circumstances—coordinate for *Hamlet* the field of action on which its character-vectors move. These lines of argument violently intersect at one of the play's major interior climaxes, after the last face-to-face confrontation between Hamlet and Claudius until the fencing ceremony at the end. At this point Hamlet's own rising power of penetration and effect is beyond question. Far more than any dilatoriness or self-doubt, it is what now defines his character not only as the dramatic agent on stage before us but as that particular agent whose words, acts, impulses most directly negotiate our full apprehension of the system of the play. In quick sequence he has struck down Polonius, thrown his old school friends' duplicity back in their faces, taunted and publicly shaken the King, and broken his power over Gertrude; indeed this Hamlet has virtually paralyzed the whole regime, which will shortly expose itself to wholesale insurrection by burying its murdered prime minister in hugger-mugger haste (IV. v. 79-84). Claudius himself is in no doubt about the potency of the antagonist he faces. "Do it, England," he perversely cries:

> For like the hectic in my blood he rages
> And thou must cure me.
> (IV. iii. 65-67)

~

As regards language, characterization, and the way things are enacted on stage, *All's Well That Ends Well* may seem a long way down from the peculiar excitements of *Hamlet*. Certainly its long-term critical and theatrical fortunes have been as dim, apart from one interesting interval, as *Hamlet*'s have been brilliant.[7] Since the play is still not well known or frequently seen (though a notable revival in 1958, featuring Peggy Ashcroft and Edith Evans, promptly produced a new critical respect for both its textual interest and its playability), a review of the main action may be useful:

> Helena is the daughter of a physician or magus who is dead but has bequeathed her his recipes. Coming to the French court, she pledges to cure the sickness of the King, whose doctors have abandoned hope; she offers her life in forfeit if she fails, claims choice of a husband if she succeeds. Bertram, her choice, son of a countess who has already embraced Helena as a daughter, refuses her because she is low-born and because, egged on by the braggart soldier Parolles, he wants to go to the wars and sow wild oats—there has been talk of a general debility among the French gentry which the wars are to cure. The King, being a good king, keeps his promise to Helena and forces the marriage, with reflections on how true virtue needs no title in the world but its own; but away Bertram goes, refusing consummation and setting his rejected wife the two apparently impossible tasks of (at long distance) getting a certain ring off his finger and producing a child that he is father to.

The second half of the play involves, besides the showing

---

[7] During the middle eighteenth century *All's Well* did enjoy a long season of popular favor, especially after Garrick turned it into a low farce with Parolles as hero. Restored, it has had distinguished admirers, or rather the heroine Helena has had admirers. To Coleridge she was Shakespeare's "loveliest character" (though "not very delicate," Coleridge eventually decided, shortly before the Princess Victoria came to the throne). To Hazlitt she was too perfectly sweet and delicate ever to need to blush (she does in fact blush once in the play, in a speech in which not blushing would signify the "white death" of unnaturally continued virginity: II. iii. 69-72). To Bernard Shaw, as late as 1928, she was still "too genuine and beautiful and modern"—in a word, too Shavian—for the theater public to appreciate. Yet *All's Well*, since c. 1770, has never approached the popularity of the bittersweet comedies directly preceding it: *Much Ado, As You Like It, Twelfth Night*. These and other details of the play's critical reception and stage history are given in Joseph G. Price, *The Unfortunate Comedy* (1968).

up of Parolles, a conventionally elaborate plot Helena herself devises and executes which accomplishes both tasks, getting her into Bertram's bed in the dark in place of another girl he has been pursuing; she also traps him in a sort of charade whereby it appears that he may be guilty of her death. But after he is humbled and threatened with the King's justice, Helena reappears to stand forth again, all modestly and lovingly, as his true wife.

It is commonly agreed that the play's story, which Shakespeare found in William Painter's 1566 Boccaccio, is rooted as deep in folklore as *Hamlet* with regard to its two main actions: the curing of the sick King and the capture of a reluctant lover, both to be performed by the Clever Gretel heroine. As a stage play it seems oddly constructed. In sharp contrast to *Hamlet,* *All's Well* does little to exploit its dramatic opportunities. Except for the formalized court scenes of Helena's marriage choice and Bertram's final submission, its climaxes take place off stage and are only talked about and reflected on. (Admittedly the bedding of Helena and Bertram could not be shown directly; it is nevertheless the story's decisive moment.) Toward the end Helena herself virtually disappears from the play. The court company all but stop thinking about her, and when she returns to complete the action she is given only three brief speeches, eleven and a half lines. It has frequently been argued that the text was composed in haste and bears obvious signs of negligence and patch-up; Dr. Johnson assumed this and described Shakespeare "hastening to the end of his play," abbreviating the dialogue and forcing an ending when matters had been stretched out quite far enough. Professor Dover Wilson, resolute in defending the integrity of Shakespeare's workmanship, simply decided that some low-minded, third-rate house collaborator was responsible for most of it.

But such views do not jibe with either the number or the character of the additions made to the Boccaccio frame. The important roles of the Countess and Lafew, the King's major speeches (orations really), and a subplot sturdy enough to become the core of Garrick's revision are all new material. Most important, the languge of the play is altogether distinctive and in its controlling idiom is remarkably sustained, in ways nicely fitted to the oddness of dramatic design. Indeed in what was for a long time the only performance of the play I had seen (Goodhart Hall, Bryn Mawr College, March 1963), the director's insistence on subordinating other business to a clear recitation of the Folio text strongly suggested that the problem of making *All's Well* effective on the stage is one of establishing its proper genre and dramaturgic intention. For if we take it as a kind of extended masque or pageant upon an explicit leading idea—a composition not addressed to strong dramatic excitements, yet less tilted toward allegory than the later "romances"—then the general manner of the play begins to find a good deal of justification. Its style, or voicing, embraces extremes of tone that Jonson would boldly combine in various masques and that were also emerging in Donne's new poetry of wit: stately heroic couplets, mostly end-stopped—a prosody used in *Hamlet*, apart from the "mousetrap," only for marking speech-endings and infrequently there—alongside the raciest vernacular, much of it spoken not by low life but by the high-stationed, virtue-bearing characters. Helena's own soliloquies have a riddling and introspective character that mirrors certain sequences given to Hamlet, whose warmth and courtesy in issuing instructions to his friends she also attractively commands.[8]

---

[8] A possible clue to how the play was originally conceived and understood is its classification in a 1656 catalogue of "all the Plaies that were ever printed" as an "Interlude." It is the only work attributed to Shakespeare which bears this designation: see Price, *The Unfortunate Comedy*, 76.

The fitness and integrity of the play's language have only recently begun to receive due emphasis in criticism. See, for example, Barbara Everett's excellent introduction to the New Penguin Shakespeare edition (1970), 11-13. But trust a poet not to have missed them:

> She preferred Racine to Shakespeare; I said I'd fix that
> & read her the King's cadenzas in *All's Well*
> about that jerk Bertram's father.
> —John Berryman, "Tea," *Love & Fame* (1970)

The major carrying style of the play—both in its graver passages and in those indulgently surveying that world of human misbehavior which is scorned, railed at, and sharply punished in the plays chronologically nearest it: *Hamlet, Troilus, Measure for Measure*—combines the sententious bareness of philosophic abstraction with a reconciling intimacy, and gathers to itself certain cool, philosophically subtle harmonies of a kind we hear in one of Donne's principal registers and in Marvell later in the seventeenth century, or, with Shakespeare himself, in the less pictorial of the sonnets. The characters regularly speak in a vocabulary of undecorated abstractions—time, hope, knowledge, sense, mortality, honor, wisdom, folly, nature, justice, also the "all" and "well" of the title; they generalize their reflections through an aphoristic "we" and "our," and are given to observing themselves in action or when about to act, like characters of Brecht's announcing their own typifying qualities. So the King, checked by Bertram's refusal of Helena, first raises the appropriate verbal placard ("My honour's at the stake . . ./ I must produce my power": II. iii. 149-150) and only then starts issuing reprimands and fresh decrees.

It is thus fairly in keeping that the word "virtue" is sounded four separate times (along with one adjectival "virtuous") within the first hundred lines of the play. Each time it has a different resonance. The blend in these opening uses repeats in miniature the range of meanings active in *Hamlet*. The sense of chastity is not immediately introduced; but that off-color argument about virginity between Helena and Parolles which began to be embarrassing sometime in the later eighteenth century, and which opens with a trope about blowing things up that equals anything in *Hamlet*, locks this vernacular meaning in place directly following those first hundred lines. There we have heard of "virtue" (1) as the King's personal offering to his subjects, whereby a widowed countess may find a surrogate husband and her son a second father; (2) as a name for those properties of personal being which, uncorrupted, generate goodness but when crossed with "an unclean mind" turn inward traitor; (3) as a positive force within Bertram of the same kind as the "important blood" he has inherited (III. vii. 21);

(4) as a soldierly courage which in some men will turn quite bloodless under an adverse wind. As the play progresses, the word effectively becomes—again as it does in *Hamlet*—the special property of the protagonist and of her devices for gaining her ends. The Countess's praise of Helena, seemingly dead, as "the most virtuous gentlewoman that ever nature had praise for creating" (IV. v. 9-10) tells us she is now to be recognized as, in life, a bearer and in some sense origin of all virtue. It is a role Helena herself has already casually assumed, when she formally wishes "a fair and virtuous mistress" to each of the Lords she does *not* take as husband (II. iii. 57-58), and reaffirms when she extracts needed assistance from one of the King's men, saying, "I put you to/ The use of your own virtues" (V. i. 15-16). And it is, of course, the role defining her initial entrance into the central action of the play: the physician's daughter from the borderlands of the realm with her life-restoring, kingdom-steadying medicines.

Virtue in use, virtue as a force linked to natural secrets and working the most potent effects, virtue as both champion and prize in a contest of powers where personal character and dynastic kingdoms are alike tested for their resistance to corruption and life itself rallies against the attack of death: this is what *All's Well* is "about," the ground of meaning on which it joins its chronological partner *Hamlet*. (Both, we notice, open with the occasion of mourning, the figures of greatest virtue dressed in black, and with a casting about for the proper means of recovery.) They would be an excellent pair of plays to alternate in repertory—a highly practical idea, as it happens, since *All's Well* very nearly reproduces the main cast of *Hamlet*; you could give your Hamlet a needed rest on the odd night and let the others in your main company move across to precisely corresponding roles.

There is the French King, who has all Claudius's power but, once cured, has it all for the good. Gertrude of *Hamlet* becomes the Countess of *All's Well*, again mother to the disturbed young lord of the play; mother also, by self-election, to its true protagonist. That young lord, Bertram, slips over into the good-bad Laertes role, falling into just those young-ruffian scandals abroad that Polonius outlines in advance to Reynaldo (*Hamlet*: II. i. 17-71) and coming to the same decisive last-minute repentance. Even the Ghost is spectrally present, as Bertram's dead father, whose commemorated virtue, and sorrow at current derelictions, overshadow the rising generation (I. ii. 26-63). Meddling Polonius becomes the antic Lafew, precise custodian of reputations and the rules of behavior; the gravedigger is now the Countess's clown, whose comparably Saturnian wit, though it produces answers that "serve all men" and "fit all questions" (II. ii. 13-20), leads him to choose at last "the house by the narrow gate" (in his touching final speech: IV. v. 50-52); while Parolles combines and pulls back toward the center of the play the affectation of Osric, the supervisory duties of Reynaldo, and the initial bellicosity of young Fortinbras. Diana of Florence is a faithful Horatio in assisting the protagonist, and Helena herself an Ophelia transposed to the very center of things and made a free, self-determining agent (though sharing with Ophelia the burden of loving someone "out of [her] star"). Her *alegrìa* is at the opposite corner from Hamlet's melancholy but like it is subject to imputations of unwarranted ambition—she brings them against herself (I. i. 90; III. iv. 5)—until her graciousness in action proves them false. Like Hamlet, Helena appears to us as a deviser of corrective plots and a maker of valuable actions, one who invents life and fortune as she goes. In curing the King she works with such instruments as were bequeathed to her. Thereafter her remedies are all drawn from her own resources, and it is with these that she accomplishes the promise of the play's title—the same formulaic promise, incidentally, made twice in *Hamlet*, where, as we hear it spoken first by Claudius ("All may be well"; III. iii. 72) and then by mad Ophelia ("I hope all will be well": IV. v. 68), it patently is not fulfilled.[9]

---

[9] There are several odd echoes of this sort. One of Ophelia's songs is about someone wearing "cockle hat and staff," emblems worn by pilgrims to that shrine of St. James Compostela where Helena pretends to have gone. With the cue of Helena's name the clown Lavatch begins singing ironically about the

There are also correspondences in primary theme. The main
complex of themes in *All's Well* may be stated fairly briefly,
though their articulation is continuous in the play's taut push
of argument. Virtue, defined in itself as a full creaturely integrity and in its effects as a life-restoring potency, is at the center
of a cluster of related ideas: civil probity, as against courtier's
affectation; honor and honesty, as against self-division and
self-betrayal; fulfillment of being according to "nature" or
"kind";[10] a savory health or harmony in persons and in states;
true as against false ways of inheriting; generative as against
sterile sexuality; and finally a power of self-engendering life
that answers to providence but makes its own way before, and
holds time and nemesis at bay by claiming for itself no more
than what is lawfully its own (I. iii. 102-105; II. v. 79-82).

Helena is the main bearer of these arguments, although
nearly everyone in the play, even the miscellaneous French
lords enlisted for the foreign wars, speaks pointedly to one or
another of them. She herself must first establish her essential
"honesty," and this is complicated insofar as she admits to
being a climber to a higher astrological as well as societal
sphere (I. i. 85-89) and a familiar of very mysterious potions
and powers. That Shakespeare, in locating her "virtue," was
alluding directly to the technical business of Hermetic magic
and Paracelsian alchemy is beyond question. Helena explains
to the wary King that her magus-father particularly impressed
on her the value of a recipe embodying the "triple eye" wisdom
of Hermes Trismegistus (II. i. 105-109); in the scholarly era of
Frances Yates and company, who can doubt the form and
pressure of that designation? The whole rising action of the
play turns on a series of alchemical and medicinal metaphors.

---

same episode in the matter of Troy, Priam's death, which Hamlet will ask the
first Player to recite.

[10] The explicitly sexual sense of both words is well established and persists
in out-of-the-way precincts. Among a scattering of seventeenth-century locu-
tions in the speech of "Nate Shaw" (b. 1885), the unlettered black-American
autobiographer of *All God's Dangers* (ed. Theodore Rosengarten [1974]), is
the term "nature-course," for the sexual act itself.

The ailing King fears prostitution by "empirics" (II. i. 119-122), but Helena, for whose virtues the Countess has claimed from the beginning the improving quality of "simpleness" (I. i. 44), assures him that her practices derive from "simple sources" (II. i. 139-140). Being expert in such matters, her astrological banter with Parolles over the precise "composition" of *his* "virtue" (I. i. 190-205) is in no way surprising.[11]

The King receives Helena like a love-applicant, answering her suit with the promise of a husband. When he recovers, he more than recovers. Lafew reports that he is now "lustier" than "your dolphin" (II. iii. 26: no doubt the standard English joke about how it is in France). Sexuality and its right resolution is front and center in *All's Well*, very much as in "The Phoenix and the Turtle," though of course our inert clinical word for the matter was not in Shakespeare's vocabulary. The vaudeville routine of Helena's first exchange with Parolles—in which virginity is threatened with the fate either of being sat down before and blown up or of rotting into itself like a mite-infested cheese (I. i. 110-164)—breaks off in an astonishing ten-line aria about what thing it is that a true lady offers her lord; something that is itself "a thousand loves" and a whole family-commonwealth-cosmos of benefactors (one of them a phoenix) that will keep him on edge until he is destroyed with sweetness and then comfort him with a festival of silly love names (I. i. 165-176—and is the text here possibly less corrupt than editors have assumed?). She sets a just value on her virginity yet without that disturbing insistence which touches, at least to our ears, Isabella's talk in *Measure for Measure*. So it

---

[11] Typically this Hermetic-Paracelsian motif is repeated with comic emphasis. Against the King's suspiciousness Lafew evokes medicines whose "simple touch" would raise King Pippen (dead a mere eight hundred years) and make Charlemagne himself write love letters to this Helena, this "Doctor She" (II. i. 72-80). With Bertram and Parolles, Lafew laments the neglect of these genuine arts by latter-day "philosophical persons" (II. iii. 1-24)—persons in historical fact who, in another dozen years, with Isaac Casaubon's learned exposure of the fraudulence of the Hermetic texts, will successfully undermine this last stronghold of the old science.

is Helena herself who identifies virginity as the "white death" that might "sit on [one's] cheek for ever" (II. iii. 71), and she cheerfully, womanfully, surrenders it when the time comes, a time she herself has adroitly contrived. Virginity is for her like the arts and medicines she commands, a gift rather than a possession, and this is what ennobles her, even though she dismisses the matter by characterizing herself as one who "cannot choose/ But lend and give," in the role life has provided her (I. iii. 214-215). In folklore terms she is the play's donor-figure, and she is also its regenerative scion; in both respects she displaces the male agent—the King, young Bertram—normally assigned these functions.

"I am not an imposture," she alertly pleads (II. i. 155), but she can play parts and work what the Elizabethans called "practices" as effectively as any. When she overcomes the King's *ex officio* resistance, it is by ascending, first, into language of high Christian piety (II. i. 136-154) and then into sybilline incantation (II. i. 160-168) of a kind that T. S. Eliot, faced in *The Cocktail Party* with the same dramatic need to move his verse into a richer register, had to borrow from Shelley; later she pronounces a spell for Bertram's safety specially compounded from the elements of lead, fire, and air (III. ii. 108-iii). This matter of role-playing and possible imposture is the marrow of her interesting link to Parolles in the play, who is in more than one way her antitype; for besides being a figure always getting ready to act but never acting, Parolles is the broad-comedy carrier of that disease of affectation from which all France is allegedly suffering. This disease surfaces in a style of absurdly mannered talk among Bertram and his friends (of the kind Hamlet plays at with Osric), and so Bertram's part, too, fits into the theme of integrity, of living in false or true relation to one's proper self—living, as we might say, away from one's natural virtue.[12]

---

[12] A suspicion that even the heroine may be infected is characteristically acknowledged by Helena herself. The Countess says to her (just as Claudius and Gertrude complain to Hamlet), you grieve too much for your father, people will think you are merely affecting this sorrow. Helena's answer, virtually a

Parolles, in keeping with his name, is all words and no body. His soul is his clothes, Lafew says, a nut without a kernel (II. v. 43-44), and he occasions some of the trimmest wit in the play. His anti-eponymic "I love not many words" (III. vi. 84), after Bertram accepts his claim to be a man of action, is struck off his much-noted Falstaff side. But Lavatch's superb riposte to his patronizing "Go to . . . I have found thee"—"Did you find me in yourself, sir, or were you taught to find me?" (II. iv. 32-34)—enters a comic dimension more purely Parolles' own, and the play's. For he is also the occasion for serious projections of the play's major themes, above all the theme of an existential integrity and health. "Is it possible," First Lord asks, that such a man "should know what he is, and be that he is" (IV. i. 44-45); a question which, two quick scenes later, joins itself to the Lords' head-shaking over Bertram's misbehavior, when First Lord exclaims, "As we are ourselves, what things we are! " and Second Lord replies, "Merely our own traitors," streams overflowing ourselves into vileness (IV. iii. 19-25). When trapped, Parolles is not merely exposed as a stock *miles gloriosus*. In a veritably Brechtian or Beckettesque turn he develops a bottom-of-the-barrel pathos and dignity, within his unchanging nature, that bypass the whole dubious military and court world and become the sharp shadow of Helena's formally tested worthiness. Threatened with hanging, Parolles pleads, "My life, sir, in any case! . . . in a dungeon, i' th' stocks, or any where, so I may live" (IV. iii. 241-245). From the main action of both these plays (for it fits the world of *Hamlet*, too) he draws an argument that takes all the edge off his humiliation—"Who cannot be crushed with a plot?" (IV. iii. 325)—and moves on to an oddly touching self-reconcilement: "Cap-

---

précis of Hamlet's to the King and Queen, is also her first speech in the play: "I do affect a sorrow indeed, but I have it too"—a riddle she explains a moment later in a way seemingly to her discredit. She is not thinking of her father, she has quite forgot him (of course she hasn't; she holds his most precious bequest in her pocket), her imagination is now all on the apparently unattainable Bertram (I. i. 48-58, 79-83). The dramatic correspondence of this scene to the opening of the first court scene in *Hamlet* is manifest.

tain I'll be no more/ . . . Simply the thing I am/ Shall make me live."

> Safest in shame! Being fooled, by foolery thrive!
> There's place and means for every man alive.
> (IV. iii. 330-339)

That at least is honesty, and it is aimed in the right direction: the maintaining, the continuance (to each in his own way) of life itself, or of the real thing within that makes life. For the bearer of genuine virtue something more is required. Yet what this is lives by the same logic. Parolles' new ethic is that morally equivocal one described in chapter II (above pp. 51-52): living according to one's given nature, whatever that happens to be.[13] Quite remarkably Helena herself has a major speech to the same point. "Say thy prayers," Parolles has curtly ordered her (going on to provide a formula for the trap she will eventually set for Bertram: "Get thee a good husband, and use him as he uses thee": I. i. 213-215). Her soliloquy in response anticipates, for all differences of tone and context, the disturbing self-reliance asserted by Edmund and Iago; she takes up Parolles' first recommendation here precisely as Edmund takes up Gloucester's maundering about the influence of the stars, and Iago Roderigo's complaint that what is sensual in his constitution must determine his behavior. No, she says, appealing to higher powers is proper but it is only supplementary. We ourselves have the shaping of our lives and fortunes:

> Our remedies oft in ourselves do lie,
> Which we ascribe to heaven. The fated sky
> Gives us free scope, only doth backward pull
> Our slow designs when we ourselves are dull.
> (I. i. 216-219)

---

[13] Helena has seen from the first that some such perverse harmony of being is constitutional with Parolles. His vices, she remarks, are his principle of life; they "sit so fit in him" that they will stand by him and hold him together when all soldierly valor has bled away (I. i. 102-104).

Our "slow" designs: Helena possesses all along the perfected patience, the fitness of means to purpose, that Hamlet
stormily advances to. Since she intends, the Countess prophe-
sies, to claim "only as much love as she finds," "[t]here is more
owing her than is paid, and more shall be paid her than she'll
demand" (I. iii. 102-105). "I wait upon his will," she says in
reply to Bertram's initial rejection (II. iv. 54); I'll "eke out"
what "my homely stars" have so far confined me to (II. v. 74-
76); and it is because she neither "persecute[s] time with
hope," as the King had done under his doctors' regimen (I. i.
14-15), nor too hastily "answer[s] the time of request," as Parolles had urged in the matter of virginity (I. i. 155), that in the
crisis—and this is our last view of her until the rapid close—
"though time seems so adverse and means unfit," she carries
on at just that pace of action and effort which her own means
are best suited to (V. i. 25-35). The clinching lines here are difficult to paraphrase efficiently but are decisive to our formed
sense of her qualities, and not less so for the echo of Parolles'
words two scenes earlier:

> I will come after you with what good speed
> Our means will make us means [i.e., the means to
>   maintain or continue with].

Helena's work in the play has been, through an inventive
constancy and perseverance, to give dramatic substance to a
line from her confident early speech about freedom and fate—
"Who ever strove/ To show her merit, that did miss her love?"
(I. i. 226-227): a line too often singled out as summing up the
whole story. (By itself it sounds morally wishful.) If there is any
concrete occurrence that makes the callow Bertram begin to
seem worthy of her—and this has been an interpretive sticking
point, despite the not inconsiderable details of his rank, good
looks, and reported "honourable service" in the wars—it is
that he, too, within the perverse license of comedy, has exhib-
ited remarkable constancy, though with the wrong lady.
(Originally he was one of those " 'younger spirits . . . whose

constancies/ Expire before their fashions' ' ": his own father's complaint, as the King remembers hearing it: I. ii. 60-63.) The mother of Florentine Diana—the plot's admirably helpful and self-possessed "other woman"—remarks that this Bertram "persists" in his suit "[a]s if his life lay on't" (III. vii. 41-43), and he himself affirms what under the right circumstances would be exactly the right thing: "Say thou art mine, and ever/ My love, as it begins, shall so persever" (IV. ii. 36-37).[14]

Helena all along has felt sure of Bertram's native honor and of the promise of steadiness in him. He has "important blood," she points out (III. vii. 21), taking that as a weight in the behavioral scales which may be counted on. Here, too, her consciousness of the play of energies and forces outpaces, in the event, the wisdom of any particular utterance about them. One of (to us) the most attractive arguments advanced in *All's Well*, as in the great central oration by the King on what virtue and honor really are (II. iii. 117-144), is that the act or property itself creates the value we give it, not the title or pedigree—if you took our bloods, the King says, and mixed them up, you would quite confound ordinary distinction of persons. Yet like any folklore-rooted comedy (consider *Tom Jones*) *All's Well* is quite unembarrassed about having the moral point both ways, and we see that true virtue never hesitates to effect its natural alliance with fine blood.[15] Helena's dower to her unready husband, in this play about the beauty and yet Machiavellian te-

---

[14] Bertram's final couplet accepting Helena is critically notorious for appearing to make his submission dependent on still further disclosures:

> If she, my liege, can make me know this clearly,
> I'll love her dearly, ever, ever dearly.
> (V. iii. 315-316)

But I see no reason not to read that "if" as adjunctive ("seeing that she has made all this clear to me") rather than conditional ("only if she can convince me of the truth of this"), which shifts right around both sense and tone. The lines, moreover, double the rhymed "ever" of Bertram's earlier vow to Diana.

[15] Such overdetermination, we recall, is constitutional to natural existence, though it is also a great part of what makes natural existence eternally problematic to reason and judgment.

nacity of life's essential renewal, is thus not only her own rare virtue. It is also to have brought to active life in him his birthright male inheritance ("flame" and "oil": I. ii. 59) from that exemplary father of his, whom the King has so particularly eulogized.

But except for Helena's forthright and poetically telling avowal that when, that once, they lay together she found him "wondrous kind" (V. iii. 309-310: again, the sexual sense in unmistakable), Bertram's coming to virtue is still mostly a promise as the play ends. If he makes the grade, it will be Helena's doing, just as the whole play—the curing of the King, the accomplishment of the tasks, the setting out of a frame of argument in which even the farce of Parolles gains an exemplary logic and seriousness—is chiefly Helena's doing. The action is, to our eyes, as the chief character's peculiar virtue has had power to make it. Two last words on this point. The first is by G. Wilson Knight, a little carried away by the play's lovely spirituality but as always acutely perceptive in following the text, who said of Helena what, since Romanticism, has traditionally been said of the character of Hamlet above all others: "Her consciousness functions on the plane of Shakespearean poetry itself" ("The Third Eye," in *The Sovereign Flower* [1958], 143). The second is Lafew's, who first persuaded the suffering King to try his luck with Helena on the grounds of her amazing "wisdom, and constancy" (II. i. 84) and to the end plays out his role as the play's registrar of values. " 'Twas a good lady, 'twas a good lady," he says, when Helena is thought dead: "We may pick a thousand sallets ere we light on such another herb." To which the oracular Lavatch replies, "Indeed, sir, she was the sweet-marjoram of the sallet, or, rather, the herb of grace" (IV. v. 13-17).[16] No hyperbole, it seems, would be too extravagant, but one which is both homely and transcendent is taken to be the most fitting.

---

[16] The exchange sets up one more intimation of essential meanings. Five stage minutes later Lafew is back using, with characteristic double entendre, the same words for Dame Fortune, "who of herself is a good lady and would not have knaves thrive long under her" (V. ii. 29-32).

~

What is true of Helena under comedy's free and generous privilege also holds for the hero of *Hamlet*. That quality in Shakespeare which nineteenth-century adulation assigned him
above all other authors, his godlike power of origination, is
singularly active in Hamlet's part, and it is made palpable in
the two standard ways: in what we see him doing and, of
course, saying, and in what is said about him by everyone else.
In the pulsations of the play's clash of "fell and mighty opposites," Hamlet generates the developing action in ways that
Claudius himself particularly identifies. A series of speeches
through the middle scenes both confirm the sense of Claudius's
shrewdness and determination and, rising in intensity, testify
dramatically to Hamlet's advance. It is the King who dismisses
the Polonius-Gertrude notion that Hamlet is merely lovesick;
it is the King again who first names that "something in his
soul" which hints of danger, and at once decides on his exile to
England (III. i. 162-175). After the "mousetrap" is sprung,
Claudius's apprehensiveness grows expectably sharper. For a
while he still raps out orders and determines policy, yet all in
defensive reaction against a counterforce that scene by scene is
felt as gathering fresh strength. That "something" in Hamlet's
soul is now, to the King, a general "hazard" that "doth hourly
grow/ Out of his brows"; it is a "fear. . . . [w]hich now goes
too free-footed" (III. iii. 6-7, 25-26: note again the bodily substance these phrases are given). With the killing of Polonius,
Claudius's words for Hamlet grow audibly more frantic and
move toward the climaxing image of the hectic in his own
blood, an expressive run that starts with a line which, stepping
up into abstraction yet keeping colloquial speed and directness, can be heard as choric for the whole play—"His liberty is
full of threats to all" (IV. i. 14). It gives us another strong clas-
sifying word for what from the first has drawn imagination
after the vivid hero.[17]

[17] Twice again Claudius invokes the liberty and moral authority gathering to
Hamlet as the play proceeds, and acts with Machiavellian resourcefulness to

For the character Hamlet is, or has become, a free unitary force attacking us everywhere with the consciousness that the world is indeed a booming, buzzing system of "occasions," all capable of "informing" against whatever agent or focus of action is in the ascendant. This unitary force is the outward manifestation of the prince's *virtue*, in our root sense, and it has, in relation to conventional moral wisdom, the appropriate ambiguity. Princely virtue of a copybook kind is also directly claimed for Hamlet: those courtier's, scholar's, soldier's qualities listed by Ophelia as lost in him through madness, and the nobility and sweetness, according to Horatio, and capacity for soldierly kingliness, according to Fortinbras, that are lost in his death. More inwardly, his virtue is associated with that famous melancholy of his—and the verbal evidence is there, dramatically accented, to indicate that Shakespeare, reworking the component of madness in the protagonist bequeathed him by tradition, was thinking directly of the properties and effects of natural melancholy according to reinforced sixteenth-century thinking on the subject.[18] The Warburg Institute scholars have spelled out with particular emphasis the conjunction, in Renaissance ideas of melancholy, of medieval sloth or acedia with Greek conceptions of the character of creative genius and heroic accomplishment—see especially R. Klibansky, F. Saxl, E. Panofsky, *Saturn and Melancholy* (1964); the key passage in Aristotle's *Problemata* is given on pp. 18-29. As regards one tough old problem in Hamlet's behavior, his harshness with Ophelia, a solution along these lines (or at least a further com-

---

turn them to his own advantage. In an oral memorandum on his realm's woes he specifies to Gertrude that Hamlet is to be considered the "most violent author/ Of his own just remove" (i.e., his dispatch to England under a death warrant: IV. v. 80-81). In plotting the fencing match Claudius points out that Hamlet will not be likely to inspect the foils for poison, being himself "most generous, and free from all contriving" (IV. vii. 134-36). This last detail Claudius knows is not true as regards himself, but it remains something to be counted on in all other respects.

[18] Bridget Gellert Lyons, *Voices of Melancholy* (1971), has a chapter on the centrality of the ideology of melancholy to both dialogue and plot in Hamlet. See also Laurence Babb, *The Elizabethan Malady* (1951).

plication) may be offered. The melancholy temperament, as it
enters its special estate of madness, suffers a hot-cold intensi-
fication of lust; in particular it fears the cold despondency after
sex that follows on the loss of warm fluid and propulsive air;
thus, to retreat from sexuality would be, to a mind tormented
by melancholy, a first-order act of self-defense, and recom-
mending life in a nunnery would not necessarily be totally unsympathetic or hostile. Some such argument might also apply
to Hamlet's tirades to his mother against bed games.[19]

But in the general progression of the play, our main sense of
Hamlet's *virtue* does not depend on notation of this kind. It is
established dramatically, and poetically. In action it is that
quickness of response and, to the end, unexhausted resourcefulness—his soliloquies berating himself for failing to act are,
after all, major dramaturgic actions—which come forward as
soon as Horatio tells him about his father's ghost (in dialogue
Granville-Barker rightly praised for acceleration and nervous
drive) and which in the last crisis are still the means he acts
with. Pasternak, whose criticism of Shakespeare is unrivaled in
our century, describes Hamlet's characterization as first of all
a matter of rhythm, a musical progression in which "the very
pulse of his being seems to be made audible" ("Translating
Shakespeare," in *I Remember*, tr. Manya Harari [1959], 129).
This progression comes over the play whenever Hamlet enters.
His frequent doublets and triplets are the simplest form of it
("Thrift, thrift, Horatio!" or "Words, words, words"); more

---

[19] By the middle of the play Claudius, too, may be suffering from melancholy—the tyrant's melancholy. His sluggish thoughts are earthbound, cannot
follow his heaven-directed words.

Lore about melancholy may support other details in the Ophelia passages.
Walking in the sun, usually understood as risking conception, is also standard
therapy for cold melancholy, an affliction Hamlet would hope she might be
spared ("Let it not happen that she, too, must walk in the sun and show herself
prey to such conceptions as have overtaken me"). Other traditional cures for
melancholy, still alive in Keats's mind two hundred years later, are to feed
"deep, deep" on one's raving mistress's "peerless eyes" and to glut melancholy
on flowers, which absorb tears as they absorb rain. Or was Keats, in the *Ode*,
directly remembering, synthesizing, the *Hamlet* details?

generally, it is a propulsion of voice either forward or in an abruptly different direction, as if into another key, as his thought continually expands its "reach" and "range."[20] As a quality of personality it combines energy and courage—compare Horatio's faltering response to the Ghost's entrance in I, i to Hamlet's in I. iv and I. v—and that rapidity of judgment and rich decisiveness of speech (an unusual amount of it, for heroic drama, in the play's agile prose) which set Hamlet apart from every other character. Most typically it is felt as a moving out to meet, to absorb, to continue beyond the occasions which activate it.

And it is repeatedly a matter of vivid dramatic action and contrast. Among all the others who take their places and follow their course in the play—with outreaching force, like Claudius, or with pitiful self-absorption, like Ophelia—it is Hamlet himself who acts with steadily increasing adequacy

---

[20] A half-hidden but traceable motif, about moving across the entire frame of human experience and then breaking beyond it, speaks to this fundamental design. It begins early: Hamlet immediately sees that whatever the Ghost's embassy means, our thoughts will be driven in its presence "beyond the reaches of our souls" (I. iv. 56).Claudius's stress on the free ranging of Hamlet's madness (III. iii. 2) and his words about Hamlet's dangerous "liberty" extend this motif; Polonius contributes vulgar reductions about "taints of liberty" and the "flash and outbreak of a fiery mind" as regards Laertes (II. i. 32-33), also a casting "beyond ourselves" which is the present age's objectionable fashion (II. i. 111-114). Pasternak boldly responded to it, playing on the literal sense of "ecstasy," in picturing Hamlet's "manner of staring into the distance of the unknown whence his father's ghost once summoned him and where it may at any moment speak again."

The accompanying poetic rhythm is one that can be active in the dialogue when Hamlet himself is not—though the most concentrated instance of this involves the character most in sympathy with Hamlet and occurs in the one scene prior to Hamlet's own initial appearance. It comes with Horatio's lines in I, i, from the quick humor of "A piece of him" (in answer to "What, is Horatio there?") and the iterations of "Tush, tush" and "Speak, speak, I charge thee speak!" to the speech of his which effectively completes the scene and which T. S. Eliot picked out in the essay "Poetry and Drama" as a climactic instance of "musical design" running beneath all incidental poetic and dramaturgic effectiveness (*On Poetry and Poets* [1957], 76-77).

and freedom.[21] If the outward progression of the plot is toward the framing of a moment when the King's atrocious guilt is clear not only to Hamlet but to everyone else, so that action against him can proceed openly and freely and with, in political terms, a self-evident legitimacy (the design the old story has in both Saxo Grammaticus and Belleforest, fully explaining Hamlet's delays), the interior progression is the fashioning of a hero who will prove equal to that moment. So we see him, as the play develops, continuously in action. It is Hamlet alone who turns openly to everyone in his path and speaks warmly and fittingly to them all, the players, the courtiers, the soldiers on watch, the young men and scholars, the sea pirates (so we hear), and the churchyard rustics; who stands forth as a praiser of excellent men though always willing, out of the same precision of regard, to give the retort courteous or countercheck quarrelsome; who appears on the battlements, at sea, in the pit of graves, or out on frontiers where ignorant armies march by to death for an eggshell. In every case these are actions which, as he opens himself to the existence of others, authenticate him as a dramatic agent, a figure of responsive force, and equally as a pattern of the fit and seasoned ruler-designate, the soul of the continuing commonwealth. (Marjorie Garber touches on this aspect of the play, though only in terms of its hero's moral profile, noting how he subsumes the major qualities of those around him: "Like Laertes he can be gallant and impetuous; like Horatio, prudent and studious; like Fortinbras, princely and courageous; like the First Player, expressive and emphatic; like Old Hamlet, resolute and royal; even, like Claudius, unscrupulous and sly": *Coming of Age in Shakespeare* [1981], 201). So too it is Hamlet who in the play's voicing regularly lifts and extends the argument into the furthest structure and reason of things, as if fulfilling his own admonition:

[21] Harold Rosenberg also sees Hamlet as a framer of actions who becomes "historically" equal to the plot into which he is cast: "The Stages: Geography of Action," *Act and the Actor* (1970). See also Erich Auerbach's paragraph on *Hamlet* in *Mimesis*, tr. Willard Trask (1953), ch. xiii.

Sure He that made us with such large discourse,
Looking before and after, gave us not
That capability and godlike reason
To fust in us unus'd.
(IV. iv. 36-39)

To Pasternak again, Hamlet is never more himself, more alive
and potent—and Shakespeare is never grander—than when he
turns with violence and an oath against his friend Horatio (his
first decisive physical act in the play, it sets the form for his
last) and wrenches away to confront, and interrogate, the terrific image of his dead father:

O! all Shakespeare perhaps is simply in this:
That Hamlet converses freely with the Ghost.[22]

This Hamlet rhythm does not subside with the quieting into
patience of the last act. Its urgency and directness are still dominant in the charged verse of Hamlet's sea-tale to Horatio
opening the long final scene (V. ii. 4-55). Trimmed to prose, it
propels his extraordinary last words in private ("Not a whit;
we defy augury": V. ii. 219-224—a speech of staggering clarity
and dramatic beauty). And it continues undiminished to the
moment of his death (V. ii. 332-358). The consequence is an
ending which, though littered with dead bodies, seems to me
different in feeling from the end of any other tragedy of Shakespeare's. That difference is consubstantial with the ascending
authority—moral, civil, dramatic—of the hero himself.

---

[22] The lines climax the poem "To Briusov," written in 1923 on the fiftieth
anniversary of the older poet's birth, in which Briusov's genius is imagined as
a "house-spirit" and surrogate father whose words rebuke the vulgar official
ceremonies in his honor and teach his living descendant not to submit child-
ishly to lies and unappeased grievances, yet not, despite adversities, to die
either—"it may be easier to live." The lines were quoted, but without reference
to the whole poem, by Andrei Sinyavsky, "On Boris Pasternak," *Encounter*
(April 1966), 49. In the Russian original the second line ends with its periodic
weight falling on the word "Hamlet: "That with utmost simpleness speaks out
freely with the Ghost Hamlet." I am grateful to Rachel K. B. Douglas for supplying, and translating, the full text of the poem.

Great tragedy ends, we are told, with the sense of a terrible reduction in the human force that has acted and suffered before us, a reduction also of the prospects that remain. The ending of *King Lear* is the great instance in English, and Edgar's last couplets express it with the utmost spareness: "We that are young/ Shall never see so much, nor live so long." *Coriolanus* ends with a dead march, *Antony and Cleopatra* in cold Octavian severity, *Othello* with heavy hearts and its demidevil strangely unsubdued, *Macbeth* with a bloody head on a pike and the diversionary relief that goes with the extermination of a butcher. *Hamlet* ends instead on a crisp half-line, with clear martial orders and a fresh peal of guns. The scene is "dismal," as the English ambassador says, and terrible explanations remain to be given, though now it is only the "unknowing world" that requires to be told "how these things came about"; the actors, the audience, know all. The real hectic or poison at large in the play has been fully purged and in the one way possible, by a counteragent whose sum of virtue is unreduced by it even as it stops his breath; a new regime is mandated to succeed, one that has been visible on the fringes of the play all along, undergoing its own parallel discipline of preparation; and the hero himself has accomplished his mission and passed on to future times a legacy of virtue which is now formally completed and made unassailable by the seal of princely legitimacy.[23] At last he rules, though now (like Mar-

---

[23] In an uncut performance, the Fortinbras passages take their place in what plays as a tragedy of the rising generation (the class of '98 at Wittenberg, so to speak). By the end Rosencrantz, Guildenstern, Ophelia, Laertes, and Hamlet are dead, and Horatio has been kept back from suicide only to serve as bearer of their story to the world—but Fortinbras remains to assume directly from Hamlet himself the "readiness" to act and command in every appropriate way. Arguments that he, too, is a usurper and that Hamlet has bumblingly delivered over the kingdom to a hostile power come from considerations outside the articulated world of the play.

So in the main do psychoanalytic interpretations, which tend to cut away the political and dynastic dimension of the play's system of meanings. What Ernst Kris identified in the character Hamlet as "a dangerously submissive attitude to his idealized father" (quoted in Garber, *Coming of Age*, 200) can as

vell's sea-embroiled hero) "in story only," having recovered a space where his father's and the realm's terrific ghost can rest and be silent—and having in the process historically altered, by advancing it in self-apprehension, European imaginative consciousness.

---

well be taken as a legitimating respect for the principle of authority he will himself be called on to embody; an office as difficult to accommodate, perhaps, as that of "heaven's justicer" but as vital a test of fully realized virtue.

CHAPTER FOUR

"What Do Other Men Matter to the Passionate Man?": *The Charterhouse of Parma*

". . . when men and women did her bidding, they did it not only because she was beautiful, but because that beauty suggested joy and freedom."
—Yeats, "The Trembling of the Veil," V, iv

With a new chapter and a new text it is worth restating main positions. First: the great subject of literature—the subject of subjects—is virtue, in the root sense of primary human capacity or potency; a property of being which can be realized in collective and communal form as well as in exemplary individuals but which in either case will be different in kind from teachable moral goodness (even when understood as the realizing force within any such goodness). Second: as virtue in this root sense regularly eludes the expectations of scheduled understanding, the most affecting representations of it in literature may be correspondingly problematic to critical reason. They will seem more or less of an embarrassment, or worse, to school philosophies—if only by surpassing philosophy in their appeal to creaturely assent, to our participatory grasp of experience itself.

These propositions seem suspiciously well illustrated by Stendhal, not only because of his tenderness as a writer to the sheer anarchy of human personality or his self-advertising assertion that "it is almost impossible to write well without recalling at least indirectly truths that are a mortal offense to power" (*Promenades dans Rome*, entry for October 20,

1828). Stendhal is also that classic modern writer of whom one admiring critic can say, as regards his greatest novel, that the author himself "does not believe in the story he is telling," and another, that the formal scheme of *The Charterhouse of Parma* is so "patchy"—"really little more than six or seven *bravura* scenes" arbitrarily connected by the barest sort of "functional narrative," the "rickety machinery" of cloak-and-dagger melodrama—that rather than catching you up in a convincing imitation of human life, it continually makes you ask, why *do* I go on with it? what is it that keeps me "wanting to know what happens next in this scattered work?"[1]

The *Charterhouse* lends itself even better to an exploration of what really happens between writers and readers if I take account of my own most recent experience of the book. As I came back to it for a new trial of working principles, it seemed substantially different from the book I had been counting on. It seemed more disturbing in its performative license, less affectively appealing. (For one thing it fairly literally confirmed, this time, the remark attributed to the Canon's nephew in Stendhal's preface "To the reader": "have a care! this story is anything but moral. . . .") It disconcertingly resisted much of what I thought I wanted to say of it. A sort of celebratory ap-

---

[1] The first judgment is Nicola Chiaromonte's in *The Paradox of History: Stendhal, Tolstoy, Pasternak and Others* (1971), 19; the second is Michael Wood's in *Stendhal* (1971), 158, 174, 177. There is a singular readability about critical writing on Stendhal, which rarely fails to take on some part of its subject's distinctive charm and imaginative élan. Among readily accessible titles the following may also be recommended: Robert M. Adams, *Stendhal: Notes on a Novelist* (1959); Margaret Tillett, *Stendhal: The Background to the Novels* (1971); Geoffrey Strickland, *Stendhal: The Education of a Novelist* (1974); Robert Alter, *A Lion in Love* (1979); Jean Prévost, *La Création chez Stendhal* (1942); Jean Pierre Richard, *Stendhal et Flaubert: littérature et sensation* (1959); Gérard Genette, "Stendhal," *Figures II* (1969); and the relevant chapters in Erich Auerbach, *Mimesis* (1953), Martin Turnell, *The Novel in France* (1950), Harry Levin, *The Gates of Horn* (1963). The great scholarly reconstruction of the Stendhalian universe is Henri Martineau's, in a lifetime of explorations and improved editions. Everyone in or out of France who writes on Stendhal is necessarily in his debt.

proach I had had in mind, though with due qualifications, began to seem inappropriate.

But such an experience is as instructive, critically, as any
other. In this instance it may reflect not simply one particular
reader's normal changeableness.[2] There may well be something volatile and elusive in the character of the book itself;
something perhaps common to all Stendhal's writing and registered in the exceptional amount of lively and free-ranging
commentary he has received and goes on receiving. It is as if,
no matter how many good and true things have been said
about his rendering of human experience, or his own sensibility, or his discursive-aphoristic grasp of the forms of reality, he
retains a power to surprise the next round of readers and to
convince them that something essential to the whole performance remains critically undefined; some *intrigue intérieure*
(Valéry's phrase) that has not yet been properly honored by
even his most fervent admirers. The greatest works of literature, Jean-François Revel has remarked, are indeed "like those
[great] queens who regularly had last night's lover executed at
daybreak"; that is, they are nothing if not punctual "in laying
out their periodic ration of stone-cold critical corpses" ("Fore-
word," *On Proust*, tr. Martin Turnell [1972]). If it is characteristic of most critical systems, as Revel goes on to say, that
they tend to make all the works to which they are applied too
much resemble one another, whereas art itself is at the core "a
matter of differences," then the *Charterhouse* may be that
most useful of offenses against imperializing critical perspectives in being a work that is fundamentally different, not to say
antithetical, with each new open-minded reading.

Different except (again to speak personally) in one central
respect. From my own first reading of it—I was seventeen and
simply fell in love both with its heroine and with the whole im-
pudent Stendhalian dream of a special gallantry and intoxica-

---

[2] Or unreliability. More basic, I suspect, than "unreliable narrators" to the
general problematic of prose fiction are unreliable readers, not least those who
read mainly on salary.

tion of life to be known and shared by some "happy few" (a party whose invitations to life-membership would surely arrive quite soon)—the book has always seemed oddly flawed in several important aspects (self-preening, morally careless, and in execution both cursory and repetitious) and yet irresistible as a whole, as well as in those six or seven bravura scenes. At the least it is a novel that compels anyone bent on critical system-building to maintain a flexibility sufficient to embrace these experienced differences, this power of resistance even to preconceptions it was itself initially responsible for.

~

One other thing remains as it has always been with the *Charterhouse*, and that is the brilliance and dash of its opening pages.[3] They have the synoptic efficiency of a Mozartean overture (which may indeed have been one of Stendhal's compositional models). From the first sentence—describing the entry of "that young army," already triumphant and commanded by a modern hero fully the equal of any known to the classical world, into (as it was for Stendhal) the sacred North Italian city of Milan, which immediately wakes up, like a princess of legend, from two and a half centuries of torpor and madly embraces a whole "new and passionate way of life"—a contest of values and energies is set in motion that spans the totality of active life. So we note how, moving from the Napoleonic drum-roll of that first sentence into details of private jokes circulated fifteen years later at the expense of powder-headed legitimists, the opening chapter systematically shows this conflict operating within each of the two great orders or spheres of *virtue* that Stendhal is concerned with and that I take all great literature to be concerned with: the civil or political, the virtue (or lack of it) of governors or their surrogates and of whole peoples and states, and the private or personal,

---

[3] Citations of the text of *The Charterhouse of Parma* are to the translation by C. K. Scott Moncrieff, completed in 1924.

the capacity for an inward release of passion and directed energy that each of us is, ideally, born to.

In that first chapter the "daring and genius" of the French liberators are said to restore overnight the innate gallantry of the Milanesi, who have been "enervated" by the long night of despotism and clerical repression and reduced to a shameful impotence, under the Austrians, by bargain-rate exemptions from military service. The gaiety and youth of this revolutionary army whose commanding general is understood to be, at twenty-seven, its oldest member bring a frenzy of happiness and pleasure into Lombardy. At once the population divides into two moral camps which remain divided through the ebb and flow of French and Austrian power during the next fifteen years and into the counterrevolutionary retrenchment following Leipzig in 1813. On the one side are the people of courage and gaiety, amiable in spirit, serene at heart, who are by nature lively, candid, and impulsive, and given to explosions of laughter at everything solemn or ridiculous; these are all qualities the novel's heroine in particular is invested with as soon as she is mentioned. (It is also specified that at the historical moment in question she is exactly as old as was Stendhal himself, a first sign of the author's personal stake in his story.) Those in this first party throw in their lot with the liberating army. They thus have the common people on their side. When Austrian repression returns, they quixotically give up fortune and security and take their stand, at whatever cost, with the now beleaguered forces of revolution. Against them are all those paralyzed by fear, or avarice, or invincible mediocrity, who cling to received doctrines and go on powdering their heads in order to set a forceful example of resistance to novelty and change. All who are "old, bigoted, and morose" flock to this second party, whose happiness comes when the police are out arresting every man of spirit within reach.

There is no question, in this archetypal liberal fantasy, which side the author and his readers, happy though few, are to be on.

But a novel which merely took sides in this self-privileging

way would become tiresome and dishonest, however buoy-
antly begun, and Stendhal did not write such a novel. In the
story he does unfold, the credit allowed his children of light is
by no means untarnished. Though the book begins in gaiety
and liberation, the narrative realities it ends with are of the
stuff of tragedy. The young lovers and their love-child are as
barrenly dead as the protagonists of *Romeo and Juliet*, and the
superb heroine has not only lost the particular happiness she
most cherished but has suffered the humiliation bound to be
most galling to her; it is not less galling because her own passionate recklessness has brought it about. She has also, in the
course of things, carried out an act of merely personal revenge—a state murder, no less—as barbarous as anything attempted by her retrograde enemies. Correspondingly her
lover, the adroit Count Mosca (whose age matches Stendhal's
when he was writing the novel; clearly the author distributes
himself among all three of the principal characters) has been
trapped by *his* special combination of political and personal
virtue, Machiavellian craftiness and schoolboy generosity, and
has made by his own standards amateurish errors of policy.[4] It
has been a point in Mosca's favor that he has decent regrets
about the execution of two liberals during his political apprenticeship as a Napoleonic officer in Spain, yet he has now got
sixty more honest patriots killed while suppressing a revolt
against Parma's tyrant prince, a revolt instigated and financed
by his own vengeful countess-to-be. On top of this we soon
hear him endorsing in so many words the chilling logic of the
Final Solution—his model is the St. Bartholomew massacre—
as a means of stabilizing the regime in power.

Thus the acts of revenge, murder, betrayal and self-betrayal
that stand in opposition, in this novel, to the ideal reign of gallantry and civilized pleasure are committed by the party of the
Happy Few as well as by their contemptible antagonists. That

[4] Robert M. Adams points out (228) that Mosca is said to be forty-five in
the year 1815 but fifty-six when the action comes to a crisis in 1821. The shift
confirms the critical point: Stendhal himself turned fifty-six in January 1839,
inscribing the preface with his exact birth date.

is a narrative reality which no amount of repetitious phrase-making about their gaiety and generosity, their turning radiant with passion or mad with joy, can paper over. These bitter, profoundly compromising events take place, moreover, not because some superior force of necessity requires them but because the most attractive characters make gratuitous mistakes, mistakes we are required to understand as the negligent overflow of their virtue.

Erich Auerbach, in his memorable account of Stendhal in *Mimesis*, proposed this moral equivocality as the measure of Stendhal's "modernness," describing him as the first important writer to incorporate fully into his treatment of character and event the modern, post-Revolutionary vision of reality itself as unstable and intrinsically changeable, and as continuously reacting upon men and women not simply by way of external nemesis (the old *fortuna* to which *virtù* stood opposed) but through an inward infirmity of being. As Auerbach observes, however, there is no historicism of the high nineteenth-century sort in this apprehension of things. Stendhal's characters are not the determined products of irreversible historical situations but free beings who leap into these situations through the force of their own desire, their own excited dream of life. An intuitively precise apprehension of the weight and pressure on individual spirits of modern high-speed societal changeability was beyond question a main part of Stendhal's actual power to reach those readers of 1885 or 1935 he pretended to be writing for; and improvising sociological explanations of human behavior amused him as much as identifying psychological patterns and reducing them to laws and maxims; but the vitality of his major characterizations is differently derived. It has to do rather with their full narrative freedom to create for themselves an individual destiny (a legacy in fiction that Gide and Proust, in their different ways, labored to maintain against an even more constricted future). The very capriciousness of these characters' struggle against external determination makes them perhaps even more representative of modern history's sustained assault on the human self. The silliness and waywardness of dramatic detail that even Stendhal's best writing lapses into are fairly subsumed within this broader narrative economy. Stendhal is one of the prime inventors of the modernist escape routes, in narrative design, of comic absurdity and of a disturbingly inverted anti-heroism. What Goethe learned as a novelist from Diderot and Sterne and what in Laclos and Sade is expressed (at least to my foreign ear) in the harshness of overinsistence, Stendhal registers casually, as if by instinct and simply for its own sake and for the pleasure he himself finds in it.

Stendhal, we know, came relatively late to the writing of his full-scale novels. He wrote them rapidly—the *Charterhouse* was dictated in seven or eight weeks (nine or ten, he told Balzac a year later: letter of October 16, 1840)—and made up the linkages and forwarding details of his borrowed plots as he went along, very much as his protagonists are shown contriving on the spur of the moment the sequences of their affairs. This atmosphere of improvisation, with all its risks to seriousness and coherence, seems to me fundamental to both the vitality of the narrative and the show of virtue in the principal characters. But the extraordinary mastery and originality of *The Red and the Black* and the *Charterhouse* are not likely to have materialized in thin air; and it is in certain writings in other modes more than in earlier attempts at fiction (such as *Armance* in 1827) that Stendhal's conception of the structure of human experience is tried out in full and given detailed, proto-narrative definition. The "physiology of love," as he called *De l'Amour* in 1822, is the first work in which human capacity is itself the main subject—that is, is addressed as such and not refracted through historical biography or art history or travel description.[5] In *De l'Amour* and again in the autobio-

---

[5] *De l'Amour* also sets out the expressive strategy he will follow in the novels, with its insinuating appeal to a certain kind of reader without whose imaginative collaboration the job of presenting and explaining his subject would be impossible to bring off. Readers who have not already experienced the master passion of love—it is suggested that they are the sad majority—will simply be made angry by this book (so he added in a second preface in 1834). They will

graphical *Henry Brulard*, written after *The Red and the Black*
but before *The Charterhouse of Parma*, the equivocal and contradictory character of all that men and women most intensely
desire, and the capacities which are the agency of such desiring, are as minutely registered as we find them to be in the major novels.

～

The description of love in the opening pages of *De l'Amour* reaffirms the central Socratic myth. Love is a "madness" of
being, a "soul-sickness" (first preface), or a distracting fever
that lifts us out of ourselves as if into an altogether different
sphere of existence (chs. iv, v).[6] It transforms spirit and sensibility as completely as the condition of grace supposedly transforms the soul in Christian thought. But as with grace this
completeness of inward transformation, as Stendhal presents
it, is combined with a certain indistinctness in the realm of ordinary consciousness. The mind is not simply moved by a
uniquely powerful emotion; it "becomes an emotion in itself"
(ch. xiv). Love brings pleasure through a fullness and intensity
of sensation, but also (as opposed to the emotions of sublim-
ity) through the intimacy of the relationships it sponsors (ch.
ii). Its spirit is "tender, generous, ardent," or (Stendhal adds)
"as it is commonly called, *romantic*" (ch. iii); actions undertaken in its spell have the charm of "unconstraint," of "a
boundless confidence and a sweet familiarity" (ch. vi). In this
way love is preeminently self-delighting. Those gifted with it
habitually endow its objects "with that imaginary charm of
which they have just discovered an inexhaustible supply
within themselves" (ch. xxii). Love's chief antagonists in life
are vanity (the "national passion" of the French) and that ter-

---

come "to suspect the existence of a form of happiness" which they have missed
and which modern life has made more and more difficult to get through to.

    [6] The best English version, followed here, is that "translated by H.B.V. un-
der the direction of C. K. Scott Moncrieff" and available in a Doubleday An-
chor edition (1957).

rible ego-pride which is actually fear—nothing else, Stendhal remarks, can explain "the horrors of M. de Sade's *Justine*" (ch. i). The passion of hatred, however, in the degree that it is spiritually justified (which frequently it is), is not a mighty opposite of love but a complementary force obeying similar laws of development (ch. vi).

Above all, love is a passion, a burning concentration of sensibility and imaginative attention that, as Stendhal extends his analysis, proves comparable also to the activity of mind of the world's supreme artists, for it is that one passion "all of whose developments are inherently beautiful" (ch. 1). At the same time it distorts perception: "The moment he falls in love, even the wisest man no longer sees anything as it really is." Bodily transformations take place—"an incipient madness, a rush of blood to the head, an upset of the nervous system and of the brain center"; as analogues Stendhal entertainingly proposes "the ephemeral courage of a stag and the train of thought of a soprano" (ch. xii). The first consequence of love is extreme quixotism in personal behavior. "Anything the lover imagines becomes actual reality so far as its effect on his happiness is concerned."[7]

The analogy here is not only to the absurdities of madness but to the behavioral ambiguities of artistic making; and in *Brulard* in particular Stendhal gives an account of the essential unbalance and exaggeration of the writer's mind that looks ahead to Flaubert's and modernism's myth of the writer as a unique species of behavioral monster. This analogy is borne out in the famous doctrine of *crystallization*, which, as presented in *De l'Amour*—beginning in the second chapter—divides into two distinguishable processes. It is the *modus operandi* by which love sets about working its intense effects; it is also that preexisting capacity of mind that makes this action possible. Crystallization thus has the same double character,

---

[7] Small wonder that the discovery of *Don Quixote*, in the gloom of *bien pensant* Grenoble, marked for the author of *Henry Brulard* "perhaps the greatest epoch in my life": *Vie de Henry Brulard*, ch. ix.

an intrinsic quality and an outgoing power, that the idea of *virtue* has persistently maintained in vernacular consciousness. It has also the same physicality. The action of crystallization is irresistible, and it is irresistibly expansive and accruent. Through it the mind, in love, absorbs into itself every new experience or observation that in any way touches this new inward determinant of thought and sensation; through it the mind can impose itself forcibly on the most difficult or apparently unpromising new circumstance.

For this reason crystallization proceeds continuously as long as passion itself continues (ch. vi). It also overreaches, doubling back on itself—and here we come directly to the potentially tragic equivocality at the heart of Stendhal's narrative vision (and the element of generative excess that regularly marks the operations of *virtue*). The lover's appetite for new proofs which will augment passion leads him to doubt the value, even the reality, of the proofs he has already acquired, and so what Stendhal calls "second crystallization" begins (ch. ii); perversely this becomes more important than the first, which so far has been wonderfully agreeable. But now the lover would rather dream of continuing at some time in the distant future to attract the woman he loves than receive from her in the present anything she can offer him (ch. iii). At this extremity crystallization becomes self-mutilation. Through a passion of doubt (and of compensation for doubt) matching its creativity step for step, it destroys portions of its own already achieved organization of life.[8]

The severe irony within this description incorporates, indeed pivots upon, Stendhal's famous law of radical disappointment; a law implicit in the question, "Is what I desired no more than this?" and spelled out at circumstantial length in the autobiographical *Brulard* (which abides by its author's principle that the chief reason for writing is the pleasure it brings

---

[8] The perversity in this differs from the aristocratic kind that rules in *Les Liaisons dangereuses*. It is, as regards immediate pleasure, at the expense of oneself rather than of others.

you only by extending recollection to the moment of his arrival with Napoleon's army, in the beautiful spring of 1800, into the earthly paradise of Milan).[9] *The Life of Henry Brulard* (tr. Catherine Alison Philips [1925]) is a chronicle of two sets of discoveries: (1) what life in the world really is, and what odds it poses against achieving happiness, and (2) what the human self really is, as an agent seeking to fulfill its own best vision of life and finding out along the way its bottomless talent for self-frustration. Against memories of a bourgeois-provincial childhood in Grenoble—an ambiance that seems now not "dangerous" but merely "disgusting" in its hostility "to the slightest impulse of generosity" (ch. ix)—Stendhal holds up a suitably frivolous vision of the ideal society. It will be "a salon of eight or ten people, where all the women have had lovers, where the conversation is gay and full of anecdote, and where they drink a light punch half an hour after midnight" (ch. xxix). But he undergirds this easy formula with an entirely serious declaration of ethical value: "In my opinion, a man ought to be a passionate lover, and at the same time he ought to carry joy and movement into every company where he finds himself" (ch. xxxix).

Brulard continually draws the line between the moral qualities conducive to this vision of happiness and the qualities inimical to it; also, between those few among the memoirist's teachers and companions capable of imagining such a life and the unfortunately much larger number (like his father and nearly all his actual teachers) dismally immune to its appeal. One exception, the political Jacobin who taught him algebra,

[9] Gerard Genette argues that as the *Charterhouse* begins precisely where *Brulard* breaks off, with the French entry into Milan, the two books compose in effect a fictional autobiography. Stendhal himself—in the guise of the impoverished young Bonapartist lieutenant and commoner, Robert—thus becomes Fabrice's father. I don't suppose it disturbs this pleasing argument to point out that two different military episodes are in question here, Fabrice's conception taking place in 1797, not 1800. What matters is that Fabrice, at Waterloo in June 1815, is exactly the age of Stendhal at the fortress of Bard in April 1800.

"filled my whole soul" with the matter-of-fact exactitude of his demonstrations (ch. xxxv). By contrast, a childhood friend who becomes in due course a peer of France and a stalwart of the Louis Philippe regime eventually proves only an accidental friend: he lacks the "touch of wildness," the "spark of generosity," needed to bring friendship to fruition (ch. xlii). The remarkable portrait in *Brulard* of the author's grandfather, whom he remembers as his only *confidant* within the family, is based on the ultimately unsatisfactory convergence of comparably antithetical elements—a man honest, discreet, amiable, loving astronomy as he loved Ariosto and Cervantes; yet cold and delicate in his wit and contemptuous of personal energy, of revolutionary enthusiasm, even of perfectly honorable neighbors (with a pretty daughter) whom it was somehow necessary to regard as socially inferior. But the same mixture of enthusiasm and cynicism, seen as basic to the Dauphinais temperament, becomes the secret of the author's own mature compound of "Castilian" generosity and melancholy analytical shrewdness (ch. xxi).

By one kind of example or the other, *Brulard* shows Stendhal developing a taste for personal independence and sensual pleasure—saving him, he says, from Jesuitical scoundrelism— and equally for the sincerity and naturalness, issuing in one-sided expressions of fervor, which are his prime goal as a writer. He also learns the great law of disappointment, inexorable because determined by the very force of one's original expectation. "Is [even] Paris nothing more than this? " he formulaically asks toward the end of *Brulard*. Does the thing I have so much desired, the thing I have sacrificed my life to during the last three years, inevitably bore me when I do possess it? Does judgment always become the helpless sport of those emotions which alone make a capacity for judgment worth possessing? Is passion, which begins by increasing one's intelligence but can end in stupefaction, a force that always betrays those who courageously attempt to live by it?

The discovery of these contradictions is of course not original with Stendhal. They typify the understanding of both life-in-the-spirit and life-in-the-world developed by the great line of French moralists from Montaigne forward. During his own coming of age Stendhal found them in particular in Rousseau. He speaks more than once of how *Émile* or *La Nouvelle Héloïse* saved him from hypocrisy or dishonesty or baseness, and taught him the virtue of active integrity. Eventually he puts Rousseau behind him, noting a "turgidity" (*Brulard*, ch. i), a "coarseness" in defining emotion (*De l'Amour*, original preface), besides the inconvenient fact that the works of Rousseau were a passion with his father and thus are accountable for some part of his father's perfect unamiability (*Brulard*, ch. vii). But the question set out at the beginning of *Brulard*, written when Stendhal had passed fifty—"What then have I really been?"—is precisely the question posed in the opening paragraph of Rousseau's final book, the *Rêveries du promeneur solitaire*: "What am I in myself?"[10] So too the doctrine of crystallization clinically elaborates—and complicates—a principle Rousseau offers in the second *Promenade* as the great lesson of all experience: that the only true source of happiness is in ourselves. We may add, looking as far beyond Stendhal as Rousseau was before him, that it is the psychological truth at the core of Proust's great novel.

Or rather it is half that truth, for both Stendhal and Proust would go on to say that within ourselves is the source of all our *un*happiness as well. That is a corollary the Rousseau of the *Rêveries* cannot allow himself to entertain. The perfection of style and imaginative vision in this last book of Rousseau's (written with a singular clarity and temperateness) is the perfection of a seamless paranoia, which springs up on the most trivial occasions and does not spend its force until it has become cosmic in proportion. If everything in reality, as the self knows it, proves to be unstable and in flux (fifth *Promenade*),

[10] Rather, it is almost the same question. Typically the form Rousseau gives it is static; what is to be identified is some unalterable essence. In Stendhal's version a whole progressive history is implied.

this is simply because there really is a universe of vindictive enemies ceaselessly at work, scheming to rob the self of the repose and peace it has a natural right to. For Stendhal, the thought of human infirmity defines a challenge which only augments the lover's passion, the soul's will to happiness. For Rousseau that thought is a poison and must be put absolutely out of mind (seventh *Promenade*). Both would agree that ordinary society is a realm of "embarrassment, obligation, duty" (sixth *Promenade*)—Rousseau flees it in terror; Stendhal yearns for it as the source of everything interesting in life.

For Rousseau, relishing his own benevolence, this creates a dilemma. The self's vital being, he would agree, is most active in the company of others; and doing good for others, rescuing them from injury, is a unique source of happiness. The trouble is, you invariably get ambushed by the very circumstance you set in motion. "I am no longer able to see a good act which is there for me to perform as anything but a snare . . . within which is hidden some evil or harm" (sixth *Promenade*). If nothing else intervenes, there is still the impossible problem of dealing with gratitude and with the subtle obligation which returns upon you as a doer of good not to offend your beneficiary by the least appearance of condescension. Also, you are now rigidly obliged to repeat your benefaction on demand and *ad infinitum*, so as not to disappoint expectations you yourslf have given birth to. (It comes as a relief, after very much of this ethical fastidiousness, to return to the erratic prodigality of giving and receiving alike, and of pleasure and surprise, in Stendhal's pictures of ideal human relationships.)

To Rousseau, passion itself—even the passion for good, for seeing all hearts made happy—is only hurtful, a condition of spirit always to be fled from. Rousseau dreams, fantastically, of being able to enter into the common life altogether invisibly, with godlike freedom. He drops the remark that given his native character he would have been the best and kindest of men vis-à-vis his fellows if only he had also been allowed to be supremely powerful among them (sixth *Promenade*). If the *Rêveries* projects an image of an infinitely expansive soul (*une âme expansive*: seventh *Promenade*)—an image which, as Karl Barth argued in a remarkable discussion of Rousseau, constitutes an anthropological discovery basic to the whole nineteenth-century reconstruction of religious understanding—it also invents the modern privileged-class tactic, given the instability and inequity of the common life, of refusing involvement with it. It is a refusal to risk a particle of subjective freedom.[11]

The charming lake island Rousseau retires to is thus, as described, a place of refuge for him, but it is also, by any other measure, a place of solitary confinement. As a solution to the problem of moral and civil existence it is essentially mad, besides depending on the assistance of at least twenty well-drilled servants. But to Rousseau in his calm, infinitely expandable paranoia, this solution is as logical as it is desirable, and he evokes it with sensuous and emotional conviction. And Stendhal's youthful heroes are clearly responsive to its appeal. Both Julien and Fabrice discover that there are indeed times when solitary confinement in a prison cell resolves every wordly difficulty, and the heart actively yearns for it.

~

But there is a difference. Happiness, for Rousseau, is not happiness at all unless it becomes permanent and unbroken as a condition of life. The human self cannot live without this permanency; and the escape or retreat into the island of self described in the *Rêveries* is for the great purpose of preserving the integrity, the singleness of creaturely being, which alone assures the fulfillment of virtue. Only by escaping the "theater of the human world" with its vanity and treachery can we find something to love which will not, as the encounter progresses, transform itself into something hateful. That something is un-

[11] ". . . often I abstained from some good work that I had both the desire and the power to perform, fearful of the subjugation of self [*l'assujetissement*] which in the aftermath I would have to endure if I thoughtlessly gave myself over to it" (sixth *Promenade*). Karl Barth's analysis is in *Protestant Thought from Rousseau to Ritschl*, ch. II.

peopled nature. Only nature receives without vacillation our restless capacity to expand our affection, and purges it of that compulsive pride which cleverly disguises itself as love of justice and is the last stronghold of the self's vain struggle with an infinitely malicious world (eighth *Promenade*). True happiness, to Rousseau, is finally a state in which even selfhood is no longer required of us and individuality vanishes into a beneficent—i.e., inert—universe.[12]

Rousseau's essential prayer is one that ordinary life allows you only in certain peaceful intervals which, because they are snatched from you so quickly, leave the heart more anguished than before, being full now not only of regret but of rekindled yearning. It is the prayer, "Would that this moment might last forever" ("Je voudrais que cet instant durât toujours": fifth *Promenade*). When the same prayer is voiced in Stendhal's *Vie de Henry Brulard*, as in fact it is shortly before the narrative's end, it comes instead in the very middle of the violence, the confusion, the *personal* embarrassment (being matched at seventeen against seasoned veterans) of the April 1800 campaign into Italy. It is at just this moment of tension and danger, with the French army unexpectedly blocked by the cannon of the fortress of Bard, that the author recalls himself wishing "that this present life might last forever" (ch. xlv).

Happiness for Stendhal is the impersonal release of feeling and spirit under a maximum of difficulty and constraint. (So beauty is famously, for Stendhal, the promise of such happiness.) And perhaps the perfected antithesis to the dream of life recorded in the *Rêveries du promeneur solitaire* is the double

---

[12] But even with nature one must be careful. Rousseau decides against studying the mineral and animal realms, since these involve you with the apparatus (and requisite human personnel) of quarries, furnaces, laboratories, and hammers, or else with traps and cages, stinking cadavers and frightful skeletons; that is, you find yourself once more involved, assembling your specimens, with other people and with reminders of mortal infirmity. Only the calm unresisting realm of plants can "purify imagination"; only there will you find a spectacle that never betrays devotion. Fortunately Rousseau seems not to have heard of Venus's-flytrap and the like.

dream—at once excursionary and historical, memorializing beauty and virtue together—projected in Stendhal's own book of escapist peregrination, the *Promenades dans Rome* of 1829. The *Promenades* was published, we note, just a year before *The Red and the Black*; I am inclined to agree with the judgment of Margaret Tillett, one of the few commentators in English to pay much attention to it, that in this casually assembled, money-making improvisation, Stendhal established, "minutely and elaborately, the spiritual climate of the novels to come."

It would take more space than is practicable here to give a proper account of the *Promenades'* merits.[13] My own sense of them is no doubt immoderate; I first read the book (following, though I did not know it at the time, the example of young Henry James a hundred years earlier: letter to Alice James, November 7, 1869) at the start of a four-month stay in Rome, when it seemed to me quite simply the best guidebook ever written. This was not only because, early on, it firmly advises *against* buying guidebooks at the start of your visit and thus poisoning your mind with other people's opinions. Rather, the thing to do is to roam about at random and see what is before you *without thinking about the duty of seeing* (Stendhal's emphasis: entries for August 10 and 15, 1827). The book as written is substantially fictitious. Cast as a consecutive journal of a twenty-month visit, it was actually put together in Paris, most of it cannibalized (with none too strict a regard for accuracy of detail) from other guidebooks and histories, from various of Stendhal's earlier writings on Italy, and from the recollections

---

[13] The most accessible English version is one intelligently abridged and translated by Haakon Chevalier as *A Roman Journal* (1957). Jean Prévost, defining the technique of the book as that of a *guide romancé*, nevertheless notes its differences from Stendhal's earlier writings on Italy: it is less an "initiation into happiness" than a "lesson in wisdom." Scornful of standard historiography, and advising his tourist-reader to believe only in monuments he actually touches, Stendhal—as Prévost describes him—had intuitively arrived at our own latest *annaliste* or Foucaultesque method of "opposing archaeology to [conventional] history": *La Création chez Stendhal*, 126-133.

and notes of a cousin of his who had originally intended to make his own book out of recent Italian travels. It is nevertheless in one great way the most truthful of guidebooks, not only offering vivid descriptions of Roman life and history but tracing out the psychological dynamic of the modern traveler's own treasure-greedy ordeal of estrangement and—if he sticks it out—eventual restoration.

In this way the narrative provides another analogy for the long process of the lover's passion, and for the writer's (or any historical agent's) wavering pursuit of his purpose. In each case there is a headlong quest for new truth and new pleasure, an arduous and frequently tormenting discipline for monitoring responses, and an exacting effort at self-continuance in each of these roles; all to the end of maintaining that openness and readiness of spirit without which the whole game—love, active creation, foreign travel—must be lost.[14] The narrative scheme of the *Promenades* thus follows the basic arc of Stendhalian experience. From keyed-up anticipation and a first ecstatic broadening of sensation, the party of travelers slips into a phase of discomfort, restlessness, mutual irritation, and a general despair of ever getting deeper into their mission; and it is only when both these stages have been traversed and absorbed, nearly halfway through their long visit, that in a sort of "inner revolution" they discover that a true passion for Rome has crept upon them so that, at last, "no detail" of the

---

[14] Early in the book we come on a highly practical warning about the traveler's need to separate himself from his companions at regular intervals in the tour, making side-excursions, going his own way and letting even his closest friends go theirs without excuses, so that the correspondingly volatile undertakings of friendship and of assimilating foreign ways are not sacrificed to each other. The implied critique of sustained friendship as a potential danger to the life of imagination and sensibility is one we find elaborated in Proust's novel, also in a notorious passage in Thoreau's excursionary *Week on the Concord and Merrimack Rivers*, where there is a characteristic warning that two seemingly natural avenues to virtue—sympathy and imaginative curiosity—may be deeply at odds. The perils of intimate friendship is in fact one of the great Romantic themes. As with others like it, precedent may be found in Scripture, particularly the Epistles.

city's life and history is "too severe or minute for us" (June 30, 1828, July 5, 1828). In a curious way the book takes on, through such notations, the character and rhythm of a conversion narrative.

As to Rome itself, it is as much the now moribund government and civil order as the famous past that interest Stendhal and generate the distinctive moral atmosphere we recognize from the great novels. Also, the historical Rome that does command his interest is not that of classical antiquity but the much nearer Renaissance city of Machiavellian popes and masterly artists and, coincidentally, of the first assaults of modern European imperialism on the old Mediterranean order of city states and independent principalities. (The sack of Rome in 1527 by a French army of German and Spanish mercenaries is vividly described.) Rome, where religion, art, and empire have all incomparably flourished, is the greatest of cities for assessing the power and consequence of human energy. By comparison there is something paltry to Stendhal about Paris under the Bourbon restoration. The *Promenades* thus stops early to celebrate the palpable creative force of a Saint Teresa (whose letters reveal a true Stendhalian protagonist, "all passionate sensibility and no affectation") and, in the numerous churches dedicated to her, the unique force of Mary herself ("the finest invention of Christian civilization," Stendhal comments). It celebrates equally Raphael's "tender, generous soul" and the Roman (specifically, Trasteveran) openness, ferocity of spirit, and disdain of affectation of Raphael's Fornarina, whom the painter is said to have loved "with constancy and passion" (entries for August 20 and 28, 1827). The Rome of its churches and painters allows Stendhal to deploy for his French audience a familiar structure of oppositions: between French critical intelligence and Italian energy of feeling, seen as morally superior; between the corroding wit of Voltaire and the thirst for beauty of Raphael; between the vanity and affectation of the Parisian, with his dryness of heart, and the Roman's admirable willingness to appear simple-minded and ridiculous for the sake of what he loves; between the

gloominess of a national population that remembers having
once won for itself, in 1789, political control of its life and future, and the perfect absence of gloom—as opposed to passions of grief or rage—in the "scoffing, satirical" Romans,
since "one must have some first inkling of hope in order to be
gloomy" (February 28, March 11, 1828).[15]

The oppositions and paradoxes that, to Stendhal, Rome peculiarly abounds in have all been intensified by the events of
1789 and after. The Rome of 1827-1829 is still under the fist
of the Popes (whose devotion is not to the Gospels but to the
Council of Trent and the Counter-Reformation). Rome is thus
that contemporary seat of power where the liberalizing forces
of nineteenth-century society have penetrated least. It is also
where the rampant instability of modern civil existence has
been the plain condition of life for centuries past. The real state
religion, in Rome, is fear of change. But change is precisely
what at any moment is most likely to happen next. The machinery of Roman government limits each regime's rule, no
matter how absolute, to roughly eight or ten years (the prince
of the Church elected by his jealous peers is always elderly);
thus the life-expectancy of each new Pope, the termination of
his regime, the advent of a successor, are everywhere the
preemptive topics of conversation. The one thing Romans can
predict with any certainty is that all present lines of force and
favor will soon be completely rearranged. (The realistic maxim
is simply, "The successor will be worse": January 27, 1828.)
Each regime's power, while it lasts, is absolute, unpredictable
in application, and capable of any enormity in its own defense.
Rome is that modern European city, Stendhal remarks as he
stands before an inscription commemorating not the victims
but the perpetrators of the St. Bartholomew massacre, "where
assassination is publicly honored" (March 7, 1828).

The consequence is a population that in order to survive

---

[15] A structure of paradoxes, too, such as in the early Christian fanaticism
that produced "exaggerated encomiums on the state of virginity" but also won
for woman the right "to negotiate as an equal" and bargain for "a free and
independent life" with the man who seeks her in marriage (June 21, 1828).

must be ready for anything. By necessity, inventiveness and improvisation become its life-or-death vocation. "Take at random," Stendhal proposes,

> one hundred well-dressed Frenchmen walking across the Pont Royal, one hundred Englishmen walking across London Bridge, one hundred Romans walking along the Corso; choose from each company the five who are most remarkable for courage and wit. Try to recall things exactly. I claim that the five Romans will have it all over the French and the English; and this will be so whether you put them on a desert island, like Robinson Crusoe, or at the court of Louis XIV, charged with carrying out an intrigue, or in the center of a stormy session of the House of Commons. (June 9, 1828)

This will be so, he explains, because neither the Englishman, blessed with a relatively just and stable government, nor the Frenchman, supremely advanced in polite civilization, has been obliged like the Roman to "make up his mind, at least ten times a month, in small hazardous cases that can very well lead him to ruin, or even to prison and death." In these circumstances quick wits and inexhaustible energy are at a premium, and it is best that their exercise be unconstrained by ethical scruples. So too it is perfectly natural for a population with no historical experience of administrative justice to be preoccupied with mechanisms of revenge—refinements of the famed Italian *vendetta*—and Stendhal unfolds story after story, from history and current gossip, of exquisitely contrived poisonings and long-meditated intrigues ending in violent death, until you are well persuaded that apart from building gorgeous churches and painting magnificent frescoes, *this* is the occupation through which Rome has brought human capacity to perfection.

Paradoxically it is the modern era of liberal revolution that provides the best context for defining—by antithesis—the supremacy of unchanging Roman virtue, even though this era threatens Rome and all Italy with a new ordeal of instability and suffering. How alive still, he exclaims, is "the soul of this greatest people on earth!" "Against the Romans one can make the same objection as against Napoleon. They were not infrequently criminal, but never has man himself been greater" (August 16, 1827). But the Napoleonic regime itself, which lasted in Rome from 1802 to 1807, has given the city a fatal glimpse of "modern civilization." In the Roman soul the sheer orderliness of French rule has grown into a "colossal memory": "For five years an odd idea was current in Rome: namely, that it was possible to obtain something from a prefect without making payments to his mistress or his confessor." The liberalism of the Enlightenment has given French thought and French practice "the right of succession in Europe; Napoleon and the Republic have renewed this right. France has a certain thing called the *Charter*: Russia and Italy will weep until they, too, have a charter" (September 28, November 4, 1827). But when liberty does come, Stendhal felt obliged to ask, will it be welcomed? Will it not, in a hundred years, destroy all feeling for the arts, for beauty, for wit and grace? Consider the case of republican America, he kept saying (June 25, 1828, and *passim*), though not without the puzzled respect of a man who had elsewhere seen all he could stomach of dynastic violence and cruelty.

～

Meanwhile Rome, as Stendhal presents it, remains that milieu where life and survival are most continuously at hazard but where anyone passionately interested in life's fulfillment would most wish to live. It is also where the Rousseauist dream of a perfect integrity of being, of virtue achieved in separation from a corrupted and corrupting world, is soonest exposed as fantastic and absurd.[16] Rome thus performs an essential serv-

---

[16] Except at the two extremities of power: with its secure possessor and with its helpless victim. "It seems to me," Stendhal remarks, speculating about the new papal regime whose election in the spring of 1829 brings the book to a close, "that one can be oneself in two situations in life, when one is nothing and when one is everything" (April 1, 1829). Yeats, as in *A Vision*, worked

ice for Stendhal (as does Italy in general) in completing the long process of "de-Rousseauizing" his judgment; the same process, incidentally, that Julien Sorel will undergo in *The Red and the Black*. The understanding that carries Stendhal beyond Rousseau also carries him back toward the radical insight of Montaigne, who in his essay "Of Virtue" described the quality under discussion as no more than a transient passion, brief fits of energy followed by prolonged relapses. Anyone is momentarily capable of *virtue*—which to Montaigne is principally courage, or *fortezza*—insofar as he is human: "except order, moderation, and constancie, I imagine all things may be done by an indifferent and defective man" (Florio translation). According to Montaigne, virtue is no more than a function of our "fantasy," our conception of ourselves, and such conceptions have no constancy; or if they do, it is likely to appear ludicrous. Montaigne's one example of perfect constancy in virtue is the absurd Pyrrho:

> if he had begun a discourse [he] would end it, though the party to whom he spake were gone: and if he went anywhere, he would not go an inch out of his path, whatever let or obstacle came in his way; being kept from falls, from carts or other accidents, by his friends.

Stendhal in his own satirical vein is capable of this degree of characterological skepticism. His improvised reflections on human baseness and corruptibility have, frequently, a toss-of-the-head cynicism that can become as tiresome in reading as any patched-up scheme for tolerating the intolerable. It is the expressive counterpart to a manipulative indulgence, as novelist, in comic-opera escapades to fill out awkward gaps in the main action—such as, in the *Charterhouse*, the labored episode of Fabrice's duel with Count M——, ending the first half of the novel, or much of the role provided for the Republican

---

through to the same sort of analytic diagram but construed it differently. To Yeats these two situations, or phases, are the two in life that wholly transcend natural selfhood.

poet-fanatic Ferrante Palla. But at the center of his novels' main sequences of action and emotion, Stendhal's vision is more generous and more subtle. It is true that setting the *Charterhouse* in a petty Italian principality where, after Napoleon, fears of Jacobinism supply the rationale for every state policy, and schemes of intrigue and revenge account for all other motives while at the same time keeping public life in unabated turmoil, creates the opportunity for facile ironies about civil and political behavior that are entertaining enough as they flash by but perhaps too predictable to carry any great weight of meaning or truth: all of which undercuts critical attempts—beginning with Balzac's enthusiastic celebration of the book as a New Machiavelli—to make the case for *The Charterhouse of Parma* as an anatomy of modern political wisdom.[17] But the ironies following upon its main characters' passionate and generous pursuit of the phantom of happiness seem to me of a different kind. They are both more humanly profound and, in sequences of dramatic conflict, more surprising and original.

The *Charterhouse* is, I think, most truthful exactly where it is most rhapsodic and idealizing. It forthrightly demonstrates (and in the process puts in jeopardy our sentimental regard for the protagonists) that there is no such thing as a steadily dependable virtue, public or private. What there is instead in the novel's expressive climaxes is more or less of vital force from the natural constitution of things; more or less, that is, of the inborn human capacity to act, at need, with competent energy and to sustain action, for the time required, against odds. In the narrative design of the novel, such energy and extended competence are allotted to all the leading characters on both sides and not alone to the privileged protagonists. A first result is that the contest between the two sides is both fairly joined and dramatically interesting. Moreover, where this capacity

---

[17] This is not to dismiss the obvious satire on Congress of Vienna political attitudes, ridiculing their paranoia about change and reducing them to comic-opera triviality.

for *virtue* is most alive, it is shown spilling over into that self-excess which was identified (in Chapter I, above) as verifying the reality of the thing itself. The consequence is a further squaring of the dramatic odds, since the conflict is shown to be inward as well. The common truthfulness as well as affective warmth with which Stendhal treats the chief bearers of the burden of virtue is his imaginative trump card. It seems to me at the heart of that ethical and psychological poetry which is his greatest invention and his enduring distinction as a novelist.

The politically anachronistic, comic-opera setting of the *Charterhouse* serves very well these deeper purposes. (Interestingly, when Stendhal set the action of *Lucien Leuwen* directly within that modern political order which after 1830 he most despised, the *juste milieu* of Louis Philippe, he ran into basic narrative difficulties.) Italy, in the *Charterhouse*, offered him what it offered Hawthorne twenty years later in *The Marble Faun*, a milieu romantically apart from major nineteenth-century history yet fully exposed to contemporary winds of change; and he had the advantage over Hawthorne (the author, an art-historian friend once remarked, of the second best guidebook to Rome) of knowing Italian life from closer inside. The Parma of the novel is much like contemporary Rome in the *Promenades*. It is a world doing its best to seal itself off, holding fast to its own intricate rules and requirements. Yet it has already experienced the impact of revolutionary change, and cannot give up the taste it has acquired for the new excitements even as it goes in terror of their recurrence. One central premise of the story is that neither of Parma's two successive Princes can abide the thought of the dullness of court life if the witty and vivacious Bonapartist heroine removes herself from it. More than once it is her threat to live out her life somewhere else that forces concessions from her enemies.

Revolutionary values hang threateningly over Parma, and Stendhal's allegiance to them, however shaded by irony, is fundamental to the triad of practical considerations establishing the public environment of the story. The inexhaustible capriciousness of Parma's rulers—with the hypocritical Ernesto IV it derives from a vigorous appetite for manipulation and revenge; with the young, Rousseauishly sincere Ernesto V, from an absurdly misapplied moral perfectionism—is the primary component of this triad, and it is explicitly contrasted to the startling "constancy" of the Napoleonic administration (ch. 9). As in Rome, despotic capriciousness is the great obstacle to happiness for those within its reach, a condition repeatedly signalized by the metaphor of sudden storms which transform the political atmosphere and force reassessment of all existing assumptions and plans. The second framing consideration is summed up by Count Mosca, the senior hero, in defining to his beloved Gina—whom he is immorally counseling to marry for convenience the aged and rich Duke of Sanseverina—what under such conditions the task before them really is: "We must take some decisive action [here in Parma] if we wish to spend the rest of our lives in an enjoyable fashion and not grow old before our time" (ch. 6). As the public world of the novel is constructed, it would be profoundly unreasonable to set any other practical goal; to propose, that is, some grander or more heroic conception of happiness. Combining the first and second considerations gives us the third, which is that surviving in Parma's civil order while pursuing the legitimate goal of personal happiness is essentially a game. You study the rules, which you accept as you accept those of whist, and you apply yourself to making them work to your advantage.[18]

The novel's main story spans the life of its second and younger male hero, Fabrice, love child of an Italian marchesa and a Bonapartist lieutenant. Conceived in the aftermath of that springtime march into fabled Italy, Fabrice himself springs into action in the novel by rushing off, at sixteen, to join the

---

[18] The character in Stendhal's fiction who acts most successfully on these principles, mainly because he is almost without vanity in his mastery of them, is Lucien Leuwen's father, the banker and national legislator whose only real weakness is that success too quickly bores him. Coming easily, it makes him a trifle negligent. So he never quite anticipates the passionate constancy of his son's imprudence.

emperor at Waterloo. This long episode fixes him securely within the party of true virtue, but also turns inside out the whole idea of conventional heroism by presenting the great battle itself as a disorganized scrimmage whose participants, including its commanding generals, have little idea what is happening. Was what he had seen and taken part in really a battle, Fabrice asks, and if so, was the battle really Waterloo? In fact it was not—what he had actually seen of it—Waterloo proper; nor is Fabrice himself the book's real protagonist, as Napoleon-worshipping Julien Sorel is the protagonist in *The Red and the Black*. (He is, though, something more than the *Charterhouse*'s "juvenile lead," to take issue with a formulation in Michael Wood's excellent study of the Stendhal "world.") The real protagonist is Fabrice's aunt Gina, the Countess Pietranera, Duchess of Sanseverina, and finally Countess Mosca—Fabrice's aunt but not blood-relation, it should be kept in mind. I can be fairly brief now in speaking about her and about the rest of the novel, for those earlier works of Stendhal's I have been examining, in particular the *Promenades dans Rome*, have already given us its organizing themes and dramatic reasons. What the *Charterhouse* adds is a wonderfully fluent richness and vivacity of orchestration and, of course, the unifying power of a sustained story.

It is Gina's "Roman spirit," we are told, that gives her energy and consequence as an agent in the story; a woman—as she is described by the candid, simple girl who becomes her rival and successor in Fabrice's heart—"of so remarkable a capacity for action, so superior an intelligence, so terrible a will" (ch. 20). In another attempt to define Gina's force of being, Stendhal draws on the behavioral ideal formulated in *Henry Brulard*. She in particular has the prized capacity to bring "animation" into the company around her and, by taking part in its activity, introduce into it life and motion (ch. 15). Like Stendhal's Romans, she is passionate, forthright, incorrigibly impulsive, and not scrupulously moral, not at any rate by North European standards. Certainly she has in full measure the Roman appetite for vengeance. When she loves, she loves generously and unselfishly—her hatreds are her selfishness—and she knows how to make others love her. Her impact on various lesser figures in the novel, including servants and followers, is what regularly produces those *bel canto* duets and choruses of reciprocal nobility which it is well to have some tolerance for if you are traveling the course with Stendhal.

These qualities also cause, expectably, a lot of trouble. Mosca's comment that Gina's impulsiveness invariably upsets even her own best plans is somewhat too round—he makes it under the shock of discovering her deep "instinctive" love for Fabrice—but it is a fact that during the rescue of Fabrice from the Parma prison her "ardent imagination" takes a hundred excessive precautions which, arousing suspicion on all sides, are of "an incredible imprudence" and jeopardize the whole escape (ch. 22). Such ardor of imagination is another of her "Roman" qualities, especially as it feeds the will to revenge. The Romans' appetite for the *vendetta*, Stendhal wrote in the *Promenades*, is based simply on the vividness of their imaginations. Unlike the circumspect French, they are quite unable to put out of mind any strong feeling, most of all the feeling of fear. It is because Gina, reacting in fear, instinctively humiliates Ernesto IV while contriving a state pardon for Fabrice—because at the decisive moment her superb outrage overflows the occasion and she acts "at random, and for her own immediate pleasure" (ch. 14)—that the Prince, whose own passion for revenge is untrammeled by nobility of spirit, is moved to betray his pledge to her and to throw Fabrice's life in jeopardy again. Her counterstroke is simply to have the Prince poisoned; then, in a splendid bravura scene, she turns loose all her wit and energy of spirit to persuade the dowager Princess to burn the evidence that would implicate her in the assassination. But in due course she pays for this, too. The same impulsiveness unnecessarily traps her, in saving Fabrice a second time, into a pledge to the new princeling to take him once as her lover: a submission (an *assujetissement*, to borrow Rousseau's bitter word) that requires her, less for honor's sake than for self-appeasement, to exile herself from Parma for the rest of her days.[19]

In her rare combination of grace and soldierliness, and in her embattled grief, Gina is Stendhal's repayment of his imagination's youthful debt to Ariosto's Bradamante—in *Brulard* he remembers the pain of having no one "to talk to about my tender admiration for [her]" (ch. xl)—and there are in fact a number of correspondences between the stories of these two heroines. But the suffering that Gina's natural character brings down on her is matched in the experience of Fabrice and Mosca. All three pass through nights of anguish and soul-wretchedness that, with the two older figures, carry them briefly (again as in Ariosto) to the edge of madness. Stendhal's irony, Nicola Chiaromonte remarked, "spares neither youthful impulsiveness nor worldly wisdom." We might add that it particularly does not spare the middle-aged impulsiveness of the worldly wise, with which, in Gina's case, it is at once most tender and most severe.

Yet this picture of an equitable distribution of happiness and suffering within even the charmed circle of virtue is not strictly accurate. Fabrice, in his youthfulness and half-fabulous origins—the child, so to speak, of that legendary drum-roll in the opening paragraph—does appear to be treated as a character with special indulgence. Formally he exists, to a degree, in a different kind of story, one ruled by other conventions than those of a skeptical realism. Like a ballad hero he is gifted in essential matters with unfailing good luck, though it is frequently delayed in arriving; he leads in the main a charmed life. Even its early end has the privileged charm of folktale sym-

---

[19] Stendhal is explicit concerning the fault, or lacuna, in Gina's power of imagination when, in despair that Fabrice will be poisoned during this second imprisonment, she overlooks the objective fitness of this possibility as a consequence of her own act. A woman brought up in the Protestant north of Europe, Stendhal comments, would have seen the connection at once: "I was the first to use poison, now I am perishing by poison." In Italy, however, "reflections of that sort, in moments of passion, appear in the poorest of taste . . ." (ch. 25).

metry. Prison itself, the most fearful of specters along the borders of the Austrian empire (within which looms the dreaded Spielberg), is not prison for him. Waiting for his daily glimpse of the prison governor's daughter and looking out to the sunset-gilded Appennines with the moon rising behind him over the Alps and the Lombard plain, he exclaims in that most familiar of Stendhalian cadences, "But is this really a prison?"[20] Michael Wood comments shrewdly on the repeated instances of "sexual good fortune" contrived for Fabrice, beginning with his conception and birth in the new heaven of liberated Milan. His aunt's prophecy (ch. 2) that women will "make his fortune" proves accurate in the event, while his early tutelage with the astrologer Prior Blanès (modeled on the benign grandfather of *Brulard*) introduces a narrational context for the profusion of signs and omens marking out a distinguished path for him through his brief life.

Everywhere Fabrice moves and acts, guardians come forward to offer assistance. He in turn seems, all unconsciously, to return a portion of this increase of virtue to those around him—as when, at Waterloo, his embarrassments call forth that nobility of soul among various women which constitutes, Stendhal remarks, the "beautiful side" of the otherwise irritating French national character (ch. 4). In Machiavellian Italy the natural generosity of ordinary people comes to life in his presence and is regularly there to see him through. He has been lucky even in his Jesuit schooling. This, Stendhal explains, fixed him early in habits of thought that are extremely useful in places like Parma, in particular the habit, as regards politics and morals, of "not paying attention to things clearer than daylight" (ch. 12); he thus avoids the hypocrisy of spirit which even Gina can slip into when her passion is upon her. From first to last Fabrice remains "innocent and simple" (ch. 23)— to the point, Mosca necessarily feels, of a certain youthful

[20] Stendhal's recurrent use of towers and prisons—places of extreme isolation which are at once a mortification and a release—has attracted a good deal of interpretive comment. See, *inter alia*, Stephen Gilman, *The Tower as Emblem* (1967).

"cruelty" of spontaneous self-assertion (ch. 10). So the deaths that end the book (writing to Balzac, Stendhal explained that this was the ending he had in view all along) are precipitated by a natural but impolitic "caprice of affection," Fabrice's insistence that his infant son live beside him every hour of the day so as to take, hour by hour, the place of the child's mother (the prison governor's daughter, now the Marchesa Crescenzi). For in the *fabliau* resolution of their story, he may now visit her—as he regularly does, with transports of joy—only at night and in the dark, so that they do not violate their sacred vow never to *see* each other again.

These final details have a catch-as-catch-can quality in the telling, and Stendhal hurries through them in a few synoptic sentences as if no longer intensely interested in the emotions involved.[21] For us the key matter is simply that the peculiar virtue of youth and blood, with its birthright gift of passion, remains to the end of the *Charterhouse* what it has been from that clarion first sentence—and what of course in the process of life it must always be, whatever the cost in disappointment or suffering to the no longer young—a privileged quantity which, although no more to be spared in the full cycle of experience than any other moral or spiritual element, justifies merely by its existence everything that happens under its spell. It is the part of human virtue that has least to do with any reasoned discipline of self-reflection or moral understanding—the part that is renewed, that crystallizes, biogenetically—and there is little question, I think, but that to the childless Stendhal its claim is absolute.[22]

---

[21] Professor Martineau transcribes marginal notations in Stendhal's hand claiming that his publisher has compelled him to squeeze into a very short space what was originally a much more detailed closing sequence (see Strickland, 225, 285n). Perhaps so. . . .

[22] A point given general support by Northrop Frye: "Of course, the real natural aristocracy in all ages, the society of those who are genuinely entitled to leisure and privilege and consuming the goods produced for them by others, are the children" ("The Problem of Spiritual Authority in the Nineteenth Century," in *The Stubborn Structure* [1970], 249).

Supplementary Considerations

(1) On the politics of the *Charterhouse*: Assumptions that the novel endorses anti-Jacobinism or any other reactionary politics seem to me to mistake the temper and pitch of Stendhal's narration. It is true that the republican poet-revolutionary Ferrante Palla has more than a touch of comic-opera extravagance about him; Mosca wearily tabs him as "a lunatic—[though] a genius," and he is most spirited and decisive when executing Gina's intemperate designs. But when, after the defeat of his (and Gina's) revolution, Palla departs for America, Stendhal allots to his farewell letter the shrewdest political observation in the book. "Besides," Palla writes, "how is one to create a Republic without Republicans?" As well as a good deal of actual history the remark anticipates by a century and a quarter a whole acclaimed generation of American Revolutionary historiography.

(2) Stendhal as feminist: That Stendhal's most moving inquiry into the trials of virtue turns on the case of a woman is not out of keeping with his other work. The Romans of the *Promenades* share the condition of subjection which is woman's lot in modern society, despite compensatory advantages; and in *De l'Amour*—though it is a masculine analysis—he recognizes that the unfair weight of social opinion upon women, the one-sided demand for moral respectability, is a substantial complication:

> Women, therefore, have to be very much more cautious. By virtue of their way of life, all the intellectual movements in which the birth of love consists are with them more delicate, more retiring, gentler and less decided; they are therefore more disposed to constancy; consequently they must find it more difficult to arrest the process of crystallization once it has begun. (ch. viii)

(3) The Stendhalian aftermath: One of the first, so far as I know, to grasp the depth and scope of Stendhal's psychological-experiential vision was Baudelaire, who in the ending of a

profoundly serious poem, "Le Rêve d'un curieux," borrowed
the central Stendhalian formula, taking it a step further into
the mythology of modern death itself:

> J'étais mort sans surprise, et la terrible aurore
> M'enveloppait.—Eh quoi! *n'est-ce donc que cela?*
> La toile était levée et j'attendais encore.

CHAPTER FIVE

"Why Does One Thing Happen and Not Another?": *The Man Without Qualities*

"The other self, the anti-self or antithetical self, as one may choose to name it, comes but to those who are no longer deceived, whose passion is reality."
—Yeats, *Per Amica Silentia Lunae* (1917)

"J'ai horreur de tous les métiers."
—Rimbaud, *Une Saison en enfer* (1873)

In a critical excursion emphasizing not only the subject and agency of *virtue* in imaginative literature but the categorical priority of this subject in any work of more than sentimental interest, the reasons for including as a twentieth-century instance the major work of the Austrian novelist Robert Musil can begin with its memorable title. *The Man Without Qualities*: the representative human creature in his essential being, stripped of all that ordinarily screens him from the fundamental process and task of existence. (The male creature, of course; but in relation to the masculine oligarchies of fifty and seventy-five years ago, releasing a male figure from the protective cover of specialized function and consciousness is the more radical experiment. Also, as will be remarked, Musil's amplifying narrative encompasses the feminine as well, in several modalities.) A long novel which accomplished its promise to fix this subject of subjects into a clarifying narrational order would seem to offer itself as an indispensable modern classic. For what else unifies, intellectually, the chaotically expansive modern age if not a spreading awareness of the free, necessar-

ily reflexive anthropological factor in every projected scheme
of either action or understanding?

But bringing *Der Mann ohne Eigenschaften* into the general
argument of a book written in English requires extra preparation, for Musil's unfinished masterwork remains, in Great
Britain and North America, the least known and least assimi-
lated of the great modernist undertakings in prose fiction. (In
the United States only one of its three completed parts has ever
been published.) One consequence is that its title may instead
work as a subtle discouragement, in seeming to point to an abstract and more or less actionless field of interest. An un-
daunted new reader, however, discovers soon enough that
chapter by chapter an ordinarily concrete discrimination of
human qualities and consequences still prevails, and that the
novel's titular hero is not at all a characterological blank but
an active, resourceful participant in life. With an intelligence at
once objective and sensual in its determinations, he comes forward first of all as a man strongly attracted to any occasion in
life promising transcendence of ordinary constraints and the
renewal of seemingly foreclosed possibility. In short he may
even be that rare and much looked-for phenomenon, a fictional hero fully adequate to our own indeterminate time.

But the uncertainties in Musil's critical reception have not
been accidental. *The Man Without Qualities*, in the differently
extended versions different editors have proposed, is a work
whose textual history complicates every judgment. Notebook
intimations of it date from Musil's adolescence, but when he
settled down to the project in his mid-twenties, after the considerable success of a first novel in 1906, he discovered—"several hundred pages along"—that he was not ready to carry it
through. Resuming work in earnest after 1925, he brought out
the first two main sections on schedule in 1930. The long opening out of the third section, constituting a second full volume
(and virtually a new story), followed in 1933—as promptly as
Joseph in Egypt would follow the first two volumes of Thomas
Mann's concurrent prose epic. For the remaining ten years of
Musil's life nothing more appeared in book form. What passes

now for a third volume is made up of posthumously published
materials of which only fourteen short chapters—there are
ninety such additional chapters, in their first editor's arrangement—were completed and revised by Musil himself; these
fourteen do not even complete Part Three of the announced
four-part scheme. Of the remainder a great deal represents
much earlier stages of composition or else alternative projects
that Musil had abandoned. There is good reason then for arguments that Musil did indeed lose his way, discovering the
book to be uncompletable as planned. (One Musil authority
concluded that he had forgotten the plot.) "Fiction is living
ethic," a late notebook entry characteristically proposes, but
the ethical and behavioral problematic that issues from Musil's developed perception of things, though foreshadowed in
all his earlier writings, has this time—the argument would
go—been all too fully absorbed into the compositional design.
As a result that design became unresolvable, as indeterminate
as the master vision it was intended to convey.[1]

[1] Data about Musil's career along with descriptive introductions to *The
Man Without Qualities* are available in English in the compact forewords by
Eithne Wilkins and Ernst Kaiser accompanying their three-volume translation
of the 1930 and 1933 texts (1953, 1954, 1960: an announced fourth volume
translating the posthumous materials has not appeared); in Burton Pike, *Robert Musil: An Introduction to his Work* (1961); in Frederick G. Peters, *Robert
Musil: Master of the Hovering Life* (1978). David S. Luft, *Robert Musil and
the Crisis of European Culture, 1880-1942* (1980), is to date the fullest account in English of the ideas Musil shared with others of his European generation. Hannah Hickman, *Robert Musil and the Culture of Vienna* (1984), has
a narrower focus but fills a blank in both Allan Janik and Stephen Toulmin,
Wittgenstein's Vienna (1973), and Carl Schorske, *Fin-de-Siècle Vienna*
(1980). John Simon's Afterword for the Signet edition of Musil's early *Ent-
wicklungsroman, Young Törless*—properly, *The Bewilderments of Boarding
School Pupil Törless*—gives a balanced overview of Musil's accomplishment.
The long chapter on Musil in Lisa Appignanesi, *Femininity and the Creative
Imagination* (1973), is an excellent review of major narrative themes and cov-
ers (as does Pike) fugitive works like the two plays of the early 1920s, *The Enthusiasts* and *Vinzenz and the Woman Friend of Important Men*. John Mc-
Cormick's lively chapter on *The Man Without Qualities* in *Fiction as
Knowledge* (1975) opens with a helpful account of the textual confusions
since Musil's death.

Such conclusions have a way of becoming self-confirming, disposing of the critical problem by establishing reasons for not really exploring it. Musil had from the beginning, as a writer, a fine capacity for biding his time and for resisting premature resolutions. Apparently he expected to live into his eighties, as his father had; despite a warning stroke in his mid-fifties, he maintained a vigorous physical regimen meant to safeguard this encouraging patrimony. Also the climate of the 1930s, throughout Europe, must be given its due. Berlin, Musil's second home, became insupportable under Nazi rule, and in 1938 *Anschluss* drove him into further exile in Switzerland. His publisher, royalties, and regular working environment were gone; an income supplied after 1932 by the Musil-Gesellschaft was cut off; applications for foundation help were rejected—he seems, in short, one more victim of the climactic 1938-1945 nightmare. Yet it must also be said that a first authority for thinking that his difficulties with *The Man Without Qualities* were intrinsic is Musil himself. For what is to be made of a narrative running to over a thousand dense pages of authorized text and hundreds more of drafts, fragments, pro-

---

My own quotations are from the excellent Wilkins-Kaiser translation, except when a point about the exact tenor of Musil's phrasing calls for the most literal rendering possible. Citation is by book or "part" and chapter: I, 1, and so forth.

With posthumously printed materials I have been helped by the excellent French and Italian editions. The first, translated by the poet Philippe Jaccotet, follows the 1953 text assembled by Adolf Frisé (reissued with revisions in 1970); the second, translated by Anita Rho with an introduction by Cesare Cases, uses the different arrangement proposed by Wilkins and Kaiser in 1962 on the basis of their own researches and those of Wilhelm Bausinger in his Tübingen thesis (1961) on textual problems in *The Man Without Qualities*. Both the novel and its author have been the subject of a series of *Times Literary Supplement* articles over several decades. Those of October 28, 1949, July 6, 1956, September 23, 1960, and March 15, 1963 are especially valuable. But in the issue of November 30, 1979, D. J. Enright once more presented Musil as a writer awaiting proper discovery. There is, it should be said, a thriving Musil industry in Germany and his native Austria: a Musil-Gesellschaft, a Musil-Archiv, an annual *Musil-Studien* and *Musil-Forum*.

visional extensions, and contradictory variants, whose author—at the moment his second volume was in press—made
this notebook entry on the whole undertaking: "What the
story that makes up this novel amounts to is that the story that
was supposed to be told in it is not told."

I doubt there is any short way to decode that opaque remark. But if we begin *The Man Without Qualities* braced
against apprehensions that our ordinary interest in sequential
narrative will have to be suspended, we are in for a nice surprise. There is "story" in abundance. By the middle of the second part upwards of twenty-five solidly defined characters
have been set moving through distinct episodes, occasions of
suspense, passional convergences and ruptures, toward a set of
terminations at least as definite as those to be found in *Ulysses*
or *The Counterfeiters*. At any rate, given the novel's relative
unfamiliarity, a summary of this rising action seems the likeli-
est way to start.[2]

~

The story proceeds along two main tracks, one psychological
and moral, the other civil or political, treating of affairs of
state and of public order. The two run parallel throughout.
Whatever further authority is claimed for Musil's text is thus

[2] The changing response of as alert and generous a commentator as Frank
Kermode can serve as an index to the experience of reading Musil. In a 1960
notice of *The Man Without Qualities* Professor Kermode, noting loose comparisons to Proust and Joyce, remarked, "I suppose it would be reasonable to
say that Musil had as much sheer brain as the two of them together," but "as
a novelist, he is simply not to be thought of in their company." Absorbed in
purposes "not very intimately related to narrative," Musil is identified as "the
interesting limiting case" ("A Short View of Musil," *Puzzles and Epiphanies*
[1962]). Five years later, introducing the novellas and stories of Musil's middle
career, with an interest sharpened perhaps by his own fresh explorations in
The Sense of an Ending, Kermode spoke of Musil as unquestionably among
"the great twentieth-century novelists," if still "the least read." "When it becomes the custom to read and value him it will seem surprising to nobody that
one speaks of him as belonging to the same class as Joyce and Mann."

not to be separated from his mainstream realism, his circumstantial grasp of the imprint on even the most insulated private
lives of great suprapersonal juxtapositions and antagonisms.
Characteristically, locale and epoch and the manner of life
they foster are precisely specified in the book's first paragraphs. The time is the late summer of 1913; the place, Vienna.
Equally characteristically, Musil at once plays down the topical aspect, observing that "no special significance should be attached to the name of the city." That comment leads directly
to a first strong statement of what Musil (sharing modernism's
premise that the art of our era is necessarily a city art) sees at
the heart of all existence and is conceptually—and architecton-
ically—challenged by:

> Like all big cities, [this one] consisted of irregularity, change,
> sliding forward, not keeping in step, collisions of things and
> affairs, and fathomless points of silence in between, of paved
> ways and wilderness, of one great rhythmic throb and the
> perpetual discord and dislocation of all opposing rhythms,
> and as a whole resembled a seething, bubbling fluid in a ves-
> sel consisting of the solid material of buildings, laws, regu-
> lations, and historical traditions. (I, 1)

From this alone we could make a one-sentence précis of the
questions *The Man Without Qualities* sets out to explore. If
such indeed is the medium of our existence—a perpetual dis-
location, a uniform but untraceable "sliding forward" (*Vor-
gleiten*) into extensions, self-oppositions, disorienting blank-
nesses—how precisely is the creature man to make a
consequential life in it, and how is that life to be properly represented? But we would not yet have begun to sense the cast of
mind, the curiosity and openness, that distinguish Musil's fictive inquiry from, say, the repetitive parables of a Hermann
Hesse.

Without delay important characters appear—or seem to.
First, in deft outline, Ermelinda Tuzzi, a sumptuous dumbbell
who is the ambitious consort of an Imperial Permanent Secretary and who under the Platonic soubriquet of Diotima

(whether reminding us of the *Symposium* or of Hölderlin's *Hyperion*, the irony of the allusion does not wear out its welcome) rules the capital's chief intellectual salon, and beside her the smoothly impressive Arnheim, business magnate, diplomat, master intriguer, and Superman of Letters, who as possessor of all publicly rewarded qualities and talents helps define by contrast the protagonist's divergent course.[3] But are these two really themselves? Musil's text turns to expository teasing almost before it has material to tease with. Described as having "their initials significantly embroidered on their underclothing" and their grasp of their importance fixed equally fast "in the exquisite underlinen of their minds," they are in fact supposed to be somewhere else at this moment and not in each other's company at all. Do they go about the city streets, impressing each other with sociological statistics, under the illusion of being immune to the processes of existence just defined? Evidently they are persons to be wary of. Then, very promptly (the over-all scheme opening out in runs of short chapters, with rapid cross-cutting), we meet the protagonist himself. He is Ulrich, whose youthful determination to become "a man of importance"—as soldier, then civil engineer, then theoretical mathematician—has now given way to the momentous project of a "year's leave," a "holiday from life" (I, 13; II, 62). He has, it is said, the appearance of "a man who has learned renunciation" yet knows neither "submissiveness" nor "infirmity" (I, 2). With such a man, we are allowed to think from the first, any specific act of renunciation may well register as essentially creative, and life-affirming. (Somewhat later we hear that even while carrying out the researches which won respect among mathematicians and scientists, this Ulrich had already decided that "there was only one question really worth thinking about, and that was the question of right living": II, 62.)

[3] The model for Arnheim was the unfortunate philosopher-statesman Walter Rathenau, whose assassination in 1922 came to be seen as foreshadowing the fate of the Weimar Republic.

A well-populated core society now rises up around Ulrich. Needing help at this moment of change in his life, he has risked a renewal of dependence on his worthy father, a professor of law and adoptive aristocrat widely trusted as counselor of state. He sheds one mistress and acquires another who is much more entertaining; this is the inwardly chaste and infinitely seducible Bonadea, whose own appetite for distinction has got displaced into limitless sensuality. Her meetings with Ulrich allow Musil to reassert at intervals the minute attentiveness to erotic experience, its rhythms and sequences as surprising as they are inexorable, that marks all his earlier fiction (attentiveness strengthened by a clear understanding that this "great disrespectful love-suffering capacity"—*die grossen rücksichtslosen Liebesleidenschaften*: III, 25—is only an extreme form of the human restlessness brought about by any active continuance in life). At the same time Ulrich renews contact with two friends of his youth, Walter and Clarisse, now locked into a discordant marriage and wholly at the mercy of the qualities and accomplishments that first bound them together: he a drifter through several of the arts, saved from psychic breakdown by changeableness itself; she a new woman of the pre-1914 era, free-minded but without proper occupation. Hypersensitive, fanatic, sexually vengeful, and, at the core, mad, Clarisse is one of a subset of the disoriented or else insane whose presence in the novel sustains both levels, the political and the psychological-moral, of its long narrative démarche.[4]

With Walter and Clarisse, Ulrich becomes absorbed in the criminal case of one Moosbrugger, a psychopathic murderer obsessed by visions of a universal orderliness that "by some strange inversion he felt . . . had its origin in him, although he knew it was imposed upon him" (II, 87: a clear evocation of the *Unheimliche* as a category of experience). Moosbrugger's plight draws out Musil's special gift for the perspective-frac-

---

[4] If this opening synopsis suggests some wearying obstacle course of expository complication, let me enter here a flat endorsement of John McCormick's remark that for all the novel's digressiveness it really "does not seem long to read."

turing, category-dissolving metaphor. The man's "huge and powerful body [does] not quite hold together"; "sometimes the open sky peered right into his skull"; the object of juridical disputes as confused as the medical verdicts on his condition, he exists in the story "like an uninhabited—and invisible— coral island in an endless sea of analytic discourse" (II, 110). Moosbrugger, though appearing infrequently, is an extraordinary fictional invention. An autonomous system of "wild but obstructed possibility," he is monstrous only in the perfection of instincts common to all men and women (and children). He thus becomes a measure of all others' condition of being. "If mankind could dream collectively," goes one of Musil's pithiest sentences, "it would dream Moosbrugger" (*müsste Moosbrugger entstehn*; Moosbrugger must take form, or break out: I, 18).[5]

The question of what the civil order can conceive of doing with such a person provides one of several crossovers from private existence to the public realm. The patchwork Austro-Hungarian empire—wittily described in its unfathomable contradictoriness as consisting of an Austrian part and a Hungarian part minus the Hungarian part (II, 42), and resolute in a policy of remaining "the second weakest among the great powers" (I. 8)—is itself a major narrative focus. That it was still somehow at the center of European destiny during the novel's time frame, yet had vanished almost beyond imagining a decade later when Musil began writing his book, is primary to his controlling vision, which strikes me as more substantially political than is usually taken account of. The virtue or

[5] There is a conspicuous parallel between Moosbrugger and Franz Biberkopf, the manic-depressive working-class hero of Alfred Döblin's *Berlin Alexanderplatz* (1929), who has the same spasmodic rage for order. Biberkopf's moronic obsessions, however, rise more directly from class subservience, and he winds up as a factory gateman drugged on obedience and order.

Correspondences between Moosbrugger's pattern of consciousness (and Musilian psychology in general) and the turn-of-the-century psychological "elementarism" of Ernst Mach and others are explored by Judith Ryan in "The Vanishing Subject: Empirical Psychology and the Modern Novel," *PMLA*, October 1980.

force of being emanating from great national and supranational societies is as much in question in Musil's novel as is the free anthropological factor, the imprint left by the human presence itself stripped of all restrictive "qualities."

Thus it is in no way incidental to Musil's intention that at nearly every stage of the novel the protagonist, though more and more absorbed into his "holiday from life," moves familiarly among characters privy to the highest decisions of state. Through friendships with the benign *éminence grise* Count Leinsdorf, with Permanent Secretary Tuzzi (an honest cynic grumblingly submissive to his wife's affectations), and with General Stumm von Bordwehr (an imperial staff officer with the gruff good sense of the invincibly guileless), as well as with Diotima herself (his cousin) and thus with the hovering Arnheim, Ulrich is drawn into the great Collateral Campaign, or *Parallelaktion*—Musil's word makes explicit the Campaign's political refraction of the novel's metaphysical riddling. Preeminently, in this polyglot empire whose present ruler's interminable reign dates from the aborted revolutions of 1848, the great task of state policy is simply to reassert its own artificial existence. (The mysteries of Austro-Hungarian nationhood are, Musil suggests, "at least as difficult to understand as those of the Trinity": II, 42.) Conceived as a unifying instrument, the *Parallelaktion* becomes when initiated a catalyst of dissolution. Under its stimulus all sorts of slogans, ideologies, guru sects, youth cults, schemes of regeneration, plans for the total reconstruction of man and society—not omitting, if required, the elimination of misfits, starting with the Jews—burst into the open (see II, 89-90, and later chapters on the proto-Fascist student zealot Hans Sepp, the guru cynic Meingast, the arriviste poet-prophet Feuermal, and the chameleon new-journalist Meseritscher).

Some of these schemes, like Arnheim's self-consciously Goethean cerebrations or the treatises on sexual science and human unity that are Diotima's favorite reading, claim consonance with imperial goals. (It becomes Diotima's *idée fixe* that mankind can be helped "only if dealt with couple by couple":

III, 34.) Others are dead set against these goals or else mania-cally indifferent. Taken all together, Musil comments, the phe-nomena in question signalize nothing less than the dethroning of the established "ideocracy," the intellectual support system holding up European civilization. Trouble of another sort is brewing in the hard-edged aggressiveness of the empire's up-start rival, Wilhelmine Germany. It is known that five years hence, in 1918, Germany will stage a great festival celebrating the thirtieth year of the Kaiser's reign. Therefore Austria-Hun-gary (or Kakania, Musil's cheerfully indecent renaming) must celebrate the seventieth year of the reign of the senile Franz Jo-seph. It must do this for more than merely the honor of the thing; without great counterefforts a "second Sadowa"—the terrible defeat of 1866—would be threatened.

As the novel's short first part ("A Sort of Introduction") comes to an end, the *Parallelaktion* has been launched. The comedy of its progress is on show throughout what follows. Even with the change of narrative direction in Part Three, when Ulrich is reunited with his long absent sister and begins his interior adventure in earnest, political affairs are only par-tially displaced; and in the final pages Musil published in book form, some sort of climax seems at hand. The phrase, "A Great Event is under way" (literally, *ist im Entstehen*) supplies the first half of the title of four of the last five chapters (III, 34-38). It is also entirely in keeping that as this Great Event ap-proaches, "no one notices it" (III, 38). More than one irony operates here, but the overwhelmingly obvious one—it is now early summer, 1914—has been in place from the beginning. Everything that happens in the public realm of the book hap-pens, for its reader, in the immense shadow of 1914-1918.

The wit, the social and psychological acumen, the pathos, the narrative counterpointing, the metaphoric unexpectedness, the maxim-rich capacity for self-definition, the fluent yet abrupt shifts in register and perspective, the sense that behind everything some transforming revelation is preparing—all this is continuous in a text whose performative virtue does seem to me to generate its own acceptances (as Coleridge asserted the work of genuine imagination will always do). The question of how Musil might have completed *The Man Without Qualities* deserves scrutiny, and I will return to it; but it is not, I think, decisive to the question of whether the work left to us succeeds as a novel. (Do we ever really worry about the incompleteness of *Tristram Shandy*, or of *The Castle?*) As continuously as any other modern work on the grand scale, *The Man Without Qualities* embodies that "thought adventure" which in D. H. Lawrence's view can alone give weight and force to the business of writing fiction.[6] There are limits to what commentary can do to substantiate such claims. But some concrete indication of what reading Musil is like is worth attempting, not only for those who do not yet know him.

The self-contained chapter—with, usually, some ironic title—is the particular unit of his effectiveness, and it is impracticable to quote whole chapters. Otherwise, a first choice

---

[6] The outward expression of this in Musil is the densely essayistic texture of the narrative, corresponding to that "Essayism" (Ulrich's "chosen expression": II, 62) which is simply the experimental plasticity and venturesomeness of life itself, phenomenally considered. Musil's narrative style represents an attempt to be faithful to two things: this (to us) infinite plasticity, and the paradoxically "unique and unalterable" figures imprinted by it on the mind. If the narrative is basically representational, it is also meant to be philosophically answerable. Musil's own essayism, so understood, is not an affair of independent philosophic wisdom. Nor is it "that irresponsibility and semi-finishedness of mental images known as subjectivity." Rather it reflects something universal in phenomenal experience: the fact that everything encountered for the first time "behaves as if it were perfect" but soon makes known to us its participation in energy fields whose fixed state is one of "invisible but never-ceasing transformation" (II, 62).

In the next-to-last chapter of Part II (II, 122) this necessary alternative to the narrative orderliness we ourselves impenitently crave is also called the "lyric." However named, "precision" is its overriding value, notwithstanding the living infinitude of change and indeterminacy. We may note that this ideal precision prompts Ulrich at a later point, in explaining what is valuable in writings by certain mystics, to speak with admiration of Stendhal (III, 12).

might be the conventionally narrated ten-page account (II, 63) of Bonadea's high-minded second seduction of a now reluctant Ulrich through appeals to his absorption in the Parallelaktion and the Moosbrugger affair (neither strategy works) and then, successfully, through soliciting his help in the removal of a flea (identified as favoring the same bodily areas as a lover). A serio-comic reprise of this chapter ("Bonadea or the relapse": III, 23)—in which conversation swings round from the Diotima-Arnheim world of quality-trafficking to Ulrich's departure with his sister into a different life, thus bringing three of the four leading women characters into a single extended focus—exemplifies the novel's compositional balance and pliancy. Or we could cite the free-standing episode (II, 40) in which Ulrich, metaphysically drunk on his resolve to shed the burden of "qualities," is arrested on the street and compelled in a district police station to acknowledge that whereas the State normally appears to a man accustomed to its privileges as a sort of "hotel in which one was entitled to civility and service," it can suddenly become that place where the same man is not asked even once about the work that has "brought him honor in the world." (The episode marks a new stage, of "statistical disenchantment," in the self-audit through which Ulrich realigns his life. Ironically, the immediate result is his appointment by Count Leinsdorf as the Parallelaktion's honorary secretary.)

Most original and beautiful of all, I think, are certain chapters in the third part—like III, 24 and 25—telling of the passage of Ulrich and his sister-double Agathe across the borders of any world where measurable, saleable qualities remain determining. (In its dismissal of worldly valuations, the new ethic they begin to enact retains more than a trace of aristocratic, *symboliste* arrogance.) The special force of these chapters, their wavering conversational rhythms laid across a palpable erotic undertow, may well derive from Musil's own exploratory uncertainty as to the sort of lovers he meant Ulrich and Agathe to become. The interpretive problem here typifies some of the difficulties commentary on Musil has gotten into and is worth stopping to consider for a moment. Unquestionably in the spectacular manuscript chapter "Journey to Paradise" (III, 94 in Frisé's edition) a physical consummation occurs, and is frequently cited as the plainest of narrative facts for the work as a whole. But Wilkins and Kaiser, following the lead of Wilhelm Bausinger, show that this chapter is from a much earlier stage of composition—as early as 1920 and not later than 1925—in which (1) the protagonist is not "Ulrich" but "Anders" (Man? Other?), (2) he and Agathe are twins in biological fact and not merely in their own speculative fancy, and (3) the idea of a "man without qualities" has not yet materialized out of a cluster of more melodramatic possibilities. Even in this early draft "Anders" at the moment of consummation speaks of the event as incidental to what is really taking place between the pair. Conceivably it is the one way to put behind them an obstinate sensual distraction. Shortly after, the narrative specifies, they resume separate bedrooms. And there is evidence that in the middle or later 1930s the chapter itself was dropped from Musil's working scheme.[7]

In shorter compass a good deal of Musil's special flavor may be caught in the elaboration of a very different love duet, between stately Diotima and polymath Arnheim, and of the critical factor of "soul" in so momentous an event. Their liaison will become adulterous soon enough; for the moment, though, they are seen behaving with sublime restraint. The chapter in question (II, 45) bears the promising title, "Silent encounter

[7] See Eithne Wilkins, "*Der Mann ohne Eigenschaften* and Musil's 'Steinbaukastenzeit,' " *Oxford German Studies* (1968); also Ernst Kaiser, " 'Der Mann ohne Eigenschaften': Ein Problem der Wirklichkeit," *Merkur* (July 1957), and the book-length study by Kaiser and Wilkins, *Robert Musil: Eine Einfuhrung in das Werk* (1962). Admittedly it is only in some late notes and revisions that Musil appears to have seen (if he did) another way through his story besides physical incest—to be followed, for Agathe if not for both, by suicide. But it seems reasonable to think that nothing essential to Musil's primary purpose hangs upon these overt plot dispositions. For one thing the idea that possible or imagined events are as real to consciousness as those actually occurring, and are equally consequential, sets its mark on everything Musil wrote.

between two mountain peaks." Speculations about all passional existence quickly take charge of the exposition and are allowed all the space they need. Yet I think it will be seen that the narrative advance is not deflected by these interpolations; in any case, no more than with Proust do we abandon the bluff comedy of satiric representation:

> But . . . something was there that made this man who hobnobbed with American tycoons and had been received by emperors and kings, this nabob who could offer any woman her weight in platinum, stare spellbound at Diotima. . . . For this "something," here once again the word "soul" must be used.
>
> This is a word that has already appeared frequently, though not precisely in the clearest of connections. For instance, as that which the present time has lost or that which cannot be combined with civilization. As that which is stirred, not only into repugnance, by a murderer [the Moosbrugger theme]. As that which was to be set free by the *Parallelaktion*. As religious meditation and *contemplatio in caligine divina* with Count Leinsdorf. As a love of metaphor and simile with many people. And so on. Of all the peculiarities that this word "soul" has, however, the oddest is that young people cannot pronounce it without laughing. Even Diotima and Arnheim were shy of using it without qualification; for that someone has a great, noble, cowardly, daring or base soul is something that can just about be asserted, but to say outright "my soul" is something one cannot bring oneself to do. It is distinctly a word for older people; and this can only be understood by assuming that there is something that makes itself more and more felt in the course of life, something for which one urgently needs a name, without finding it, until in the end one reluctantly makes use of that which was originally spurned.
>
> And how then is one to describe it? One can stand still or move on as one will, the essential is not what lies straight before one, what one sees, hears, wants, takes hold of, and

masters. It lies ahead, a horizon, a semicircle; but the ends of this semicircle are joined by a sinew, and the plane of this sinew goes right through the middle of the world. In front, face and hands look out of it; the sensations and strivings run along ahead of it; and no one doubts that what we do there is always reasonable or at least impassioned. That is, circumstances external to us demand our actions of us in a way that is comprehensible to everyone; or if, involved in passion, we do something incomprehensible, that, after all, is still something with a way and a nature of its own. But however completely understandable and self-contained it all seems, it is accompanied by an obscure feeling that it is merely half the story. There is something the matter with the equilibrium, and man advances in order not to sway, like a tightrope-walker. And as he advances through life, leaving behind him what he has lived through, a wall is formed by what is still to be lived and what has been lived, and in the end his path resembles that of a worm in the wood, which can twist any way it likes, even turning backwards, but always leaves an empty space behind it. And this dreadful feeling of a blind space, a space cut off behind all the fullness, this half that is always still lacking even although everything has become a whole, is what finally causes one to notice what one calls the soul.

One thinks it, feels it, has premonitions of it all the time, naturally, in the most various kinds of surrogates and according to one's temperament. In youth it is a distinct feeling of uncertainty, in everything one does, as to whether whatever it is is really the right thing. In old age it is amazement at how little one has done of all that one actually intended. In between it is the comfort of being a hell of a chap, efficient, and a good sort too, even though not everything one does can be justified in every detail; or that after all the world isn't what it ought to be, either, so that in the end all that one has done wrong still amounts to a fair enough compromise; and finally some people even think, away out beyond everything, of a God who has the missing piece of themselves in His pocket. Only love occupies a special position in all this; for it is in this exceptional case that the second half grows on. The loved person seems to stand where otherwise there is always something missing. The souls unite, as it were, *dos à dos*, so making themselves superfluous. This is why after the passing of their one great youthful love most people no longer feel the absence of the soul, so that this so-called foolishness fulfills a meritorious social function.

Neither Diotima nor Arnheim had ever loved. Of Diotima we know this already. But the great financier, too, possessed a—in a wider sense—chaste soul. He had always been afraid that the feelings he aroused in women might not be for himself but for his money; and for this reason he lived only with women to whom he, for his part, gave not feelings but money. He had never had a friend, because he was afraid of being used; he had only business friends, even if sometimes the business deal was an intellectual one. So he was wily in the ways of life, yet untouched and in danger of being left on his own, when he encountered Diotima, whom destiny had ordained for him. The mysterious forces in them collided with each other. What happened can only be compared to the blowing of the trade winds, the Gulf Stream, the volcanic tremors in the earth's crust; forces vastly superior to man, related to the stars, were set in motion between the two of them, over and above the limits of the hour and the day—measureless, mighty currents.

At such moments it is quite immaterial what is said. Upward from the vertical crease of his trousers Arnheim's body seemed to stand there in the solitude of God in which the mountain giants stand. United with him by the wave of the valley, on the other side Diotima rose, luminous with solitude—her dress of the period forming little puffs on the upper arms, dissolving the bosom in an artfully draped looseness over the stomach and being caught in to the calf again just under the hollow of the knee. The strings of glass beads in the door curtains cast reflections like ponds, the javelins and arrows on the walls were tremulous with their feathered and deadly passion, and the yellow Calman-Levy volumes on the tables were silent as lemon groves. Reverently we pass over their opening words.[8]

The fullness of notation in this passage, and—for all its digressiveness and jokiness—the human energy of response it bears witness to at every diagnostic turn, are wholly characteristic. Even when at the mercy of forces "vastly superior," human selfhood, we are insistently reminded, is protean and dynamic and reaches out to perfect its given formation. The variations of behavior brought forward simply in the first full paragraph of this narrative tableau reach into half a dozen distinct levels, or reaction-systems, of experienceable virtue. In rapid series reference is made to busy interpretations of the character of the present age, to the profound psychological attractions of the obscene or forbidden, to the factor of fraud and false promise common both to grand state policies like the *Parallelaktion* and to the private fixations of dignitaries like Count Leinsdorf, to the fictionality and arbitrariness even of ordinary language use, and to—implicit in all the others—the ingenuities of evasiveness the human self continually produces in its life-abiding impulse to self-completion.

Here as elsewhere what is most vitally representative about Diotima and Arnheim is their ability to slide from one point to another in what they do, or wish to do, without being responsibly present during the actual crossing. But there would be little advantage in merely abusing them and the qualities they embody.[9] In Musil's governing conception they exemplify

---

[8] A later chapter about this same pair (II, 105: "Being sublime lovers is no joke") exemplifies those recapitulations and re-enactments of familiar material that are not the least of one's rewards in reading, and re-reading, Musil.

[9] On this point it may be assumed that Ulrich speaks for the author: "One can't be angry with one's own time without damage to oneself" (I, 16). Ulrich's expressed view of Arnheim, not without some envy for the man's self-possession, is finally unsparing: "He is always overestimating the happiness it is for time and space to meet with him in forming the present moment" (II, 69). The tone here helps prepare us not to take undue alarm during a mo-

laws of behavior which every systematic inquiry discloses. For at the heart of Musil's undeflectible vision is a volatile disconnectedness not only between reality and consciousness but, so far as we can see, between any one moment of existence and even the one most directly succeeding it. What we call reality is never more than provisional; a first truth about it is always that it could just as well be "otherwise." Musil's authority as a writer is in persuading us that this vision, at once imaginative and conceptual, rises altogether naturally from our observation of life; his art, then, is in keeping this vision continuously active in particular passages and expository figures. Thus, for example, the grammatically peculiar title of the novel's long second part (which takes us through to the moment when Ulrich's break with the world of "qualities" begins in earnest): *Seinesgleichen Geschieht*—Things Equivalent to It Come to Pass, or, in the translators' idiomatic rendering, "The Like of It Now Happens." And thus, too, the whole pattern of emphasis and detail in the nineteen chapters of the "sort of introduction" (*Eine Art Einleitung*) constituting Part One, chapters brilliantly outlining the paradigmatic society from which the man without qualities plans his escape.

This society has its own self-serving formulas of explanation, which Musil ruthlessly parodies. (Like the supreme Vienna *feuilletoniste* Karl Kraus, he commonly strikes his targets by describing them in their own language.) New methods of thought have descended on the world, so it is claimed, and are causing an "unfathomable transformation" (I, 11). Everyone who makes a living professing knowledge of the soul— "clergy, historians, or artists"—agrees that "mathematics" is

---

ment near the end of Part Two—a moment strikingly like Hamlet's crisis of impulse in finding Claudius at prayer—when Ulrich during a climactic interview with Arnheim self-consciously rehearses a temptation to stab the man in the back and rid himself for good of this self-appointed mighty opposite. Arnheim in his double role of state counselor and munitions magnate has been trying to coopt Ulrich by offering a job that would not only bring him under surveillance but also, in some hidden corner of Arnheim's brain, bind him into the obligations of a son.

responsible. The rationalizations of mathematics have entered modern life like a *daimon* and destroyed all its balance, making man simultaneously "lord of the earth" and "slave of the machine." The best to be said for man's behavioral condition in the present century is that it has metamorphosed into "an immense new, collective ant-like heroism" (I, 2). Or so it must appear from the new "psycho-technical point of view," from which the qualities possessed by world geniuses and champion boxers are not only much the same—cunning, courage, precision, and an exceptional "combinatory ability"—but are not different from those to be found in a champion race horse; a "race horse of genius" in the idiom of the age (I, 13). (Under this psycho-technical lens the value system of traditional civilization looks "simply comical": I, 10.) What we know from the first about Ulrich is that he has already worked past these pseudo-explanations. But understanding has brought with it neither power nor freedom; it merely reveals that he is himself at a dead end. "He saw wonderfully clearly," Musil writes, "that . . . he had in himself all the capacities and qualities favored by his era; but the possibility of applying them had for him somehow got mislaid." Hence the "year's leave" he now proposes, "to seek the most exact use of his capacities" (I, 13).

Again the condition defined—a complexly acquired yet unavailing personal resourcefulness—is universal. Every inhabitant of an actual world, Musil writes in a remarkable extended figure, "has at least nine characters: a professional one, a national one, a civic one, a class one, a geographical one, a sex one, a conscious, and unconscious, and perhaps even too a private one" (I, 8). But though he "combines them all in himself, they work to dissolve him." They pour through him and leave behind a tenth character which somehow renders inactive the other nine, being "the passive fantasy of spaces unfilled." A maxim adapted by Ulrich from Emerson—a favored early source of confirmation, along with the Anglo-American moralists generally[10]—sums up the law of perpetual displace-

[10] ". . . Ruskin, Carlyle, Emerson, Thoreau, C[h]anning (Selfculture) . . .":

ment that is involved. It is simply that every specific human accomplishment can get eclipsed (*übertroffen*: I, 10; "beat hollow" might be an idiomatic equivalent) by the next. To Ulrich all mankind, more certainly in this century than ever, is on an expedition to no discernible end. Unless inclined to settle for mere "travel fantasies" (*Reiseträumen*: I, 8), it must accept the burden of conducting life "on interim principles"; it must meet the demand for clear answers with a simple "not yet" (I, 13). It must truly live, that is, in imagination—through a "sense of possibility" coordinate with and yet surpassing the "sense of reality"; through a sense of uncreated alternatives, things not yet realized but implicit in any conceivable formation of the real; through a sense above all of what would be required of the self to live in the consciousness of "what is not" as well as of "what is." In short, mankind must live in acceptance of an idea Ulrich had once propounded in a school essay (nearly getting expelled for it): that "even God probably preferred to speak of His world in the subjunctive of potentiality . . . for God makes the world and while doing so thinks it could just as well be otherwise" (I, 5). An ethic of pure possibility, we might call it, if Musil's philosophic identity were our central concern—or had been his. But, as with a later philosopher-turned-novelist, the undervalued Iris Murdoch, Musil's choice as a writer was not for philosophic definition but for the "living ethic" of fiction, and he asks to be tested first of all on this ground.

His originality at any rate is not in the paraphrasable substance of the hypotheses and judgments turned over in such passages as I have been citing here. Their moral skepticism and naturalism are common across a broad sweep of modern writing.[11] What is immediately distinctive is rather Musil's angle of

---

Tagebücher, Aphorismen, Essays und Reden, ed. Adolf Frisé (1955), 95. Frisé dates this notebook entry to 1905.

[11] So, too, is their audible Nietzscheanism. More or less inevitably for a writer of Musil's generation, Nietzsche dominated his early reading (though his direct teacher was the philosopher and physicist Ernst Mach, subject of his doctoral thesis at Berlin in 1908); at any rate there is more than a trace of

entry and the experimental equipment he brought with him. Characteristically the bruited explanation that mathematics (or science, or technology) is the transforming demon of contemporary civilization is covered with irony even as it is set down in the text; the immediate point is that most of those trafficking in such explanations are themselves mathematically ignorant. Musil, by contrast, knew the mathematics, and the science generally. He was trained and practised in philosophy, in engineering, and, most significantly, in both experimental psychology and mathematical theory. As claims are advanced for the reality of a condition of being in which "what is not" is as substantial as "what is," it turns out that these claims are based in no negligible part on experimental observation and on a key analogy taken from mathematics itself.

~

The combination, psychology and mathematics, is fully in place in Musil's precocious first novel, *The Bewilderments of Boarding School Pupil Törless* (1906). In its overform *Törless* is one more novel of the slippery trials of youthful development, though it has its own way of evoking the contradictoriness of the process, the "secret, aimless, melancholy sensuality" flooding the self in adolescence. (The story, set in a school for the sons of ambitious aristocratic and bourgeois families, centrally involves an experimental scheme for the domination and degradation of one of the boys by a trio of schoolmates, among whom Törless, though not the instigator, increasingly finds himself much more than a detached observer; it is he

Nietzschean harshness and snobbery as well as fantastication in Musil's rendering of the forms of human confusion. Musil once admitted feeling that there was nothing he might write which Nietzsche had not already written (*Prosa, Dramen, Späte Briefe*, ed. Adolf Frisé [1955], 706). Yet it should be noted that when Nietzsche is invoked in *The Man Without Qualities*, the context is ironic. It is the hysterical Clarisse and the apprentice Nazi Hans Sepp who reductively swear by him, Walter and Clarisse who fight over physical possession of one of his books, the cynical Meingast who is described as descending "from Zarathustra's mountain," and so on.

who, in his own mind, becomes the real subject of the experiment.) *Törless* thus carries forward the familiar romanticist notion that the special vulnerability of childhood and adolescence may be nearer the truth about existence-in-the-world than is the ego wholeness which school training sets as its moral goal. For Törless the "something dark" within himself that words and thoughts cannot bring under control is both anguish and intoxication. Presenting itself to him as degradation, it leads to a kind of breakdown. At the same time he is drawn to the experience—to the mysterious form of it even more than to its sensual embodiment—as to nothing else in the life he knows or can yet anticipate. The whole episode, Musil specifies, will be indispensable to Törless's adult growth; it will furnish "that small admixture of a toxic substance which is needed to rid the soul of its overconfident, complacent healthiness, and to give it instead a kind of health that is more acute, and subtler, and wiser."[12]

Like several ambitious contemporaries in the novel—Gide, Mann, Lawrence—and like Dostoievsky before them (whom Musil never lost admiration for), Musil may be seen as concerned from the first to detach a persistent irrationalism in experience from the stigma of perversity, and to detach its literary rendering from Gothic (or Naturalist) exaggeration. Step-by-step notations of private feeling are a main part of this effort, which reflects the unmasking impulse at work throughout early modern writing. Discordances traditionally represented by way of the sublime and grotesque are established here in ordinary conversation. But for Musil, bringing to light what was shameful or publicly inadmissible was secondary. What interested him in *Törless* was not the scandal of adolescent homosexuality but a certain equivocality in all existence. One observed it in persons and their motives but also in objects and completed events; one observed it finally, beyond all ques-

---

[12] This is close to William James's classic differentiation of "healthy-mindedness" and the "sick soul," published four years earlier in *The Varieties of Religious Experience*.

tion of subjective distortion, in the pure world of mathematical abstraction. To minds able to see things clearly and to acknowledge what is seen, an element of the incommensurable is universal in experience. It crops up everywhere we look. What above all has tormented Törless, so he tells his fellow experimenter Beineberg (whose attitudes are conventionally blasphemous), "isn't anything supernatural at all. It's precisely the natural—don't you see?" It is, for one thing, the mere succession of our commonest states of mind, in any one of which we may find ourselves transported by feelings and perceptions impossible to re-imagine when we progress to a different state.

How do we, how does anyone, "get across" from the one state to the other? The discovery racking Törless is that there is, universally, a "lacuna" in the causality of thought itself. Studying mathematics, Törless has come upon certain peculiar units or concepts which are tame enough in ordinary use, lending themselves to all sorts of interesting tricks, but which under examination "break loose" and appear "wild and annihilating." Infinity is one such concept, easy enough to talk about and apply in specific problems but profoundly disconcerting when you try to grasp it directly. Worse yet, there are the so-called imaginary numbers, the square roots of negative integers. You can write these down, and "get across" with them from one quantity to another; yet absolutely they cannot exist. What passes as Törless's breakdown has less to do with sexual abasement than with his math master's evasiveness concerning this ontological gap, this incommensurable "second, secret life" of even the world of numbers—and with his own subsequent inability to explain to a panel of kindly school officials how it has taken possession of his thought.[13]

Metaphors of "boundary situations," "borderline experi-

---

[13] Mathematics also serves as a lever of disillusion in Stendhal's autobiographical *Henry Brulard* when the young man's algebra teacher, pressed to explain why a minus multiplied by a minus yields a plus or why parallel lines may in certain circumstances be taken as meeting, will only say, "it is the custom" and "my child, you will know later" (ch. xxxiv). Hypocrisy, young Brulard-Beyle discovers, is occupational even among mathematicians.

ences," "invisible frontiers" of understanding, openings into the incommensurable, unbridgeable gaps within what is nevertheless a perpetually moving series, are a constant in Musil's writing. And in notebook entries and manuscript fragments running from 1898 into the mid-1920s the idea is repeatedly sketched of a protagonist who will refuse all the commoner strategies for keeping this alarming vision at bay and will take on the dangerous task—sacrificial, or else openly criminal—of absorbing its mysteries into his own daily existence. As early as his eighteenth year Musil was drafting pages from the nighttime diary of a figure identified as "the vivisectionist" who would presumably knife open the hidden transactions through which the human soul enters upon its distinctive life in the world. For a time new versions of this core story keep to the note of blasphemy and transgression. Around 1918 there is mention of a novel to be called "The Devil," or possibly "The Romance of a Priest." Between 1918 and 1921 come notes and drafts for a novel to be called "The Spy" (its hero, one Achilles, is already engaged with figures named Moosbrugger, Clarisse, and Agathe); after 1921 this gives way to a more developed work provisionally called "The Redeemer" and then "The Twin Sister," with its protagonist renamed Anders. At intervals the name Robert turns up. None of these projects was completed; all in some fashion find their way into *The Man Without Qualities*.[14]

---

[14] The two plays completed and produced in the early 1920s also prefigure Musil's final scheme. *Die Schwärmer* (*The Enthusiasts*)—which has surface resemblances to Joyce's *Exiles* and Lawrence's *Women in Love*—offers a pairing of couples, Maria/Thomas and Regine/Anselm, who will reemerge partly as Ulrich/Agathe and partly in various complementary relationships: Ulrich/Diotima, Diotima/Arnheim, Ulrich/Bonadea, Ulrich/Gerda Fischel, Ulrich/Clarisse, Walter/Clarisse, to name the more important. Lisa Appignanesi's summary catches what is essential to the main action: "It is by coming into contact with this abandonment of which Regine and Anselm are capable that Thomas becomes a true visionary [enthusiast], a full man of possibility." The second play, *Vinzenz and the Woman Friend of Important Men*, presents a farcical version of Diotima's salon but as if an Agathe were subversively in

Along the way Musil published five shorter tales in which these "boundary situations" and transformations of private identity are explored within relatively conventional settings, though the writing itself is anything but conventional. Two appeared in 1911 under the common title *Unions*. The first and longer, "The Perfecting of a Love" (strictly, "The Completing of Love": *Die Vollendung der Liebe*), is a classic novella, undeviating in its anatomy of crossing and change. What overtakes the bourgeois wife Claudine is presented in two ways. It is something which, the moment she starts on her journey, begins sliding toward her from beyond herself—or from back of her in time, Musil casually establishing a precedent in her past for the adultery that becomes its outward form—but it is also something that wells up within her, displacing familiar selfhood and filling her with the antithetical sense of being, now, "indeterminate" (*undeutlich*; without meaning). Before all this has happened in reality, the "like of it" is uncovered as something that might already have happened—and so inexorably it does happen. (The man involved, a government official met on the train, is no more to Claudine than the instrument of her fixation on certain "spaces unfilled," alternative possibilities pressing toward acceptance.) The force of Musil's narration is all in the slow, rapt tracing of these all but traceless changes. Sometimes a consciousness of them comes over the protagonist "as if a door had slammed"; more often the change takes place as a sliding or gliding (the verbs *glitschen* and *gleiten* are virtual leitmotifs), a nearly imperceptible slipping off into an altered condition.

In "The Temptation of Quiet Veronica" this vocabulary becomes very nearly unbalancing. The main characters are described as gliding past each other and, in effect, in and out of each other—*abgleiten, begleiten, herabgleiten, hineingleiten, übereinandergleiten* all do service—as if entering a realm where everything possible between them must in fact come to

---

charge of it. In the hero's penchant for principled lying it anticipates Ulrich's new ethic of the intransigently experimental life.

pass. Concretely the story is of Veronica's virtual sacrifice of
self to her suicidal lover's search for a second, alternative existence, and one direct irony is that only when she abruptly retreats from the man and his obsessions can he find his way
back into substantial life. Before this happens her own sense of
self grows perilously insubstantial. She sickens in her sensory
being (a sickness objectified in feral dream-images) as if absorbing all his indeterminateness; she becomes enclosed inside
the thing that has materialized between them—this "something excessive flowing out of them" and at the same time
"curving, bulging, arching high over them"—and she will not
fully recover. It is all as abstract and indefinite as happenings
in a dream world, yet it persuasively renders not only the reality of psychic alienation but the extraordinary formative energy even that requires. The very fact that by the story's end
Veronica has moved too far from her starting point ever to return confirms a sense that this experience, too, represents humanity's power to organize, for good or ill, its own participation in the unrelenting process of life.

   In the stories published in 1924 as *Three Women* the same
narrative patterning persists, though with a greater surface dis-
tinctness and objectivity. We draw close in these stories to the
episodic-analytic mode of *The Man Without Qualities*; only a
self-delighting expansiveness of presentation remains to be
added. The most conventional in execution is "Grigia." As in
Mann's *Death in Venice* the border crossed by the story's
achievement-complacent protagonist is figured in the boundary separating northern Europe from the primitive relaxations
and energies of Italy. It is also, less decisively, a class boundary
by way of the story's remote mining-district setting (the protagonist, named Homo, has gone there as a geological consult-
ant). But in particular it is the boundary where professionalized masculine assurance and the cultural assumptions
supporting it—assumptions making up, we are told, the "common over-all soul mass" which is modern Europe—lose all
their hard purchase on reality. In contrast the complaisant
peasant woman Homo takes as mistress is protean and

amoral, a life-abiding figure within herself but a *belle dame sans merci*, in the end, for him. The second in this group, "The Lady From Portugal," also follows a scheme whereby a male protagonist's long, ambiguously resolved trial of life and selfhood has its corresponsive focus in an enigmatic woman: witch, anima, secret witness and good wife all at once, a counterforce both endangering and exalting.

"Tonka," the longest story of Musil's middle period, seems to me also the richest in narrative interest. The story again moves forward in the fashion of the events described—as a progression of "very slight experiences" that happen "all over again," that are "always there," but that eventually come to mean "the very opposite of what they had meant in the beginning." Again we are given a scientist-protagonist, a man fanatically committed to "the cool, soberly fantastical, all-encompassing spirit of technology." He is for eliminating from life everything inefficient ("emotion, poetry, kindness, virtue, simplicity"), yet he also looks forward uneasily to another, different age when at last it will "be possible to say what we ought to have *felt* about things."[15]

For this man the working girl Tonka becomes the balancing Other of antithetical possibility, for: "One knows little of oneself unless one has someone else in whom one is reflected." (A second maxim—it might have come from *All's Well That Ends Well*—subsumes this first one: "So little do we know what we know, and want what we want.") In helping him to live, yet to remain as hard and spare as if disciplined to a long journey, Tonka in her contrasting wordlessness absorbs into herself the disorder imperceptibly engulfing them: "she did not stir his soul, but rinsed it clean and smooth, like fresh water." Most of all she absorbs his emergent distrust of her. Thus the consequence of her eventual pregnancy is not only the nameless protagonist's obsession with the possibility of her unfaithful-

---

[15] Section iv; emphasis added. "The history of truth and the history of feeling," Musil would write in *The Man Without Qualities* (III, 37), "are in many ways interlinked; but that of feeling remains obscure."

ness—everything naturally dividing them confirms it for
him—but her own sickness unto death. But as she slips away,
he grows "more like himself again"; it is the *se ipse* pattern of
older myth. Also he makes a brilliant success of the scientific
speculation he has drugged himself with to balance the idea of
her infidelity—who but Musil would link these narrative factors through the mathematical figure of their each acquiring
for him a "ninety-nine per cent probability"?—and at the story's end it is "he [who] stands in the light and she [who] lies
under ground." Forgetting her except in oblique, unfocused returns of feeling, he lives on to enjoy, because of this "small,
warm shadow across his life," a certain superiority over the
lives of others; a superiority, Musil specifies, even as to "goodness." It seems to me, all in all, a remarkable story, moving
seamlessly between suggestion and explication, poetic expansiveness and narrative irreversibility, a story from the vital center of its author's speculative passion. But it is not, in any ordinary sense, a story with a moral.

~

The theorem about experience that all Musil's earlier work
turns on is stated most broadly in the title of the fourth chapter
of *The Man Without Qualities*: "If there is such a thing as a
sense of reality, there must also be a sense of possibility"
(*Wenn es Wirklichkeitssinn gibt, muss es auch Möglichkeits-
sinn geben*). But the chief characteristic of this troubling second sense—those possessing it are commonly classed as misfits, and when children display it "it is vigorously driven out of
them"—makes it hard to distinguish from its apparent opposite, for it is precisely that state of mind "which does not shrink
from reality." "It is reality," Musil continues,

> that awakens possibilities, and nothing could be more
> wrong than to deny this. Nevertheless, in the sum total or on
> the average they will always remain the same possibilities,
> going on repeating themselves until a man comes to whom

something real means no more than something imagined. It is he who first gives the new possibilities their meaning and their destiny; he awakens them. (I, 4)

This is to be Ulrich's mission in the story that follows. Treating reality not as something settled that he should seek accommodation with ("in a way comprehensible to everyone") but as an unending "task" and "invention," he will become the explorer and awakener of unrealized possibility. It is an undertaking awash in ambiguities. Self-exposure is only the half of it. Ulrich himself acknowledges that with the power this new vocation can bring, one might do "everything or nothing," become either the world's savior or an outright criminal (I, 13: an Ulrich/Moosbrugger link is thus established even before Moosbrugger appears in his own person). Midway through the long second part the Nietzschean implications of the counter-ethic in question are spelled out in detail. The qualities marking these men of possibility include—besides courage, cunning, precision—a freedom from scruple, an exclusion of moral considerations, and a spirit as willing to destroy as it is to initiate (II, 72). (Unfortunately these are qualities also available to total fools, there being "absolutely no significant thought that stupidity itself can't turn to account": I, 16.) Interestingly it is given to Walter—not stupid but febrile and unbalanced—to put a name to Ulrich's new calling (I, 17):

> He is a man without qualities [Walter explains to the ever-scornful Clarisse] . . . Nothing is stable for him. Everything is fluctuating, a part of a whole, among innumerable wholes that presumably are part of a superwhole, which, however, he doesn't know the slightest thing about. So every one of his answers is a part-answer, every one of his feelings is only a point of view, and whatever a thing is, it doesn't matter to him what it is, it's only some accompanying "way in which it is," some addition or other, that matters to him.

Over against the man without qualities stand not simply the time-serving intellectuals, the neurotics, the old-believers or

new-fanatics of what even Ulrich's father would seek out as
"the one truth and correct will" (II, 74); on any complex issue
such persons grasp at definitions that are "as round as an
egg"—or as a "hand grenade" (II, 111). There is also the exemplary class of "integral men" (*lauter Ganze*: II, 71), the men
Diotima assembles in her salon to shape Europe's future, con-
ceiving of herself as that even rarer thing, the integral woman
(*die ungebrochene Frau*; II, 24). Integral men, one supposes,
are the ethically complete. But in modern Kakania they are the
most formidable of madmen—daydreamers with a vengeance,
spokesmen and visionaries of the Whole whose passion (again
the Moosbrugger link) is to hold all existence within a single
coercive ordering. Any accurate grasp of reality they possess,
Ulrich remarks, is limited to that "one definite square milli-
meter" of knowledge which actually belongs to them (II, 63).[16]
The foremost of these Supermen is Arnheim, whose appetite
for Great Ideas is at bottom wholly practical. An idea's right
use, for him, is simply to obstruct some other idea; going armored in one's own ideas makes it less likely that someone
else's will come out on top (II, 114). To Arnheim ideas are
passports to authority and tactical advantage, belonging finally to that world of "appropriation and mastery" (*Aneig-
nens, Bewältigens*) from which, in the third "millennial" section of the novel—feeling their own thought as, instead, a
"happiness, an occurrence, a gift" (*Glück, Ereignis, Ge-
schenk*: III, 12)—Ulrich and his sister set about withdrawing.
   In Musil's scheme it is these integral men who most perfectly
resist the sense of possibility. Seeking to impose themselves on
temporality, they become instead its abject servants. The more
they try to fit the exact sum of reality to their craving for
wholeness, the more the thing itself—the unregulated flux of

---

[16] In *The Man Without Qualities* it matters who is talking to whom and in
what circumstances. This indictment of modern single-visionaries is delivered
by Ulrich with charming inappropriateness to Bonadea. As usual her mind
wanders to other subjects. Bonadea's invincible sensuality provides, at intervals, a self-contained analogue to the more destructive mind-sets anatomized
in the novel—as Moosbrugger's madness underscores them all.

events, the unfolding of actual history—swings them out into its own unaccountable orbit. It is this being reduced to "material of history" that galls Ulrich. Why, he thinks, this "abject contemporaneity," this "humanly unworthy complicity"? Instead (in the title of the chapter cited here: II, 83), "why does one not invent history," starting with one's own? At least for oneself one ought to make history, make life, rather than submit to being made by it.

But to will this alternative may only be Arnheimism in subtler form. "We are born in order to create our own kingdom," Arnheim ringingly declares (II, 112: *um uns unser Königreich selbst zu schaffen*—but Musil is unsparing; the context is Arnheim's effort to pacify his African page Soliman, who has just grasped the truth that he has been made a slave). Again the emphasis on possession gives Arnheim away. His acquisitiveness may be "sublime," issuing from a metaphysical will to have "the dignities and consequentialities of existence" (*die Wurden und Wichtigkeiten des Daseins*) in his personal keeping. It is nevertheless acquisitiveness and in the nature of things unappeasable. Indeed, Musil specifies, it is the absence of this quality in Ulrich that breaks in on Arnheim's elaborate self-possession and induces that particular dilation of acquisitiveness we call jealousy. But the sheer folly of thinking to take personal possession of the condition of being our life approaches as its finite limit, or to believe that this ultimate condition will conform to our desire for it—this is precisely the folly Ulrich now begins to see his way past.[17]

The question is not only what we ourselves, incurably finite, are capable of as persons or in the mass, but of the character and history of reality itself. We imagine for the real a component of "repeatability" (*Wiederholbarkeit*) and are morally scandalized not to find it. "How could one demand virtue from everyone [*Tugend*: moral virtue] if a virtuous act were

---

[17] An earlier passage characterizes Arnheim's philosophical ambition as the application of modern industrial principle (*Fabrikationsgrundsatz*) to "the manufacture of life" (II, 90).

not one that could be repeated as often as one likes?" (II, 85). Such repeatability, however, belongs to the secondary domain of "morality and intellect" and even more so to the world of "money" (II, 106). Reality itself, or life, or history, is something other. It carries, Ulrich sees, "an impossible condition within itself" (II, 123). For this reason the sum of reality "cannot by any means be carried to conclusion" (II, 84). Mathematics, again, supplies the best analogue. This problem of reality-as-such calls to mind, for Ulrich, a certain odd class of mathematical problems "that did not admit of any general solution, though they did admit of particular solutions, the combining of which might bring one nearer to the general solution" (II, 83). But this corresponds to what has been affirmed a paragraph earlier in the comparably absolute language of theology, a language as efficient as mathematics (Ulrich senses) for defining the general case (II, 83):

> What he had wanted to say was something like this: "God is far from meaning the world literally. The world is an image, an analogy, a figure of speech, that He must make use of for some reason or other, and it is of course always inadequate. We must not take Him at His word; we ourselves must work out the sum he sets us."

The instruments given the human intelligence for this task are language and reason. But they too participate in an elemental indeterminateness. For language is *metaphor*; and every metaphor, Musil writes—in one of several terse disquisitions on the rhetorical mode he himself brilliantly favored—contains "a truth and a falsehood . . . inextricably interlocked in one's emotions" (II, 115).[18] We deal with this muddle as we can. For practical use, unequivocality (*Eindeutigkeit*), metaphor's functional opposite, is indispensable; it is "the law of

[18] Musil's word is *Gleichnis*, which has several meanings, including *allegory* and Scriptural *parable* (*in Gleichnissen sprechen* means to speak in parables). Also it echoes the over-all title of Part Two: *Seinesgleichen Geschieht*. But the translators are surely right in taking "metaphor" as, in a discussion of language, the sense intended.

waking thought and action." Yet our necessary reliance on it is
profoundly compromising, for it acts on what it seeks to sta-
bilize as does boiling something down in order to make it serv-
iceable: "the really vital forces and spirits escape in a cloud of
steam." As a property of statement unequivocality is thus
something that "prevails equally in a compelling conclusion in
logic and"—characteristic Musilian swerve—"in the mind of
a blackmailer driving his victim before him, step by step" (II,
116). No wonder it backs us into corners. Metaphor, by contrast, is a combining of concepts by radically different means,
as in dream. It is "the sliding logic of the soul" (*die gleitende
Logik*: the participial word, formerly loose among objects and
events, now comes to a focus for Musil in the inmost mind of
man). It is thus at the root of that essential restlessness and expansiveness of spirit which—comically in the affairs of the national-imperial gallimaufry that is Kakania; sensuously and
imaginatively in the adventure shortly to open for Ulrich and
his sister—is the price we pay for being alive at all. But metaphor is also our compensation for suffering that restlessness,
our means of making unsettlement itself into something quickening and restorative. Without metaphor we would be helpless
to negotiate our own ceaselessly emergent life-interests:

> . . . whatever life holds in the way of ordinary liking and dis-
> like, agreement and rejection, admiration, subordination,
> leadership, imitation, and all their counter-manifestations,
> these manifold relations man has to himself and to Nature,
> which are not yet purely objective and perhaps never will
> be—it all cannot be understood except by means of meta-
> phor. (II, 116)

What we ultimately seek for ourselves, unless our aim *is*
blackmail, is the living fusion of these "two great halves of life,
metaphor and truth." But to reach the condition of *spirit* required, we must first endure the conviction that we totally lack
it within ourselves (II, 84).[19] Something like the great devo-

---

[19] Wilkins and Kaiser stretch things a bit in this passage by translating the

tional paradigm of *kenosis* enters the picture here; in order to achieve the "entirely open attitude of mind" Ulrich is determined to live by, there must first be an emptying out of every other—certainly of every world-rewarded—disposition. The need in any case is for a different solution to the problem of existence, a different form for that particular continuance-in-life (*das rechte Leben* is Musil's phrase) which supremely authenticates the intuition of virtue in human apprehension. A way of living is to be sought that does not leave the human self split apart into "a real half and a shadowy half" (II, 123). But what concrete form is this new life to take, among men and women, households, cities, empires? What concrete outcome would signify one's attaining it, or even coming in sight of it? In the last chapters of Part Two Musil leads his protagonist through a succession of negative climaxes. Arnheim's specious proposals are easily rejected (in a travestied temptation scene which nevertheless includes a glancing allusion to Christ's moment of uncertainty in the Garden as to what at last will be required of him: II, 121). So, less easily, is an insane challenge from Clarisse, asking him to father a child who will be the world's "redeemer" (II, 123: Musil's earlier project with that title now belonging only to Clarisse's fanaticism). Between these episodes a telegram brings Ulrich news of his father's death. The news is not shocking in itself, yet carries with it an abrupt disseverance from the assumptions enclosing his earlier life.

Returning home to oversee the business of the estate is the obvious next step. But what is to come after that, for Musil's protagonist and for the shape of his novel? What actual story, what textually convincing resolution, can be imagined for a man setting forth in search of this "other" life, this life in which not dreamily but "with all possible precision" he might stand continuously open to the self-defining, self-furthering

single noun *Geist* as "intellectuality and spirituality." But this seems a legitimate elaboration of the sense Musil has prepared for it as well as of the word's normal range of implication, even broader than that of *esprit* in French.

realm of experience he has so far approached only in certain extraordinary moments of being—"that twinkling, sliding intermutation of all the feelings there were" (II, 123)? Only, perhaps, an inconceivable and unachievable story, a story that if properly told (to return to Musil's own comment) would prove not to have been told at all. It is one thing to outline, from within familiar dialectical positions, schemes of transcendence, whether behavioral or novelistic. It is quite another to realize for them a convincing performative syntax.

~

To Musil the imaginative writer was the virtual opposite of the man bent on a definite criticism of life. In an interview of 1926 he remarked, "The real explanation of real happenings doesn't interest me." Yet he persistently characterized his effort as a journey into truth, and any particular truth would seem to require explanation of some sort. What Musil was resolved on, however, was a journey into unrealized truth, into truths the possibility of which had not yet been distinctly grasped. A notebook entry from the mid-1930s defines the task of fiction as depicting not "that which is, but that which ought to be; or"—with a characteristic further step in which a variant of some straightforward phrase, like a substitution in an equation, turns tantalizingly obscure—"that which could be, as a practical solution to that which ought to be." Musil regularly acknowledged that his conception of writing was "utopian." But he concurrently denied being concerned to prophesy any specific "reality of tomorrow." What he meant by utopia was "not a goal but a direction," not something to formulate within the argument of the work but something coextensive with its continuing realization. Writing itself becomes, ideally, utopia.[20]

Musil was explicit about his bias toward philosophic ends.

[20] These ideas and positions are efficiently reviewed in the introductory chapters of Burton Pike's study ("The Mind of Musil," "The Fiction of Musil") and of Frederick G. Peters's ("The Writer in Search of Utopia").

A "new morality" was needed, he declared in 1926, and the novel he had undertaken was to "provide material" for it and to achieve a "synthesis." For these purposes any story effectively developed might serve. No one story could be, in its particulars, more authoritative than another. What was important was that the offered synthesis, the specification of new reaches of experience, be (to the limit of current comprehension) philosophically answerable. But it would not itself be determined by philosophic prepossession. It would remain a story, a concrete manifestation of human possibility.

The problems of form involved in coordinating free philosophic exploration and the disclosure of actual experience were of course not unique to Musil. In one fashion or another they are the common inheritance of the long breakdown, for modern letters, of classical-humanist premises identifying the truths of art with the truths of scheduled reason. For German literature, especially, the association (central to Romanticism at its most soaring) of the imaginative writer with the functions of metaphysician, purifier, and sage has remained traditional, all the more so as a component of folk presentiment and folk supernaturalism has also held place to an unusual degree within major literary practice. As German metaphysics since Kant and Hegel seems uniformly haunted by the popular wisdom mythology descending from Jacob Boehme and his imaginative kind, German fiction down into the era of Grass and Handke has tenaciously kept contact with the imaginative world of the folktale or *märchen*. Whatever the historical cause—the absence in its direct ancestry of metropolitan Balzacs and Flauberts, or of the vision of national-imperial destiny organizing the great line of Russian fiction; the delayed consolidation of that bourgeois-industrial order which in France and Great Britain provided the matrix for modern realism—it may be argued that relative to developments elsewhere, the German novel has stayed conspicuously close in affective organization to its romance origins.

The central German-language precedent in fiction, as for so much else in later German writing, I would take to be Goethe, whose experiments in episodic-philosophic storytelling spanned his career. For writers like Mann and Hesse, Goethe the wisdom writer was the commanding presence, the final measure of literary ambition and honor. For Musil the relation seems more lightly borne. (In *The Man Without Qualities* Goethe realistically takes his place alongside Nietzsche as an authority figure invoked with special emphasis by fools and charlatans. Arnheim is a great Goethean.) In any event it is Goethe the remarkably freehanded experimenter in extended fiction who can, I think, shed light on the problems of assessment presented by Musil's novel in both major respects, its opening to philosophy and its textual incompleteness. The great classic in the category of the intrinsically unfinishable superfiction which becomes a lifetime's undertaking is, after all, *Faust*; and Goethe was arguably the first (after Sterne, whom he warmly admired) to conceive of a major work in which, rather than by any clear textual resolution, success comes in sustaining a continuously sufficient expressiveness, a voice and vision worth following wherever they take us—or drop us.

The fictional precedent bearing most instructively on *The Man Without Qualities* seems to me Goethe's *Elective Affinities* (1809), the title of which proposes a physico-chemical analogy as the clearest way into the story itself. If *Der Mann ohne Eigenschaften* does not allude directly to *Die Wahlverwandtschaften* there is an echo, at least, in their shared abstractness as titles (though less distinct than the echo of *Die Leiden des Jungen Werthers* in *Die Verwirrungen des Zöglings Törless*). Certainly a shared field of concern can be identified since a capacity or incapacity for particular relationships is required for any concrete address to the matter of "qualities"; how are qualities approachable except in the relations they establish or withdraw from? But it is especially on the issue of form that the precedent of Goethe's extraordinary novel strikes me as illuminating.

The Elective Affinities is a rich and subtle work, and I will not attempt to summarize the full interest of it. (It is also a "beautiful" work, as J. Hillis Miller has recently reported: see

"A 'Buchstabliches' Reading of *The Elective Affinities*," *Glyph* 6 [1979].) In the virtuosity of its concentration on a singularly compact and insulated narrative space, it may at first seem nearer in form to Musil's shorter fiction.[21] The book started out in fact as a novella but overgrew the original conception; it became one of those undertakings in which the working out of particular sequences continually generates new openings. The world of public and historical existence furnishing half the bulk of Musil's long narrative is not absent from *The Elective Affinities*—which takes place in a period of intermittent European warfare much like that in which it was written—but stands outside the main picture. By a reversal of familiar expectation, it is this public sphere that the chief male character, the estate-owner Eduard, withdraws into at moments of unresolvable private crisis. But the formal push of Goethe's work beyond its initiating design, and the sense it delivers of an effort of mind and imagination overreaching the mode of statement through which it first engages attention, are what interest me in pursuing the correspondence.

At this point an outline of the main story is needed, and I cannot myself improve on the one provided by Henry Hatfield in his lucid "guide with 'program notes' " (*Goethe: A Critical Introduction* [1963]):

> . . . Eduard and Charlotte live in leisure on their estate, in a contented if by no means ecstatic marriage. The arrival of a much younger woman, Ottilie, and of the Captain [Eduard's old friend] sets off the process of elective affinity: Eduard falls in love with Ottilie; the Captain with Charlotte; both loves are requited. Eduard does not struggle against his pas-

[21] Concerning its elegant compositional design, Victor Lange exaggerates only a little: "Almost all the principal ideas of the ensuing action are hinted at in the first two or three pages," while "each of the eighteen chapters in the first part is related in a precisely complementary rhythm to the corresponding chapter in the second part": "Introduction," *Elective Affinities*, tr. Elizabeth Mayer and Louise Bogan (1963). What should be added is that this design remains open to radical shifts both in the temper of the exposition and in its whole imaginative reach.

sion, and Ottilie, though virtuous and well-behaved, cannot conceal hers. More restrained, the Captain and Charlotte "renounce"—and soon are relegated to the background. When Eduard later sleeps with his wife, each of them has the image of the beloved person in mind; the child of their "double adultery" combines the features of Ottilie and the Captain. After an unexpected and passionate encounter with Eduard, Ottilie, distraught, lets Charlotte's baby fall into a lake on Eduard's estate; it drowns despite her desperate efforts. After its death, Charlotte is willing to divorce Eduard; but Ottilie believes that God has punished her, refuses to speak to Eduard or the others, and manages to starve herself to death. She performs an apparent miracle in death, and a credulous multitude surrounds her coffin when she is laid out in the chapel. Eduard dies soon after, and they are buried together.[22]

The setting of a story of passion and sacrificial transformation within an idealized moral and civil order is crucial to the work's unforced power. Goethe makes, imaginatively, a strong case for the claims of ordinary society: for the ordered cultivation of family relationships, of the chance at life reserved for each social type and class, and of the natural estate given in commodity to all. But he shows a like tolerance for the waywardness of the single separate spirit and its obstinate self-inventiveness (so we may note his enthusiasm in the years just preceding *The Elective Affinities* for Diderot's *Le Neveu de Rameau*, which he promptly translated). He opens his sympathetic imagination to every part of the unfolding story; at the same time he probes analytically for the laws or rules it conceivably discloses. Goethe had little of his younger contemporary Wordsworth's fear of experimental science, though insist-

---

[22] A textual ending that conceivably shaped the last sentences of that finest and strangest of nineteenth-century English novels, *Wuthering Heights*. What scandalized Thackeray and produced the moralizing sneer in chapter 67 of *Vanity Fair*—the naturalness of Goethe's poignant reversals of the licit and illicit—would surely have been understood as human truth by Emily Brontë.

ing—at the end of all experimentation—upon a humane synthesis of its findings. He remained heir to the scientific enlightenment of the eighteenth century, considering the new chemistry as direct an aid to poetic thought as astrology and alchemy became for Yeats. His novel's title is thus rightly understood as more than an incidental metaphor. But interpretation can go as much astray in following the lead of that title as it can with the poems Yeats made from his explorations into the occult. The analogy of "affinities" is indeed an element in the dialectic of experience acted out in the story. But it is not the central meaning. It is in fact something of a false lead. If Goethe puts the force of his own curiosity behind the Captain's detailed explanation of relationships in nature (Part I, ch. 4), he also puts himself behind Charlotte's undercutting comment that the unvarying example of nature does not really fit the full case of human life.

To Walter Benjamin, in his remarkable monograph on *The Elective Affinities* (1924-1925), it is this pull of explanatory parable or myth against the reality of each new textual sequence that gives form to Goethe's quest for truth in the novel. Goethe himself, in setting out his framing analogy, has a good deal more to say about "affinities" than is contained in the title phrase. The general theory, as the Captain expounds it, has three distinct phases (it is as dialectical as Stendhalian crystallization). Besides the tendency of elements in nature (1) to combine sympathetically with others, they also (2) bear vital relation to themselves, and seek to recover their original condition. But as they do not exist separately in the world, it further happens that (3) even mutually repellent elements may, helped by intermediate agents, join together within the total system, thus introducing a counterimpulse to new separations and exclusions. The more interesting affinities—as it is given to Eduard in his restlessness to remark—are precisely these more complicated and disturbing ones that bring about separations.

As in *Wilhelm Meister's Apprenticeship* twenty years before, two general systems of virtue are advanced in the narrative and set, finally, at odds. The Scriptural, and classical, myth of a choice between right and wrong paths is now a choice between competing behavioral ideals, between the life of civil obligation and the life of service to one's own destiny. In the *Apprenticeship*, theatrical performance provides the arena of choice, which is between two conceptions of the actor's métier: executing with trained skill the role assigned, or—the rarer art, though reached only by way of the other—entering into the very life and spirit of an imaginary existence through a "strength of soul" (Book V, ch. 7). In *The Elective Affinities* the central conflict develops through a multiplicity of analogies.

There is first the organization of Eduard's estate. Several early chapters take up the double business of improved husbandry and aesthetic embellishment (it plays the part of the *Parallelaktion* in Musil's broader canvas). The reconstruction of paths, watercourses, woodlands, and beautiful prospects which keeps the Captain in residence with his friends has as its goal the further refining of the owners' sensibilities, but it will also, like the discipline of household management coincidentally outlined, work to the material advantage of the whole estate, including its tenants. Efficient and attractive building, of houses and landscape monuments, furnishes a complementary analogy, the right way to build symbolizing most immediately the right ordering of human actions.[23] Education furnishes a third, by way of an explicit debate between notions that the right education is one leading to collectively useful accomplishment and the contrary notion of education as a leading forth of each self's distinctive capacity. (The girl Ottilie, her tutor warmly explains, is unable to adapt to the first system but does remarkable things when allowed to follow the second, at her own pace.) Each of these analogy-topics is explored at

[23] Karl Barth, tracing the transformations of spiritual understanding across two centuries, saw *The Elective Affinities* as a classic expression of the central idea of the age: "that idea of man . . . taking hold of everything about him and subjecting it to his will" (*Protestant Thought from Rousseau to Ritschl*, 34-35). It is worth recalling the appeal, during this embattled era, of international Free Masonry, particularly within the artisan-entrepreneurial classes.

some length, either in the author's voice or in the exchanges of the story, so that the narrative surface itself acts as the kind of "Pedagogical Province" through which, in the renewed didacticism of the second *Wilhelm Meister* (1821), Goethe's story conducts both protagonist and reader.

In the main story the two ways of virtue meet in the convergence of Eduard and Ottilie; theirs is the crucial relationship. Eduard—sensitive, impatient, constitutionally restless—has the courage of his nature as well as of his station in life. He is "frank, generous, gallant," and when to break the impasse among the four principals he self-sacrificingly departs for the wars, he acts as if in his true element, covering himself with military honor (a narrative turn anticipating what Proust would hold in store for St. Loup in the superb 1914-1918 passages of *Le Temps retrouvé*). He is also intemperate and self-serving; in one detailed episode his recklessness in pushing through a public celebration of Ottilie's birthday leads to the near drowning of a young boy of the neighborhood. Like Ulrich at the start of Musil's novel, Eduard when first seen is at a crossroads. After years at court and in the army he seeks a second life of reflection and peace and an end to all restlessness. But in the logic of the story he cannot help shedding restlessness all around him. Characteristically he rationalizes this, claiming that instability and change rule over all existence (his own patrician service to this rule makes an attractive contrast to the versions enacted by the intrusive do-gooder Mittler and by a pair of high-born profligates who descend on the estate "direct from the great world").[24]

Ottilie, deferential and self-effacing, is characterologically Eduard's opposite, yet is strongly drawn to his warmth and generosity of spirit. It is natural for her, Goethe specifies, to find congenial the "something childlike" in his moods. To Eduard her inner stillness is the purest imaginable embodiment of

---

[24] A later visitor, from England, adds the implication that the rule of restless, willful change is the rule of all modern life. By his own admission this English lord is the new man of the new age, at home everywhere and nowhere in the world, arranging his life according to the whim or accident of the moment.

the peace and rest he desires, and he turns the estate inside out
to hold her at the center of his life. At the same time this beauty
of being—her virtue, in our root sense—becomes, for all her
self-effacement, a force working changes upon others. The
bond between Ottilie and Eduard brings them happiness yet
unsettles every other relationship. But when Eduard honora-
bly departs for the wars—through a bargain with Charlotte
that appears to safeguard Ottilie's future—"an emptiness so
complete that she could never before have conceived of it"
comes over her in reaction. That rule of instability and change
Eduard embraces in the very act of seeking release from it is
deeply shocking to her as she hears it casually formulated by
new guests at the estate. Abruptly, when the full consequences
are borne in on her, she breaks the pattern. "I have strayed
from my course," she twice tells others. What she returns to is
renunciation and the surrender of life itself; the deviation with
Eduard has truly been deadly for her. Deadly at last for him,
too—despite Charlotte's conviction, profanely amending I Corinthians 13, that love can not only "suffer all" (*alles zu
dulden*) but "restore all" (*alles zu ersetzen*). As Ottilie has become his soul's happiness, he can recover her now only in
death, which soon follows.

All this comes in a narrative text alive with emblems, omens,
portents, premonitions, internal correspondences and paral-
lels. It is also a text that presses to transcend its own initiating
design, spilling over in an autonomous wisdom and truth. The
conspicuous instance—Walter Benjamin understood that it especially needed justifying—is Ottilie's diary. Over a run of
eight chapters in the second part we get six instalments of this
diary, shifting between reflections on events within the story
and independent maxims and aphorisms. Benjamin recognized
Ottilie's primacy to the story on every level, beginning with the
circle of fatality he saw it as originally enclosed within
(Goethe's task, in this view, was to free his narrative from an
empowering but restrictive mythic frame). The Daphne myth,
for Benjamin, was all too near a model for the "vegetal passivity" of Ottilie's character; and he argues in general—though I

hesitate to reduce his subtle commentary to capsule form—
that Goethe endowed her role as the story's "expiatory victim"
with a "dangerous magicality."

Just for this reason, however, the diary became a key instrument in Goethe's displacement of the underlying myth into a
freer truthfulness. Any reader can see that its free-spoken reflections are inconsistent with Ottilie's mind and character as
elsewhere delineated, and that they are spoken in Goethe's
own supervisory voice. But they are not meant to be realistic.
What they represent, Benjamin proposes, is what philosophy
would call "the ideal of the problem," a device by which the
validity of the discipline of understanding being practiced—in
this case narrative fiction itself—comes into question. They
stand, that is, for "everything [Ottilie's] existence might yet be
capable of saying" if transposed into an ideal articulateness.[25]

As such, Ottilie's diary becomes, in the second half of the
novel, a gathering place for further intuitions—of truth, of the
process of life—that the extended act of telling the story has
itself discovered. Integral to the work as a whole, it nevertheless stands apart, as if the narrative will have greater authority,
not less, if interrupted and extended in a different explanatory
mode. At any rate the diary's service seems to me nowhere
more consequential than in the closing sentences of its final in-
stalment, where Goethe gives the rule of instability and change
a final dispassionateness—and generality. "Anything perfect
in its kind," this last entry reads, "must transcend its kind [*hin-
ausgehen*: go out of], it must become other, no longer comparable to what has already been."

The always double action of virtue could not be more efficiently bracketed. As in Nature's reply to Mutabilitie at the
end of *The Faerie Queene*, the change belonging to being as
such and consubstantial with its life in the world is identified
at the last as self-change, a dilation from within each thing's
original estate. May not this rule apply equally to literary

[25] Walter Benjamin, *Goethes Wahlverwandtschaften* (1955), especially
parts I and II.

forms, giving us a way of accommodating endings that do not match, let alone resolve, their proffered beginnings? The work that satisfies us as having taken best advantage of its creative openings will not answer merely the questions it took shape from. Indeed it may not answer those questions at all. It will be seen instead as transforming the structure originally adopted and becoming (to our awareness) something cognate but essentially different, as Ottilie's diary both circumscribes and transcends the story that brought it into being—though the very idea of such new creation may point equally to an exhaustion of the energies thus released. "Everywhere," this last entry concludes, "we have to begin all over again and everywhere we would like to end."

~

The new beginning planned for the second half of *The Man Without Qualities* is positively trumpeted in the double title of Part Three: "Into the Millennium (The Criminals)."[26] The narrative means for negotiating this transformation is identified in the first new chapter title, "The Forgotten Sister" (III, 1). At the start of a new numbering of chapters, this shift to a figure barely hinted at through the novel's first eight hundred pages is a further sign that a significant boundary is being crossed. Or, more precisely, that a new factor modifying everything else is now to be introduced, for the situations and issues already in hand are by no means left behind. We continue at intervals to look in on Kakanian affairs, official and unofficial—the *Parallelaktion*, the anxieties and delusions of government officers, the corresponding anxieties of Bonadea (now attending Diotima's seminar on sexual science) and of Walter and Clarisse in their pursuit of deliverance; so one of the novel's fine cli-

---

[26] As usual, translation is chanciest with words or phrases of greatest importance; but with the German original of the main title—*Ins Tausendjährige Reich*—hindsight can make too much of a possible side-reference to Hitlerite Germany. In any case the reference would have had less force in the autumn of 1932, when this volume went to press, than it would shortly acquire.

maxes comes when the War Ministry's special delegate to the *Parallelaktion*, all the while talking imperial politics, superintends the visit of Clarisse and Ulrich to the lunatic asylum housing Moosbrugger. (The concluding grand rally of the *Parallelaktion* itself, that greater madhouse, follows directly.) Nevertheless, from this point forward what Ulrich means to become and what pattern of "right living" he will make his way toward—the question of questions, he declares in III, 24—will be known by way of his alliance with this misplaced sister, who now emerges as a figure of virtually equal consequence for the story still to be told.

It is a virtue in Musil's novel that Ulrich is not conventionally idealized. The capacity for aberration in those around him touches him, too. More than once what he takes for his own insight proves to be an idea that plausible Arnheim has got hold of or that even Diotima can blurrily reproduce. So Clarisse's "mental unrest and excitability" are on the same band as his own, however distorted the refraction; Meingast's glib philosophizing can be heard as a recognizable parody of Ulrich's exploratory notions (and of Musil's); and from the end of Part One, when Ulrich attends the final sitting of the madman Moosbrugger's trial (I, 18), the link to Moosbrugger himself is not broken. Well before that forgotten sister, at close quarters, confronts Ulrich with what is hurtful in his self-defenses, he has acknowledged a strain of "hard, cold violence" (II, 116) altogether at odds with the openness and experimentality—the "essayism"—he prizes. Such hardness fortifies his will to transcend mere certainties. But it also blocks access to this "other condition" of human response, this "methodology of what one does *not* know" (virtually the same, he thinks, as a "methodology of life": III, 14). His own nature has grown to be like "a machine . . . for continuously devaluing life," and his passion now is for it to be otherwise.

"Mathematics and mysticism" is one name Ulrich proposes for the new ethos, but Musil is at pains to distinguish it from devotional mysticism. He has Ulrich speak admiringly of the narratives of certain mystics—narratives, the proto-novelist in

Ulrich remarks, "with the strength and ruthless conviction of Stendhal's analytical probings" (III, 12)—but not of their idiom of explanation. Rather it is the mind's experience in encountering the normal, the quotidian, that is to be explored, even in the chapters entitled "Holy Conversations" (III, 11-12). As with the boy Törless, it is "precisely the natural" that baffles and excites. Addressing his reader directly, Musil specifies (III, 12) that though the way to be taken by Ulrich and Agathe has much in common with the way of those caught in God's grasp, it will be followed without any such objectively confirming faith: "They had entered upon it as beings of this world and went along it as such; and precisely this was the thing deserving notice." It may have been to secure this distinction more firmly that Musil built the second half of his novel around the relation of a brother and sister. Not only is this a relation given by life rather than being elected out of it, as is a marriage; it is that relation most immediately suggestive of the ontological accident that makes each human self the self it is, yet could just as easily have determined otherwise.[27]

Something of what overtakes Eduard and Ottilie in *The Elective Affinities* develops between Ulrich and Agathe, and something of its disordering consequence as well. Living continuously with this sister, Ulrich "for the first time quite un-

[27] No earlier work of Musil's paired a brother and sister in this way, although in *The Enthusiasts* a brother-in-law and sister-in-law briefly pretend to a blood relationship. But as early as 1908 a sister was included in a fragmentary anticipation of the great work Musil seems always to have been planning; and as noted before, "The Twin Sister" was an optional title. Plato's myth of a return to immortal life through healing the sexual division is an obvious source here but not the only source, as we are reminded by the lyric poem, "Isis and Osiris," that Musil published in 1923 (he later described it as "containing the novel in nucleus").

Concerning the "forgotten sister" and the insistence that their journey belongs to this world and to ordinary life, there is one further consideration which may have carried an imaginative weight as great as any other. Robert Musil did in fact have a sister, who died an alarmingly mythic ten months before his own birth. It is hard to think she was not a figure of significance for him: the imaginary number in his own biogenetic equation and a real presence in the economy of his coming into life.

thinkingly . . . loved his day-to-day life" (III, 28). Agathe fills a void that he has hardly understood to be there (III, 24). Simply through her physical presence, answering his own with a primal intimacy of resemblance, both his egocentrism and his coldness are effectively canceled; she "draws qualities out of me," he thinks (in a disturbingly ambiguous metaphor), "as the Magnet Mountain drew out all the ship's nails" (III, 28). The physicality of their co-existence is undisguisedly erotic. Incestuous or not, their voyage together heightens rather than sublimates everything sensually urgent.

With this emphasis we move to the heart of Musil's purpose in writing, his intention to create a work projecting (as he eventually put it) not only a "mysticism clear as day" and a realistic image of a fully "ecstatic" human society but an ultimate history of love—"the last love story of all," he summed the matter up in a much quoted phrase. An eroticism that consists entirely in animated exchange and a continual imaginative reciprocity effectively displaces the narcissism of ordinary consciousness—or so Ulrich seems to say in telling Agathe (after a scene of bathing and dressing as innocently sensual as a roomful of *après-bain* Bonnards) that in doubling his sense of self with her "second, more beautiful body" she has rendered back to him "a legitimate self-love" (*eine rechtige Eigenliebe*: III, 24). She does so the more prepotently by remaining an actual woman and sister. " 'She's my friend,' Ulrich thought, 'deliciously manifesting herself to me as a woman. What a realistic complication that she really is one' " (III, 28).

Complication indeed. As in Goethe's novel Ottilie's gift to Eduard of love and self-content takes its toll of her, so Agathe's entry into Musil's story in a comparable role brings comparable difficulties and dangers. It does not escape her that since reunion with her brother his talk, his ruminations on the theme of possibility, his projection of an authentic new "faith" that would never grow "even an hour old" (III, 12), feed more and more on *her* experience, and that her own life is being absorbed into his hunger for new understanding. Her own selfhood, however (and here she differs from quiet Veronica and wordless Tonka), strongly resists being reduced to an example. She is not to be, in Musil's scheme, merely Ulrich's emanation, the walking shadow of his breakthrough into some greater "goodness," as her name mythopoeically suggests. Indeed if either of them has already "gone out on an adventure and lost his way," the figure for the pattern of life that would accord with Ulrich's concept of "Essayism" (II, 62), it is more Agathe than Ulrich. Her own history—a dreamlike early marriage cut short by the death of her boy-husband and, in the numbness that followed, a misconceived second marriage to the pedantic Professor Hagauer—has carried her further into experience than Ulrich has yet gone. Each can look back to an episode of transformation in which the self, in love, has passed into a condition as inconceivable once left behind as it was before being entered; each has thus discovered something of the reality of the "other condition." But for Ulrich this episode (his "forgotten, though exceedingly important affair with the major's wife": II, 32) has followed the conventional scenario of a young officer's first fling at proper manhood. For Agathe it has taken the form, in her marriage and bereavement, of an unqualified giving and taking away.

So she is not at ease with Ulrich's experimentalism. Words and thoughts for her are nearer to committed actions; once spoken, they are not so easily withdrawn. "When," she says, "you talk to me like this, first this way and then that . . . it's as if I were looking at myself in the splinters of a broken looking-glass. With you one never sees oneself whole" (III, 10). And, "you always take everything back, that's what it comes to." For Ulrich the question everything else returns to is, "How am I to live?" (III, 24), and we see that a luxury of choice has somehow survived the stripping away of all other privileging "qualities." But for Agathe a different question impinges. "What am I in the world for at all?" she asks (III, 30), having already taken a new step more absolute—being criminal, and irreversible—than any her brother has yet ventured. (She has forged a change in their father's will which, by cutting her dull husband out of his rights, will also free her to divorce him.) A deeper sadness than at this point it is in Ulrich's power to feel and know overtakes her precisely as she realizes, listening to his circling words, "that she must deal with her troubles all on her own" (III, 30). A resolution for suicide that in earlier stages of composition Musil imagined as a point of arrival for both brother and sister now belongs in the story to Agathe alone, or rather—and the qualification has the pyschological accuracy Musil does not lose command of—"not actually the resolve to kill herself, but the expectation that by evening this resolve would be accomplished." (She has wandered into out-of-the-way districts full of ordinary sounds and stirrings where an impression grows that "life was complete without her"—precisely the opposite, we note, of Moosbrugger's conviction that he alone holds the world together. If mankind dreamt only individually, a new Musilian maxim might go, would it dream Agathe?)

As it happens, suicide does not round out Agathe's part in the story, though in diverting her from it Musil fell into the unwonted awkwardness of springing another new character on his story, one Lindner (he turns out to be merely another professor, much like the *bien pensant* husband she has deserted).[28] But her trial of spirit serves its compositional purpose. It intensifies recognition that an ethic based on "the infinite fullness of life's capacities"—what theology identifies as *pleroma*—is indeed an ethic of infinite risk. The Millennium itself, as earlier defined, can only be a way station. It has no more authority over the drama of human self-definition than the "compulsion and force" of life (*Zwang, Gewalt*) that drive certain men and

---

[28] Some late manuscript notes explore the possibility of Lindner's taking on further importance: he will join forces with Hagauer, he will gain the ear of Count Leinsdorf, there will be some triumph of Lindner and Hagauer together over Ulrich (see Frisé's edition of *Der Mann ohne Eigenschaften* [1970], 1572). The point seems to be to multiply the obstacles in Ulrich's path.

Agathe herself is admirably realized, but if Musil's invention anywhere falls short, it would be in maintaining a sufficient role for her after bringing her to this crisis, this limiting-case alternative—as suicide would necessarily be—to a determined existence.

women to go in search of it or "the like of it." As Ulrich sums the matter up: with any fully empowered behavioral system everything that exists is made to refer to the system's conjoined elements, "but the system itself refers to nothing. *In other words, everything is moral, but morality itself is not*" (III, 38: my emphasis). Morality is simply "order and integrity of feeling." But all one can truthfully say of feeling is that it does not lend itself to distinctions of "true" and "false"—and we recall Ulrich's earlier declaration that rationalized understandings always miss what is most intimate and distinctive in existence:

> Everything partakes of the universal, and in addition it is particular to itself. Everything is true, and in addition it is wild and free and comparable to nothing else. . . . Individual cases cannot be decided morally. (II, 114)

These last propositions, coming in the last chapter of the second published volume, have a conclusiveness that would keep its force, I think, even if Musil had gone on to extend and complete his book. In more than one way this chapter marks a climax. It brings to an end the final gathering of the luminaries of the *Parallelaktion*; and in the midst of all the high-flown ideological disputation (which now includes awareness that these schemes for harmony and peace are likely, if put into practice, to lead straight to war), it shows Agathe and Ulrich arm in arm, again acting out a retreat from the internecine world of qualities and "secretly, wildly rejoicing at being united again after their estrangement." But again other characters break in on their communion, and again Ulrich's way of speaking turns painful for his sister. Saddened, as before, she slips off at the chapter's end.

And what now might follow, other than further sequences repeating, until Musil himself lost interest, what is now firmly established as his imaginative vision? At this point a peculiar suspense strikes me as having settled over the text. It is not so much the suspense of looking ahead to the resolution of a steadily forwarded plot (something that by and large we have not been involved with, despite our interest in, for example, the great problem of Moosbrugger or our awareness of being now only days away from the pistol shot at Sarajevo). It is rather the suspense of seeing how the author will solve the problem of form and statement that through nearly two hundred packed chapters he has created for himself. Thus in the fragments and notes making up the bulk of what has been posthumously published, nothing is more interesting than certain suggestions about an ending which, instead of disposing of the characters and their problems this way or that, would have moved the whole work into a different expository register.

Most tantalizing of all is a manuscript passage from mid-January of 1942, three months before Musil's death, that bears the heading, "Epilogue by Ulrich, Conclusion."[29] In this memorandum to himself, Musil—turning over in his mind another greater war's assault on consciousness and the onset of a wholly new era in history (an era making even more profoundly unimaginable the old European order)—suggests that what is needed now is an assemblage of reflections which might, by taking full account of these transformations in world reality, help chart a path for humanity through them. But to attempt this would *not* mean giving up or breaking off his novel. Rather, he saw here a challenge that, by every ambition he had ever had for it, "*The Man Without Qualities* cannot avoid." It was precisely by way of a new scheme for an ending, "either in place of or after the 'Sort of Conclusion,' " that he would meet this challenge. He would bring the narrative forward to the historical moment in which he himself sat at his writing table, but he would not do this by narrative continuations. Merely devising new incidents would not solve anything in a work whose great theme had been from the first that whatever happens might just as well have happened in a different way. Rather, through the "Pirandellesque irony" (Musil's phrase) of a full formal merging of character and authorial

[29] The text of it is included in Frisé's revised edition (1970), 1609-1610.

voice, he would distill Ulrich's further experience, grown old, into certain final reflections composing "an epilogue to his story and to my book."

Readers who have come to terms with Musil's grand project will recognize that an ending of this sort would and would not transform its character as a text. Colloquies and monologues anticipating some such assemblage of final reflections are broadcast through the book's earlier stages, as in the full-voiced "Credo" climaxing Ulrich's "holy conversations" with Agathe (III, 12). The spread of what had begun, in 1939, as another European civil war not only to Russia and America but into the vast land and population mass of east Asia abruptly concentrated Musil's sense of a change beyond reversion in human circumstance. Coincidentally it reawakened an old admiration for the wisdom discourse of the Chinese sage and law-giver Lao Tsu. More than the specific content—for Musil would do his own thinking in his own idiom—it was the form and focus of the writing attributed to Lao Tsu that held his interest; for the *Tao* does not attempt to explain the universe so much as describe the "way" of happening within it, and the corresponding "way" to be taken by men and women through it. Where else could "essayism" find a grander prototype? And what would be more in keeping with Ulrich's, and Musil's, ground sense that in the encounter with reality the business of life is to "work out a sum" which in itself may be indeterminate, to master a "sliding logic" of imaginative adjustment, than the formulation of a new *Tao*, a *Tao* for the present age and the age ahead?

Which appears to be what this final notebook entry points to. Musil's phrasing is telegraphic: "*Wichtig: die Auseinandersetzung mit Laotse, die Ulrich, aber auch meine Aufgabe, verständlich macht, von Ulrich nachträglich durchgeführt.*" Discussion, or argument, by way of Lao Tsu? in the manner of Lao Tsu? or (most literally) directly with Lao Tsu, to be carried further by Ulrich himself? The possibilities are tantalizing. But it is the formal suitability of what is proposed that is critically important, the projected final shift from fictive narration to a species of secular scripture.

As we have seen, a comparable shift—by means of Ottilie's diary—is central to *The Elective Affinities* and the sense delivered there of a truthfulness not restricted to the circumstance releasing it. For *The Man Without Qualities* Musil's further expedient would be to place at the end a last major instance of this attention-focusing genre shift, giving it the authority of a final section or chapter. It is worth noting how many of his great modernist contemporaries used precisely this formal tactic, this alternative to narrational closure (or, equally, non-closure). The coda written for *The Confessions of Zeno* (1923) by Italo Svevo, Joyce's pupil, is a compact example, breaking off an infinitely extendable comedy of self-unawareness with a millennium-spanning vision of global extinction. In a different tonality there is the virtuoso ending of *Ulysses* itself—though the change there is really not in the mode of expression, only in voice and local perspective. (Joyce's wonderful book is full of wisdom, including critical and stylistic wisdom, but it does not itself seem to me in the category of the "thought-adventure.") A nearer parallel would be, appropriately, the last masterwork of the modernist era in fiction, Pasternak's *Doctor Zhivago*, where a sheaf of twenty-three poems forms the terminal chapter. Pasternak's other calling was of course for poetry, Musil's for reflective aphorism and philosophic speculation; but to the work of forging, for his greatest effort as a writer, an ending that would not betray the heroic openness of the work itself, each could bring a singular assurance of competence and preparation for the solution proposed.

That Musil could have written such an epilogue and made it work will seem likely enough to readers with any taste at all for his manner in prose. One doubts that it would have been presented as final truth, whatever wisdom it embodied—any more than the poems of Yury Zhivago are meant by Pasternak to mark an end to other human discourse. But there is reason enough, from our reading of the novel Musil did leave us, to imagine that in its minute particulars it would have been entirely suited to the function assigned it, and perhaps, in itself, triumphantly persuasive.

~

Lao Tzu cultivated the way and virtue, and his teachings aimed at self-effacement. He lived in Chou for a long time, but seeing its decline he departed; when he reached the Pass, the Keeper there was pleased and said to him, "As you are about to leave the world behind, could you write a book for my sake?" As a result, Lao Tzu wrote a work in two books, setting out the meaning of the way and virtue in some five thousand characters, and then departed. None knew where he went in the end. (Ssu-ma Ch'ien, *Records of the Historian* [first century B.C.], in *Lao Tzu: Tao Te Ching*, tr. D. C. Lau [1963]

Supplementary Considerations: Kakania as World State

If this conjectural ending for *The Man Without Qualities* remained faithful to its Taoist model—which mixes ethical and political wisdom in equal proportion—it would have dealt not only with the prospect of life for the unencumbered, unqualified human self but with the momentous advance of modern world history. We may conceive of it as projecting a resolution or *terminus ad quem* for the whole self-ravaged European political order (whether from the perspective of 1914-1918 or the even more perilous one of 1942); for one expression of Musil's prescience and originality is an awareness that the Europe which had plunged headlong into these final struggles for supremacy had delivered itself over to a radically transformed, and diminished, historical destiny.

Musil understood clearly the subjective distortions in every such world-political prophecy. The trouble with predictive theorizing was that it too regularly retreated, at the end, into status-determined fixations, most of all into utopian fantasies of a certain particular place "in which one would like to spend one's own life" (I, 8). In the schizophrenia of 1913 these fantasies took on, most often, a form fantastically compounded of

nineteenth-century comfort-worship (the *gemütlich* Bieder-
meier world hardened into a panicky covetousness) and futur-
istic mechanization. Utopia was now imagined, Musil remarks, as "a kind of super-American city where everyone
rushes about or else stands still, stopwatch in hand," before returning at the end of the day to relax in a sealed apartment
tower among the restoratives of "wife, family, gramophone
and soul."

By 1913 the political crisis confronting middle Europe was
not simply the competitive imperialism of rival dynasties. Polity itself had lost interior connection. Of the old Empire the remark now truly applied that if its institutional forms and practices did not already exist, it would be quite impossible to
invent them. Kakania (Austria-Hungary) seemed supremely
that contemporary state whose continuance was dead at odds
not only with the passions of its mutually contentious peoples
and provinces but with every possibility of twentieth-century
life.

Yet, given the manner in which these passions are characterized in the novel, is it surprising to find Musil writing with considerable fondness—never, though, without irony—of the old
Kakania, "that fallen yet misunderstood State that was in so
many things a model, though all unacknowledged" (I, 8)? Its
very absurdity and organizational impenetrability begin to
recommend it. Against the deadly purposefulness of the new
regimes, its relative unconcern for action beyond its borders
and its policy of spending just enough on arms to remain "the
second weakest of the great powers" are, quite literally, re-
deeming features. So too is its official preference (within limits,
to be sure, and interrupted by expedient fits of anti-Semitism)
for enduring recalcitrants and misfits rather than liquidating
them (a preference giving the problem of Moosbrugger additional importance as a test case). By 1942 Europeans had
found out several times over what worse things might be said
of a superstate than that its internal mystifications were somehow suited to the polymorph scrimmage of its constituent peoples.

Simply trying to sort out the main constitutional facts about
the old dual monarchy brings into Musil's text an odd recovery of cheerfulness and nostalgic respect:

In writing it called itself the Austro-Hungarian Monarchy;
in conversation, however, it was allowed to be Austria; that
is to say, it was known by a name that it had, as a State, solemnly renounced, while preserving it in all matters of sentiment, as a sign that feelings are just as important as constitutional law and that regulations are not the really serious
thing in life. By its constitution it was liberal, but its system
of government was clerical. The system of government was
clerical, but the general attitude to life was liberal. Before
the law all citizens were equal, but not everyone, of course,
was a citizen. There was a parliament, which made such vigorous use of its liberty that it was usually shut down; but
there was also an emergency powers act by means of which
it was possible to get along without Parliament, and every
time people began to rejoice in absolutism, the Crown decreed that there must now be a return to parliamentary rule.
. . . [Underneath all were] national conflicts . . . so violent
that several times a year they caused the machine of State to
jam and come to a stop. But in the interim or, as it were, interregnum, everyone got on excellently with everyone else
and behaved as though nothing had ever been the matter.
Nor had anything real ever been the matter. It was nothing
more than the fact that every human being's ultimate dislike
of every other human being's endeavors, something in
which we all unite, crystallized earlier in this State in the
shape of a sublimated system of protocol that might have
proved of great consequence if its evolution had not been
broken off by catastrophe before its time.[30]

[30] Returning to these mysteries as the *Parallelaktion* gets organized, Musil
provides further clarification—if that is the word (II, 42):

. . . Austro-Hungarian nationhood was an entity so strangely formed that it
seems almost futile to try to explain it to anyone who has not experienced it
himself. It did not consist of an Austrian part and a Hungarian part that, as

"Before its time": the degree of irony we allow this phrase—
would world catastrophe necessarily have crushed the prepos-
terous Kakanian system, or was there some equilibrium of self-
realization possible to it that deserves commemorating as a
least objectionable ideal?—may depend on the importance we
grant the political dimension of Musil's long argument. Is
some sort of alternative world politics at least implied in *The
Man Without Qualities*, perhaps some "politics of the next
step" matching the elusive but peremptory morality of the
"other condition"? It does not stretch matters, I think, to answer yes. Yet political divinations operate in the novel on a
mainly secondary plane of exemplification—as befits what is
understood as a secondary realm of existence, despite a capacity for destruction that in the twentieth century has become effectively total. In politics, relatively crude concepts like the
"law of large numbers," a law indifferent to personal being
and to the difficult calculus of human freedom (II, 103), all too
efficiently explain what occurs in the world at large; also, the
intrinsic inertia of the political may altogether disqualify it as
a field for disentangling the prized "sense of possibility."

Ordinary political acumen nevertheless remains, within the
overall scheme, a concrete test of any proposal for "right living." This is part of Musil's unflagging realism. When politics
gains, as it has in our century, a power of life and death over

---

one might imagine, combined to form a unity, but of a whole and a part,
namely of a Hungarian and an Austro-Hungarian sense of nationhood; and
the latter was at home in Austria, whereby the Austrian sense of nationhood
actually became homeless. The Austrian himself was only to be found in
Hungary, and there as an object of dislike; at home he called himself a citizen of the kingdom and realms of the Austro-Hungarian monarchy as represented in the Imperial Council, which means the same as an Austrian plus
a Hungarian minus this Hungarian; and he did this not, as one might imagine, with enthusiasm, but for the sake of an idea that he detested, for he
could not endure the Hungarians any more than they could endure him,
which made the whole connection more involved than ever.

Forty-odd chapters later, Kakania's character and fate are summed up in a
phrase. It was that great State which "went down to ruin by reason of its own
unutterability" (*an ihrer Unaussprechlichkeit zugrunde gegangen ist*: II, 98).

all civilization, the secondary choices it requires are curiously simplified. Everything we undertake defines itself macropolitically. Our compensation is that on this scale political choices can in fact be defined and made, though there is no certainty of our surviving any of them. (The dissenters of eastern Europe and of South Africa have shown us this.) Politics retains, in any case, the advantage to thought of coming to us in graspable form. And what there is of specifically political argument in *The Man Without Qualities* is presented in two ways: in accounts of the operative structure of the old Kakanian polity, and in the eminently novelistic rendering of a variety of public personages whose views on what is to be done are given both in synoptic form and in lengthy conversations with the eponymous hero.

The chief of these are three imperial officers—Count Leinsdorf, the principal state counselor and Ulrich's particular patron; Tuzzi, Permanent Secretary to the Ministry of Foreign Affairs and consort to the soulful Diotima; and Stumm von Bordwehr, the War Ministry's watchful delegate to the *Parallelaktion*, with his unquenchable curiosity about advanced ideas. (The Jewish banker and family man Leo Fischel makes a fourth in this group but is presented in the story as someone more acted upon than acting. Financial energy as an independent force is better represented by the omnipresent Arnheim.) Musil does not exempt these dignitaries from the flux of his satire, but he treats them sympathetically; Ulrich's own amiability toward them seems to me endorsed by the text as a whole. Measured against Ulrich's—and the novel's—further interests, all three are men of second-class intelligence, but they are of first-class civil temperament. They may look and act like fools but are honest in their folly, and now and then stumble into civil wisdom—unlike Arnheim, who lacks their liberating simplicity. In any reckoning of the action of *virtue* in Musil's novel they, too, have their place.[31]

---

[31] Most commentary on *The Man Without Qualities* presents this trio as blindly steering Kakania into the suicidal denouement of 1914-1918, but this

Among them, Tuzzi is most nearly a stereotype, though it is characteristic of Musil's interfolded narrative that at one point he is suddenly linked in Ulrich's mind—in responding to provocations with "his whole personality" (*seine ganze Person*)— to the specter of Moosbrugger, the ultimate "integral man." Ulrich, rather to his surprise, genuinely likes Tuzzi for so admirably embodying a professionalism that dismisses as unimportant anything in life not suited to diplomatic negotiation. With his own ideas stuck fast in the year 1848, Tuzzi combines a passion for correct behavior with a cynical realism about persons and motives. It has become clearer to him every day, he remarks, that, given the modern mind's tendency to make progress in all directions at once, old style check-and-balance diplomacy is more necessary than ever.

General Stumm's role involves him more directly in main situations and events, as in the *affaire Moosbrugger*. To Ulrich, Stumm has about him an appealing combination of naïveté and soldierly courage. He is genuinely studious, though modest about his own understanding and grateful when people take time to explain things to him. Assigned to monitor the *Parallelaktion*, Stumm has begun compiling a "Domesday Book of Modern Culture" where with military orderliness he inscribes the names, founders, and chief characteristics of all the ideas that have been influential over the past twenty-five years. Not unreasonably the effort has made him profoundly suspicious of the contemporary civilian mind. Only library attendants, he notes, seem to possess a reliable overview (II, 108). More important, he sees that every known ideological

---

does not strike me as Musil's main point about them. (See, for example, S. S. Prawer's summary: "Where Moosbrugger's frustration finds its release in murder, that of Leinsdorf, Diotima, and Stumm is to issue in a world war": "Robert Musil and the 'Uncanny,' " *Oxford German Studies 3* [1968], 168.) If any undertaking seems dead certain to bring on a European war, it is Arnheim's intrigue for getting control of the Galician oil fields.

One careful reader of Musil's novel has been, I suspect, Anthony Powell, who may well have adapted this and other plot details in working out a trajectory for the egregious Widmerpool in his *roman fleuve* of modern English life, *The Music of Time*.

party rages after its own dream of order and will not tolerate any other. The age itself, Stumm says, has grown "Messianic" but without increase of vision; were the Redeemer Himself to return to it, it "would hurl down His Government like any other." But eventually Stumm, too, is taken in by Arnheim's speciousness, his show of being a factor for good rather than a rogue fuse in the impending European blow-up. Also, Stumm's good sense is further put in doubt by his remark (on the last page of the novel as broken off in 1933) that the best way out might be "if some real idiot came along"—"I mean a sort of Joan of Arc," he promptly adds, but readers will already have thought of the actual alternative.

The purest old Kakanian is His Highness the Imperial Liege-Count Leinsdorf. At times Musil's humor touches him with particular sharpness. In Leinsdorf, Musil comments, "a tranquil breadth of vision" (II, 76) is sustained by "a complete absence of doubts" (II, 21), and the result can seem a breathtaking grandeur of imperception. ("We have four years ahead of us yet," Leinsdorf remarks early in 1914. "All sorts of things may happen in these four years": II, 81.) Nevertheless, in granting him political views which are of "extraordinary solidity" and have "all the freedom that goes with greatness of character" (II, 21), Musil's irony does not seem merely scathing. And when Leinsdorf is heard to remark about the great plan to put Kakania back on its legs that "a nation's legs are its established institutions, its parties, its associations and so forth, and not the salon talk that goes on in it," his conservatism seems to have the backing of the text generally, which all along, as it exposes these violent new parties and sects, has given a clear account of their organic emergence in modern history.

Thus it is that Leinsdorf, at first astonished, eventually welcomes the swarm of associations and factions springing up under the *Parallelaktion*'s stimulus. They, too, have a contribution to make to what he defines as the reality of realities in state matters—the great principle of *continuousness* (*das Kontinuierliche*). Under this principle the angriest rebels must ultimately conform to the structure of political life they are acting against (II, 120). In particular Leinsdorf welcomes the idea that "everybody should belong to at least one association." It has not escaped him that these associations exist not simply "to promote the interests of their own members [but] to obstruct those of the others" (II, 81). His reasoning does not lack subtlety. "No good has ever yet come of ideological politics," he declares. "What we must go in for is *Realpolitik*"—and *Realpolitik* in this instance means letting all ideological flowers bloom together, in one another's shade.

The historical pluralism of the old Kakania is second nature to Leinsdorf's inveterate doubleness of understanding. To every new *Parallelaktion* scheme Leinsdorf's response comes "like the swing of a pendulum that is in a different position each time but that always swings the same way" (II, 116). When opposed factions bring things to a standstill, he simply announces, "Something must be done" (*"Es muss etwas geschehn"*). Is this mindless activism? Or is it, in Musilian terms, the grand principle of possibility applied to politics? If risky, is it more risky than doing nothing at all? Is not politics itself an art of illusion and thus—so Ulrich explains the uncanniness of all art (III, 30)—"a continual creation of images that don't quite correspond to the image of life itself"? Is the Kakanian style only a "muddling through" (*Fortwurstelns*: sausaging along)? Or does it exemplify, as Ulrich himself reflects, the very "law of world history," as against the Nietzschean antithesis propounded by Clarisse, who argues that we must bend history to our conception and will be satisfied by nothing short of a coup d'état (II, 82-83)?[32]

---

[32] In foreign affairs especially, Leinsdorf's style comes into its own, as a way of keeping foreign envoys off balance. (It also helps keep the shifty new-journalist Meseritscher out of mischief: III, 35). It works all the better if the home bureaucracy is not itself sure what is really happening—or finds out that what has happened "might as well have happened in a different order or the other way round" (II, 98):

Department One wrote, Department Two answered; when Department Two had answered, Department One had to be informed, and it was usually

If the world's Clarisses had their way—the opinion is voiced by Clarisse's level-headed brother-in-law—"the world would probably have destroyed itself at the time of the folk migrations" (III, 26). By contrast Leinsdorf, alert to every ideological virus, has intuitively mastered the strategy of opposites, seeing that without it *continuousness* itself is threatened. His applications of this strategy are regularly misinterpreted; so the *Parallelaktion*, meant to preserve the Dual Monarchy in all its ancient heterogeneity, is considered by the dissident nationalities a new pan-Germanism (II, 98). There are times when Leinsdorf's vigilant efforts result in ideas he must keep "partly concealed even from himself" (II, 21). Yet it may well be that his, and Kakania's, political style comes nearer than any other to matching (1) the human mind's unceasing work of equilibration and (2) the order of Nature in its alternations of displacement and renewal, evolutionary consistency and evolutionary freedom. There is never any guarantee of success. Kakania's strategy of controlled weakness may be only sentimentally preferable to Germany's hard ambition. All that can be said for sure is that it is probably exemplary—for, Musil writes, it was at the moment when the God of history "withdrew His credit from Kakania" that He made clear to all its peoples the full precariousness of all civilization (II, 109).

Under Count Leinsdorf Kakania, as Musil evokes it, is something like parliamentary democracy as defended by Winston Churchill: beyond doubt the worst conceivable political system, except for all the others. In the indivisible world order that a writer of insight could sense opening around him in the world-apocalypse of 1942 the lost Kakanian solution has more and more the look of political realism; a "model" in-

---

best to suggest talking it over in person. When Department One and Two had agreed, it was decided that nothing could be done about the matter. And so there was always something to do. (II, 98)

No more than with Kafka's *Castle* can we tell whether the mechanisms described are the best or the worst of all possible systems of governance, or merely the evolutionary norm.

deed, though grievously "unacknowledged" (I, 8). It may not seem less so a half century later, with ethnic, religious, and ideological wars ablaze around the globe. In the inhuman default of other world-political solutions it may be one that particularly deserves reconsidering.

Musil would not be the only artist reared in the Dual Monarchy who came to think so. Here is how the painter Kokoschka looked back on it from an even later vantage point:

> ... Many people were joined together in the old Austrian Empire, each retaining its individuality, its particular aptitude, and all contributing to weld the whole "cultural commonwealth," as I would call it, into an organic unity. There has never been anything like it in history. By contrast, the British Commonwealth was a basically economic institution. In my school-class there were boys from the Alpine countries, Hungarians, Slavs, Jews, Triestines, Sudeten Germans. A real gathering of peoples. And every second master brought with him some unmistakable national element, a colouring in his voice, his manner, his way of thought. In this sense, school was a preparation for my later life, in which I became a wanderer. . . . Actually, it is a pity that the Great Powers that signed the peace terms after the First World War, having no idea of geography, broke up this unit, and could find nothing better to put in its place. But it's no use lamenting the past. (*My Life*, tr. David Britt [1974])

Further along, the Czech Kokoschka offers in support of this view the testimony (before 1914, to be sure) of Thomas Masaryk himself:

> ... the preservation of Austria in the form of a multi-national State was far to be preferred to its dissolution into a number of nation states, because this great Central European empire could offer the nationalities the best prospects of economic and cultural development—provided that it could successfully be transformed into a State composed of equal nations. (Quoted in *My Life*, 86-87)

CHAPTER SIX

The Analogies of Lyric: Shelley, Yeats, Frank O'Hara

"I say . . . it is our first business to paint, or describe,
desirable people, places, states of mind."
—Yeats (1937)

". . . a species of personal language, which institutes, which
maintains, which professes an autonomous reality felt as substantial, considered as sufficient."
—Yves Bonnefoy (1981)

An argument for *virtue* as, in the sense here proposed, literature's core subject is easiest made with narrative and dramatic
writings. Does it apply as well—this chapter will ask—to lyric
poetry? Even if we take as proven Kenneth Burke's hypothesis
that lyric symbolically encapsulates a dramatic substructure,
the relative absence in lyric of transitive particulars makes for
corresponding uncertainties in critical judgment. There is less
material to work from; actions, motives, imaginative purposes
tend to be refracted rather than circumstantially and serially
detailed; the consequence-producing scene, the full behavioral
environment, are the more completely left to imagination. (So
we commonly find sharper differences of opinion about the
success of new lyric utterance and, from one era to another, a
greater volatility in lyric reputations, which seem peculiarly liable to sudden displacement.) But this relative freedom from
circumstance and occasion also works to lyric's advantage. It
makes more immediate and intense lyric's analogizing, to consciousness, of that life of directed feeling which is the shared
medium of our experience and the first measure of our knowledge of ourselves as living agents.

Fifty years ago R. P. Blackmur thought it important, in coming to terms with Yeats's extraordinary later poetry, to point out that all imaginative writing depends for acceptance on some set of "agreements or conventions between the [writer] and his readers." What is distinctive to lyric poetry is that these are preeminently, though never exclusively, a matter of "the fundamental power of language" itself. (Novels, by contrast, as Marvin Mudrick proposed in making *character* and *event* decisive in prose fiction, may need only to be just well enough written.) Blackmur's remarks still seem to me on target; I don't believe the critical adventuring of our later time has taken us further in any essential respect. Writing from within the robust modernist myth of a poetry formally independent of its circumstantial origins, Blackmur took it as axiomatic that the words of a poem "are in an ultimate sense their own meaning." But he also recognized that "the greater part of a given work must be conceived as the manipulation of conventions that the reader will, or will not, take for granted; these being crowned, or animated, emotionally transformed, by what the poet actually represents, original or not, through his mastery of poetic language. *Success is provisional, seldom complete, and never permanently complete.*"[1]

This being so, valuations of poetry are peculiarly dependent for acceptance on a disposition to hear things in more or less the same way. There must be some willing acceptance of the formal idiom, the language of analogy, that is in use. (We have to begin *hearing* a new music before we can pronounce on its quality and merit.) But I think my broad argument about literary value and meaning can be applied to lyric, too—that is, to a literature of the single soliloquizing voice as well as to the event-structured and more concretely dialogic forms of fiction and drama. Here it will be tried out with three instances in par-

---

[1] "The Later Poetry of W. B. Yeats," *Southern Review* (Autumn 1936), reprinted in *Form and Value in Modern Poetry* (1957); emphasis added. It is worth pointing out how fully this anticipates recent preoccupation with reader-response analysis and with the increasingly troubling aesthetic premise of mastery and authority.

ticular: with, first, that arch-Romantic poet whose reputation over most of two centuries has swung to the greatest extremes of celebration and disparagement; with a second who more than any other modern-era poet in English has been held up, with sharp intermittences, as the chief test of whether in this century a major poetry is still possible; and with a third more nearly our contemporary who seems to me to have circumvented as well as anyone the solipsisms that have been his generation's protective strategy—his best poems as self-confirming on their own scale and as likely to continue giving pleasure as any written since the break-up, after 1950, of the long modernist consensus.

～

Shelley himself is our first authority for identifying at the formative center of his poetry "a showing forth, an enactment, a fresh naming of primary human capacity under the conditions taken as regulating it" (to bring down my opening formulation: p. 14). In his preface to the lyric oratorio, *Prometheus Unbound*, he made the direct claim that the "imagery" employed—meaning first the mediating cast of voices, personifications, phantoms, shapes, hours, fauns, furies, choruses and semi-choruses, spirits seen and unseen, divinities traditional and improvised—had been drawn "from the operations of the human mind, or from those external actions by which they are expressed." Poetry is thus, for Shelley, a combinatory art; if it is also mimetic or representational, what it represents are matters already formed or forming in the mind of man or (by our oldest fiction) in nature as mind apprehends it. It is thus by establishing "some intelligible and beautiful analogy" with these correlative sources of emotion and thought that poetry's "abstractions" have their power. The same emphasis returns a year or two later in the eloquent, and metacritically lucid and exact, "Defense of Poetry," where—in language notably free of any delusional "metaphysic of presence," the blanket Derridean term for the original sin of all western writing—Shelley argued that poetry's distinctive expressiveness derives from language itself, an instrument "arbitrarily produced by the imagination" and therefore having its primary relation not to material facts but "to thoughts alone."

What poetic language primarily speaks for (in the argument of the "Defense") are "the actions and passions of our internal being." "Susceptible"—in its plasticity—"of more various and delicate combinations" than are comprised by actual "color, form, or motion," this language renders back not things themselves but some "permanent analogy of things." Thus its gathered images do not answer directly to our desire for truth, which is to say our dream of cognitive harmony and of the release of selfhood into the otherness of created life, though that desire is peremptory and continuous within us.[2] They rather act out, according to "the unchangeable forms of human nature," the living ebb and flow of such desiring; and it is thus that they "participate in the *life* of truth" (my emphasis), the drama of truth-making as the central mode of human self-realization.

Such—with minor adjustments of main terms and phrases—was Shelley's declared program for poetry. Erected over the epistemological skepticism that Hume had dropped in everyone's path, it is also surprisingly modernist, if not "post-modernist." A way of writing is proposed that (in R. B. Woodings' sympathetic account) is not meant to imitate experience directly, since "what it presents has no alternative form of existence. Instead, the poet created a form modelled on human experience . . . by giving substance to the workings of the mind" ("Introduction," *Shelley: Modern Judgments* [1969]). (A cen-

[2] Yeats responded to this aspect of Shelley's enterprise in summing up his poetry as "a poetry of desire" (see "The Philosophy of Shelley's Poetry" [1900] and "*Prometheus Unbound*" [1932], both reprinted in *Essays and Introductions*). But "analogy" is the decisive word here. Might we guess, if only for the irony, that the century-long prestige of Bishop Butler's monumental *Analogy of Religion* (1736) particularly recommended the word to Shelley, the self-proclaimed atheist, in renewing the case for poetry's higher truthfulness?

tral modernist equivalent would be William Carlos Williams's projection, in final sections of *Spring and All* [1923], of a poetry that is to become "a reality in itself.") Much of criticism's chronic impatience with Shelley's practice seems to me to derive from a refusal to acknowledge the cogency and reasonableness of his theoretical position—Victorian positivism, from Bagehot to Leavis, has much to answer for on this account—and from a corollary intolerance of the expressive forms and modes, and their very considerable expressive charm, he regularly turned to.

Shelley himself is not blameless here. He coincidentally meant all his writing to teach and to legislate, to reverse historical degeneration, to help subvert poisonous dogmas and institutions; and to these ends he worked to fill up his poems with those "beautiful idealisms of moral excellence" which in the *Prometheus Unbound* preface, even while abjuring didacticism, he identified as the poet's best service to our common need to "love, and admire, and trust, and hope. . . ." He made the expression of these idealisms as impressive as he could, and in their verbal symmetries and prosodic swing they have hypnotized and roused suspicion in equal degrees. If as readers our chief concern with poetry is never under any circumstance to allow ourselves to be "manipulated," Shelley will rank high on our poetic enemies list, and we will hurry to insist that even taking into account Plato, metempsychosis, and all, there is less to "Death is the veil which those who live call life" (*Prometheus Unbound*, III, iii) than seizes the ear. But such quotabilities do not seem to me where Shelley's verse establishes its energy and force of interest. "To hope, till Hope creates/ From its own wreck the thing it contemplates" is stirringly affirmative, and audibly Shelleyan in both tone and structure, but by itself it is too exclusively a matter of words only. Words and orthography, to be exact: the shift from lower-case verb to capitalized noun merely underscores (in English) the reliance on mystification.

"By itself," however, is not how such language works in Shelley at his best. It takes its place instead in a sustained psychodrama that uses—as in the whole of the stanza just quoted from, the full-voiced close to *Prometheus Unbound*—incantation, repetition, a forwarding parallelism of syntax, and sheer expressive accumulation and abundance to secure intensities meant to match those of the fired-up human imagination itself. It is an unabashedly *affective* language, reaching for words with the strongest received associations and aiming at as substantial a recovery as possible of their emotional reference. Or, to use a term from our latter-day concern with how the mind does in fact do things with words, it is transparently *illocutionary*, and the recurrent complaint that Shelley had as a poet a "weak grasp on the actual" (Leavis's famous dismissal) breaks down in most instances on a failure to acknowledge affective desiring as every bit as "actual," and as legitimately spoken to in the arts, as anything else in the human mind's wayward life.

Of course this is not the only way poetry works. If we find, finally, a more sustained and organized imaginative power in the best of Wordsworth or in the Blake of "The Mental Traveler" (the poem of Blake's that Yeats returned to more often than any other), it may well be because the "permanent analogies of things" their poetry also executes are given not merely expostulative but, so to speak, progressive and self-bonding form. They project not only the mind's self-constituted character but its developing history, as opposed to the disclosure of already established consciousness (a disclosure that is paratactic rather than vectored) directing the "allegorical" narrative of a poem such as *Alastor*, the first long work in which Shelley's own signature seems fully secured.[3] But *Alastor*, where

[3] The first sentence of Shelley's *Alastor* preface speaks of the poem as "allegorical of one of the most interesting *situations* of the human mind" (my italics); we may note the accurate choice of a static descriptive term. Where Wordsworth's concern is famously with the mind's natural history or growth, Shelley's is with mind as a fully erected agent. Until the mind of *Alastor*'s protagonist is already packed with the plenitude of past consciousness and has become steadily "obedient to high thoughts," Shelley's account of it is cursory and insubstantial; its formation is summed up in barely eight lines (ll. 67-75).

Shelley stays closest to Wordsworth's epic narration, is formally the least distinctively Shelleyan of the major poems (and the only one written throughout in blank verse). The mode that became Shelley's own is deliberately static and celebratory. Forwarding actions and action-determined tensions and reversals are regularly subordinated to the elaboration of whatever affective state is in the ascendant. It is not at all, I want at once to add, a mode that lacks precedent or parallel in major art, though we find it more commonly in use (not to everyone's liking) outside the art of poetry proper. In expressive strategy it is poetry's equivalent to the splendid, transparently illusional arts of opera and pageant—and on this point two comments seem in order. Not only is it true that not everyone does in fact "like" opera and staged extravaganzas generally, or even feel regret at this affective—and aesthetic—deprivation. It is also rather oddly the case that people frequently take a positive pride in disliking them, and in categorically denying them the possibility of performative seriousness. (One can understand why an anti-sumptuary moralist like F. R. Leavis would prove hostile to Shelley, but there are contradictions in the violent antipathy expressed by Ruskin—who eloquently defended Dickensian melodrama—to the stage-fire that also encircles Shelley's presentations.)

The poetic forms closest to the luxuriant anti-naturalism of opera, the forms of masque and allegorical pageant of which Jonson and Dryden were the earlier English masters and Marvell in a poem like "The Unfortunate Lover" the finest miniaturist, have lapsed from practical fashion almost as completely as verse drama, despite a Tennyson's labored or an Auden's virtuoso attempts at reinstating them. They are, however, the forms Shelley was most attracted to and at ease with. He seems to have tried his hand at all their established variations and subforms: secular hymn ("Intellectual Beauty," "Apollo," "Pan," the translated "Mercury"), ode or invocational lyric ("West Wind," "Skylark," "Liberty"), tone poem (Richard Holmes's term for the exquisite "Evening: Ponte al mare, Pisa"), winter's tale (*The Witch of Atlas*: see l. 622), liturgical elegy (*Adonais*), visionary procession with guided commentary (*The Triumph of Life*), extended metaphysical apologue ("Mont Blanc," *Epipsychidion*), and of course "lyrical drama" (Shelley's own imprecise subheading for *Prometheus Unbound* and *Hellas*).[4] With each of these the unbroken profusion of illocutionary excitement is essential to the effect aimed at, a pouring forth of images and verse-sentences that through virtuosities of sound, cadence, and placarded emotion becomes the medium of its own acceptance.

The first result, with Shelley, is a performative abundance that asks to be enjoyed on its own account, though it is correspondingly more tenuous, more easily undercut by anything flat or perfunctory, than are the narrative continuities and suspensions of dramatic fiction. It is also an abundance that, when it works, validates Shelley's declared zeal for human liberty. Free poetic invention itself, in both its profligacy and its harrowing exactions, becomes a primary Shelleyan symbol. But that is only half the story. What tempers and consolidates this expressive recklessness is another performative quality that Wordsworth definitively named when—disliking almost every attitude or belief the younger poet had argued for—he looked back at Shelley not only as having "the greatest native powers in poetry of all men of this age" but as "one of the best *artists* of us all: I mean in workmanship of style."

Workmanship of style: it is everywhere apparent, and Shelley's drafts make clear that he worked as hard for it as accomplished poets normally do. It is there in the invocational overtures he commonly starts with, as in the short and then impressively lengthened first seven stanzas of *Epipsychidion* or, most originally, in the five rolling yet classically balanced *terza rima* sonnets, all but one of them invocational in voicing, of the spectacular "Ode [or prayer] to the West Wind."[5] It is

---

[4] This listing scants one whole side of Shelley's writing, the gracefully conversational or acridly satirical poetry of his Italian verse-letters and English political manifestoes. But about the effectiveness of his work in these styles there seems now little dispute.

[5] Neville Rogers' presentation of the notebook drafts for "West Wind"

there, and musical terms seem right even where Shelley has not marked them, in the lyric arias interspersing longer declamatory passages, and here a single example must serve: the eight syntactically transparent lines—each fully end-stopped (an audible shift from the *sostenuto* of enjambed sentence-compounding that leads up to them) but with their repetitions of grammar kept flexible by the slightest shifts in auxiliaries and caesuras—that open the final, voyage-away movement of *Epipsychidion*'s long rhapsody:

> . . . Emily,
> A ship is floating in the harbour now,
> A wind is hovering o'er the mountain's brow;
> There is a path on the sea's azure floor,
> No keel has ever ploughed that path before;
> The halcyons brood around the foamless isles;
> The treacherous Ocean has forsworn its wiles;
> The merry mariners are bold and free:
> Say, my heart's sister, wilt thou sail with me?

I take this to be about as close as the poetry of words can come to that most serenely enchanting moment in the literature of opera, the barcarolle *terzettino* that completes the rising action of Mozart's and Da Ponte's *Così Fan Tutti* as the lovesick young men sail off to a pretended war—it too, we notice, a lyric of rapturously shared, cosmically extended desire (*ed ogni elemento/ benigno risponda / ai nostri desir*).

Where Shelley's workmanship is least questionable is in his mastery of conventional stanza structure—which may in good part explain why the two longer poems in numbered *ottava*

---

shows that this remarkable design was arrived at as a solution at one and the same time architectural and thematic (*Shelley at Work*, 2nd ed. [1967], ch. 12). Perhaps only Hopkins, in "Spelt from Sybil's Leaves," has pushed the English sonnet nearer its imaginable limits.

Wordsworth's judgments, as our own matrix of valuation goes on changing, seem to me to outweigh Keats's better remembered but more guarded and self-referential warning about the need to "be more of an artist" and to " 'load every rift' . . . with ore."

rima and Spenserian stanzas, *The Witch of Atlas* and *Adonais*, have become his least challenged major successes.[6] G. Wilson Knight in particular, who for all his quirky absorption in metaphor and mythopoieia understood that poetry is an architectonic craft, spoke to this aspect of things in describing how, in the long fantasy of *The Witch of Atlas*, each stanza makes its own "compact, terse, usually completed statement" (*The Starlit Dome* [1941], III, iii). This is central, Wilson Knight argues, to the poem's remarkable combination of a "pith and pregnancy of wit" not far off Byron's more caustic manner with the "gossamer charm" essential to all the sustained fantastication. Illustration must again be brief but might begin with the clinching efficiency of successive end-couplets—or simply the cadenced resolution of the end-lines:

> A shadow for the splendor of her love (XIII)
> She held a woof that dimmed the burning brand (XXVII)
> Melt on the surface of the level flame (XXX—a resolution
>   Yeats may have remembered in closing the second stanza
>   of "Coole Park and Ballylee, 1931": "The glittering
>   reaches of the flooded lake")
> The swift and steady motion of the keel (XLVI)
> The spirits of the tempest thundered by (XLVIII—echoed, in
>   tetrameters, in Stevens's *The Man With the Blue Guitar*,
>   section viii?)
> To wander in the shadow of the night (LIX)
> And the dead lulled within their dreamless graves (LXIV)
> Passed with an eye serene and heart unladen (LXVIII)

—not to neglect the antithetical bite of "And threw it with contempt into a ditch" for the white-goddess protagonist's dismissal of death (LXX), or the briskly Audenesque satire on

---

[6] It was Shelley's vocabulary of "ruling symbols"—river, cave, tower, dome, star, sun, moon—that Yeats emphasized in his 1900 study, but Yeats's own deeper debt was conceivably to the Shelleyan model of the free-standing lyric stanza, and to the idea of design by means of tonally contrasted or, as at the ecstatic close of "Among School Children," suddenly fused sequences of such stanzas.

contemporary churchmen that ends, "By pastoral letters to each diocese" (LXXIII).

These effects are worth emphasizing if Shelley elsewhere raises suspicions that his wilder extravagances may be, after all, his most characteristic inventions. There *is* a distinctive Shelleyan furor of self-extending verse manufacture: a plain case, we may think, of poetic virtue running wild. At times he did, as Trelawney reports him saying, "always go on till I am stopped," and the compulsion to keep going on can seem a kind of affliction. So his own account of it in a letter to Trelawney would suggest: "When my brain gets heated with thought, it soon boils and throws off images and words faster than I can skim them off." Yet if the description of Rousseau's ghastly specter in *The Triumph of Life* as "one who with the weight/ Of his own words is staggered" seems to apply in the first place to Shelley himself, this too may be one of the ways by which he mastered what Yeats would summarize as, beyond all symbols of reference, the symbolism peculiar to poetry itself—that "continuous indefinable symbolism which is the substance of all style" ("The Symbolism of Poetry" [1900]). It would be, again, in the sweep and whirl of a self-licensing verse rhetoric that Shelley seems most to have anticipated the historic turn into modernism, through a poetry primarily engaged (despite the great phrase about poets as universal legislators) in evoking that imaginative world sacred to the intervening *symboliste* generation, "a world belonging solely to the poet" in Novalis's long-remembered phrase.

But to leave matters there is not yet to suggest why Shelley meant more than Swinburne or even Tennyson to his later peers—to Hardy and Yeats, Stevens and Auden, and even Eliot (who knew where to turn for a passage of hieratic eloquence in writing *The Cocktail Party*: Act III, ll. 464-472). Shelley's poetry *is* about living experience, experience intrinsic to the ordinary life of both the human self and, as the self perceives it, created nature. The evocation everywhere in his poems of a cosmos in continual ebullition and flux has an empirical validity independent of desire or fear. As it comes to us in the pulsations of physical description in "Mont Blanc" (carried along by an irregularly heroic rhyme scheme of intermingled couplets, quatrains, and longer suspensions), it belongs to that classicist disciplining of the mechanics of the sublime that have won for Shelley the critical epithet "Lucretian" as well as comparisons back to Dryden among his English forebears. For poetry there are, after all, only the four elements (Northrop Frye's sensible reminder); and in the general tabulation made by Humphrey House of a "rush of images based on light, sea, clouds, and mountains"—as well as in the paired recurrences of *illumination* and *burning, upwelling* and *flooding, cloud-shedding* and *vaporizing, sheltering* and *dust-strewing*—what do we have but the classic four of *fire, water, air* and *earth*, their mythic contraries all continuously in play?

It is Marvell's "masque of warring elements" ("The Unfortunate Lover"), but it has broken away, in modernist fashion, from any predetermined resolution or closure. Naturally enough this is the same mythic table of elements the alchemical Witch of Atlas performs her life-and-death experiments with: primordial forces that are beautiful when seen in isolation but terrifying in their transforming potency—their *virtue*, in our terms. And against the critical complaint that this is all "rootless fantasy,"[7] we might note that it provides the symbolic field where Shelley got his anticipatory metaphor, in the "Defense," of "the mind in creation" as "a fading coal," a power brought by outward influences to a fresh burning that nevertheless hurries on its own self-exhausted disappearance.

The concrete accuracy of that metaphor, as we unpack it, deserves comment. It is one more statement by Shelley of an active process of transfiguration and self-transformation that is normative for all being. Again and again changes of state that are also a bursting beyond the limits set to life itself are points of arrival for Shelley; the wild, self-compounding sixty-

---

[7] This was in fact Yeats's phrase for what Shelley's poetry can lapse into when (in Yeats's view) the symbolism floats free of "philosophic" tradition and long-descended meanings. Less sympathetic commentaries have made it a comprehensive indictment.

line climax of *Epipsychidion*—ending with "I pant, I sink, I tremble, I expire!"—may be only the most extravagant. Typically, too, these transformations involve more than one determining agent or agency (so that there is a reciprocation of active force) and produce more than one consequence (the total process or system is nearly always dialectical). The "fading coal" figure has a characteristic physical exactness. Renewing impulses reach the coal from outside, yet a coal not already live would not brighten at all. Each new brightening, however, brings it nearer extinction. One of the loveliest of the figurative phrases packed into "Intellectual Beauty" has this same paradoxical structure; if the Spirit of Beauty is to human thought as "darkness [is] to a dying flame," it does *not* light up the space around but leaves thought forlorn and isolated within its own remnant of vividness. Another such double-edged metaphor is of the brightest stars gaining prominence precisely as the field of their radiance (the night sky) is dulled by the first spread of daylight.

It is in these peculiar dynamics of cross-figuration that Shelley's poetry most persuades us of its purchase on essential dualities of actual life and consciousness. It seems less a "poetry of skepticism," Harold Bloom's usefully revisionist phrase for it, than a poetry of alternating affective states brought into a persistently surprising, and revealing, complementarity.[8] Everywhere there is the apprehension of an energy within—within natural phenomena, within the registering human presence—capable of co-existing with even the most terrific and obliterating concentrations of energy without. Poetic eloquence is itself a high form of this indwelling potency. (Wallace Stevens's version of this is his characterization of the human mind, and therefore of poetic imagination, as "a violence from within" answering to "a violence from without": "The Noble Rider and the Sound of Words" [1942].) But its profoundest manifestation, as Shelley writes in the "Defense," is

---

[8] See Hazlitt's not wholly unsympathetic remark that Shelley subsists as a poet "only in the violence of contrast."

the identifying force of *love*, the "going out of our own nature" toward some action or presence "not our own"—and we
observe again the participial and outreaching form of the phenomenon in question. (We observe also a characteristic ambiguity: do we, etherealized, go out from "our nature," or does
it go out from us as a force transcending and displacing our accidental selves?) There is, in Shelley, a *transformation* topos
that disturbingly doubles as a will to extinction—"Die,/ If thou
wouldst be with that which thou dost seek!" (*Adonais*, LII)—
but there is also, within it, a countervailing *emanation* topos.
Though everything created must sooner or later lose itself in
convulsive change, the state it presses forward to will be one
embryonically concealed within its original condition of being.
The fundamental law here—of an element of the autochtho-
nous in everything that lives and grows, and of transformation
as the perfecting of something already inherent—is a law for
poetry as well as for the rest of life. So in the "Defense" Shelley
clinches an argument on the self-generated character of poetry's distinctive language (and thus the impossibility of translation) by appealing once more to this infinitely applicable topos or structural formula. "The plant," he writes, "must
spring from its seed, or it will bear no flower. . . ." At this point
in the present book I hope it is not necessary to point out again
how these figures and formulations reproduce the basic definition of the force of *virtue*.

Emanation, doubling as both self-transfigurement and a will
to dissolution, fills up the whole argument of *Epipsychidion*,
as befits both the poem's odd title and the great theme of love
blazoned in its Italian epigraph.[9] But we can perhaps come

---

[9] An epigraph written by Emilia Viviani, the addressee of this—when first
printed—scandalously autobiographical performance. It translates: "The soul
when it loves is hurled forth from the created world and creates in the infinite
a world entirely for itself, very different from this dark and fearsome pit." The
equivocal definition of an ideal love partner which the poem itself offers—at
once "this soul out of my soul" (l. 238) and "soul within my soul" (l. 455)—
is matched by the exclamatory indistinctness of the role assigned its human
embodiment: "Spouse! Sister! Angel! Pilot of [my] Fate" (l. 130). As the ulti-

even nearer to Shelleyan emanation as a condition of all existence in the more conventional journey-vision text of *Alastor*,
where repeatedly it provides the form for what is seen, or
heard, or directly enacted: in night's making "a weird sound
out of its own stillness" (l. 30), in "the warm light [out] of their
own life" that suffuses a phantom maiden's limbs (ll. 175-
176), in a "brooding care" that overtakes the journeying hero
and is fed from within by his life's "decaying flame" (ll. 246-
247), in the impulse to solitude that both hides within his
"flushed cheeks, bent eyes, and shadowy frame" and hangs
about his life like cloud-refracted lightning (ll. 415-418), in the
human heart's discovery in graveside dreams of its own treach-
erously projected likeness (l. 474). Similarly, as this hero's fatal
severance from the rest of mankind comes about through pursuing the figures of an inflamed imagination, the light drawing
him deeper into destructive solitude is one that shines from
within his soul (ll. 492-493), and death when at last it comes
"on" him takes form as a forced surrender by "the hovering
powers of life" within him to their own final impulses.

If we judge by the summarizable actions and terminations of
these poems, what they are mostly about is the utter obliteration, actual or impending, of every concerted human effort
(and therefore, in our over-all terms, about the tragedies of virtue). *Alastor*'s wandering hero is not only dead but "unremem-
bered"; the supplicant of "Ode to the West Wind" asks to have
his thoughts and words scattered like dead leaves or like the
sparks and ashes of a dying fire; the poet-mourner of *Adonais*
concludes by putting himself on the same course as the poet
whose death he laments and whose transforming ascension is
correspondingly dark and fearful to him. Even in the account
of the New Man—"free, uncircumscribed ... [e]qual, un-
classed ... just, gentle, wise" and above all "king over himself"—that ends Act III of *Prometheus Unbound* (and was

---

mate love relation is a kind of reestablished twinhood, Death and Life too are
projected in the poem as brother and sister, incestuously rejoined and shock-
ingly unmindful of their proper separateness (ll. 301-304).

originally to end the poem), the last turn of emphasis is still on an ultimate subjection to "chance, and death, and mutability." All of these, though in spirit man now "rul[es] them like slaves," keep their full power to deny him the resolution he imaginatively desires. Yet these endings come about only as the overpowering force without is given reality by a complementary force within. Despite the enormous odds that Shelley himself inscribes against any such possibility, there is, in his poems, "a substance in us" (and in whatever our perception attaches to) that within fearful limits "prevails." Or, we may say, there is a "freshness" that continues to live "deep down things." Stevens and Hopkins (whom I quote here) each moved in maturity a long way off from Shelley's favored idiom but not from the binary reality his writing regularly asserts.[10]

In these reciprocations of energy that fill up Shelley's imagination of life, the source within is represented more than once by the symbol—neo-Platonic, Biblical, Blakean—of a procreative fountain. In *Adonais* Keats's spirit is imagined as flowing "back to the burning fountain whence it came" (XXXVIII), and even in "Mont Blanc," which seems largely given over to avalanches of destruction, the brisk opening account of a timeless material universe rolling over and through human consciousness leads without pause into a counterstatement of how, "from secret springs," human thought makes its own contribution to the grand process, though feebly enough and "with a sound but half its own." More typically the reactive agency, or locus of recovery, is at first no more than an indefinite space hidden away from everything awful and overwhelming, a space that may seem mere vacancy until the force of life discovered there begins its return to the visible world. Shelley's prime symbol for this residual potentiality in life, this space of continuance, is the cave—a symbol Platonic in origin but beguilingly tangible as Shelley evokes it and, given the least answering flicker of light or flame, not disorienting at all but

[10] The references are to Stevens's "Le Monocle de Mon Oncle," stanza vi, and to Hopkins's sonnet "God's Grandeur."

quite unPlatonically re-empowering. (To the "adverting mind" that orchestrates "Mont Blanc" it doubles as "the still cave of the witch Poesy"; in *The Witch of Atlas*, where it becomes the womb from which that mistress of emanation and metamorphosis springs into life—"garmented in light/ From her own beauty"—it is appropriately furnished with its own "secret" fountain.) Since in "Mont Blanc" the *cave* is not only a reinforcing symbol but, with *dome* and *river*, a prime agent in the quasi-narrative procession of effects, a superbly wrought passage forming the poem's descriptive climax can serve as a final extended instance of, at once, Shelley's formidable artistry and his panoramic address to certain actualities of experience.

The logical scheme of "Mont Blanc" is both "sublime" and simple. The enormous mountain with its glaciers and storms dwarfs the human spaces it looms over (and fitfully destroys); behind it and apart—"[r]emote, serene, and inaccessible"—is a "Power" or "secret Strength" that also floods into it and inhabits it, and thus transforms it from elemental inertness into a grand-scale portion of the eternally streaming material universe. But such Power holds a strange, trancelike correspondence with the human mind's own capacity for imaginative recreation, dependent as this may be on "influencings." Indeed, without imagination's reciprocal power to penetrate what is "secret" and "inaccessible," the mountain itself might not be sure of its substantial reality.[11] Within this grand structure of argument and analogy we come in section IV to the most sustained descriptive passage in the poem:

> The fields, the lakes, the forests, and the streams,
> Ocean, and all the living things that dwell
> Within the daedal earth; lightning, and rain,

[11] More fully allegorized readings of "Mont Blanc" have been suggested—to Shelley's first modern editor, C. D. Locock, the Ravine of Arve is universal consciousness, the stream flowing out of it is individual consciousness, and so on—but seem to me to restrict rather than enhance the poem's expressive interest.

Earthquake, and fiery flood, and hurricane,
The torpor of the year when feeble dreams
Visit the hidden buds, or dreamless sleep
Holds every future leaf and flower;—the bound
With which from that detested trance they leap;
The works and ways of man, their death and birth,
And that of him and all that his may be;
All things that move and breathe with toil and sound
Are born and die; revolve, subside, and swell.
Power dwells apart in its tranquillity,
Remote, serene, and inaccessible:
And *this*, the naked countenance of earth,
On which I gaze, even these primaeval mountains
Teach the adverting mind. The glaciers creep
Like snakes that watch their prey, from their far
    fountains,
Slow rolling on; there, many a precipice,
Frost and the Sun in scorn of mortal power
Have piled: dome, pyramid, and pinnacle,
A city of death, distinct with many a tower
And wall impregnable of beaming ice.
Yet not a city, but a flood of ruin
Is there, that from the boundaries of the sky
Rolls its perpetual stream; vast pines are strewing
Its destined path, or in the mangled soil
Branchless and shattered stand; the rocks, drawn down
From yon remotest waste, have overthrown
The limits of the dead and living world,
Never to be reclaimed. The dwelling-place
Of insects, beasts, and birds, becomes its spoil;
Their food and their retreat for ever gone,
So much of life and joy is lost. The race
Of man flies far in dread; his work and dwelling
Vanish, like smoke before the tempest's stream,
And their place is not known. Below, vast caves
Shine in the rushing torrents' restless gleam,
Which from those secret chasms in tumult welling

Meet in the vale, and one majestic River,
The breath and blood of distant lands, for ever
Rolls its loud waters to the ocean-waves,
Breathes its swift vapours to the circling air.

A first thing to say of this forty-three line section is that it
effectively divides into three sonnet-length units with one additional line (which we may identify as the singularly abstract
line, "The limits of the dead and living world"; it is the only
line in the section lacking a rhyme). The first and last of these
structural blocks keep the intermittences in rhyming of the
poem as a whole. The middle one, however, which emphatically announces the poem's major analogy ("And *this* . . .")
and begins the downward rush from mountaintop to the life-
restored landscape far below, audibly resolves into a sequence
of quatrains furnishing a prosodic frame for the precisely detailed workings—the immense release of natural *virtue*—of
the system in question. Syntactically the first unit is a single,
multiply compounded twelve-line sentence rounded out by an
unrhymed couplet, clearly set off ("Power dwells apart . . .");
the second offers a series of extended sentences that roll their
subordinate phrases and enjambments over the descending
quatrain structure; while the third, presenting the out-reach-
ing effects of the mountain system, gains emphasis through a
remarkable counter-rhythm of four-stress and three-stress as-
sertions ("So much of joy and life is lost.// The race Of man
flies far in dread;// his work and dwelling Vanish,// like smoke
before the tempest's stream,// And their place is not known"),
and finishes with another couplet, grammatically though not
phonically rhymed:

Rolls its loud waters to the ocean waves,
Breathes its swift vapours to the circling air.[12]

---

[12] I pass over in this too condensed account the enlivening alternations of
active and passive, transitive and intransitive verbs. But wouldn't Yeats have
spotted the value of abstract passives like "Never to be reclaimed" and "their
place is not known" in alternation with more sensuous and dramatic phras-

To these alternations of prosodic emphasis the physical imagery adds its own patterned balance of contraries. Here I will
comment only on the run of architectural figures, from "dae-
dal earth" through the city of ice and death and the obliterated
human dwellings to the hollowed-out caves which for men and
nature alike are the springhouses of reestablished life. Wordsworth, I think, knew exactly what he was looking at when he
made "workmanship of style" the touchstone of Shelley's
achievement. Applied to major myths of human and cosmic
self-consummation, it became a formidable poetic resource.

⁓

"And now my utmost mystery is out.
A woman's beauty is a storm-tossed banner;
Under it wisdom stands, and I alone—
Of all Arabia's lovers I alone—
Nor dazzled by the embroidery, nor lost
In the confusion of its night-dark folds,
Can hear the armed man speak."
—Yeats, "The Gift of Harun Al-Rashid" (1923)

Yeats, when he wrote his long essay on Shelley, was not yet
vitally concerned over the disparity between the period style he
had perfected in the 1880s and 1890s and an original resolve
(as later remembered) to "write out [my] own thoughts in as
nearly as possible the language [I] thought them in" (*Reveries
Over Childhood and Youth*, xxx).[13] He could still, in a com-
panion essay on "The Symbolism of Poetry," state his deter-

ings? It is a device he himself would use to extraordinary effect in the second
stanza of "The Stare's Nest By My Window" (see below, p. 263)?

[13] Quotations from Yeats's prose are from *The Autobiography of William
Butler Yeats* (1953), containing *Reveries Over Childhood and Youth, The
Trembling of the Veil, Dramatis Personae, Estrangement, The Death of
Synge, The Bounty of Sweden*; also *William Butler Yeats: Memoirs*, ed. Denis
Donoghue (1973); and *Mythologies* (1959), *Essays and Introductions* (1961),
Explorations (1962), *A Vision* (revised edition, 1956), and *Letters*, ed. Allen
Wade (1954).

mination to "cast out of serious poetry those energetic rhythms as of a man [bent on something actual] to be done or undone" and to seek instead "those wavering, meditative, organic rhythms, which are the embodiment of the imagination, that neither desires nor hates." Especially in view of Yeats's later manner this is a markedly confused, and confusing, declaration. What he was surer of after several years absorption in Irish cultural politics was that any poet who, like Shelley, pursues passion and truth and not the sentimental deceptions of the newspaper-crammed, pulpit-drilled "public imagination" must brace himself for public rejection. Shelley, in both his transcendent purposefulness and constrained overreachings, served Yeats for a time as the very archetype of the poet in post-heroic society. At the outset of his own wearying fight for an "Irish Literary Theatre" free of all parochialism, Yeats could outdo the "Defense of Poetry" itself in fervor. "Literature," he wrote in an early report on this theater's progress,

> is, to my mind, the great teaching power of the world, the ultimate creator of all values. . . . [I]t must take the responsibility of its power, and keep all its freedom. . . . [I]t must claim its right to pierce through every crevice of human nature, and to describe the relation of the soul and the heart to the facts of life and of law, and to describe that relation as it is, not as we would have it be; and in so far as it fails to do this it fails to give us that foundation of understanding and charity for whose lack our moral sense can be but cruelty. ("Samhain: 1903—The Theatre, the Pulpit, and the Newspapers")

Yeats—whose preference for Shelley over Keats as a model of poetic virtue has seemed to many a quirk of taste and personal history—did not lack the standard sense of Shelley's flirtation with vaporousness. The essay of 1900 speaks of innumerable images without the "definiteness" and "precision" of true symbols, and argues that Shelley's imperfect awareness of the structures of meaning already coded into the symbolic language he was using, and of that language's rootedness in "tradition," deprived his poetry of the greater authority it might have had. Imperfect attachment to an actual place and culture was a second great flaw within Shelley's abounding inventiveness, as it would later be, Yeats thought, for the dream-world inventions of the generous-minded William Morris. Describing his own deep attachment to the Sligo of his boyhood, where he had returned each summer of his London years, Yeats recalled an early conviction that "if Morris had set his stories amid the scenery of his own Wales . . . if Shelley had nailed his *Prometheus*, or some equal symbol, upon some Welsh or Scottish rock, their art would have entered more intimately, more microscopically, as it were, into our thought and given perhaps to modern poetry a breadth and stability like that of ancient poetry" ("Four Years," xiv: Morris, despite his name, was not in fact Welsh).

By 1912 and after, when, with new models like Donne (in Grierson's influential edition) and the hard-edged tutelage and practice of Ezra Pound, Yeats was consciously amending his own style—with results praised for their "hard ruggedness" by Forrest Reid in 1915, in the first book-length study—he could acknowledge an element of the "unhuman and hysterical" forced on Shelley by modern civilization's retreat from the physical candor available to Donne in the Renaissance ("The Tragic Generation," xiii). Other such reservations are spread across Yeats's later prose and letters, as are a number of remarks acknowledging Keats's rare artistry.[14] But one aspect of

[14] Yeats would not be the first or the last poet to write his own concerns into his judgments of others. Much of his seeming coolness toward Keats—in *A Vision*, though Keats in Phase 14 (as Helen Vendler notes) stands as near as Blake in Phase 16 to the crucial Phase 15 of fulfilled subjectivity, he is also seen as deficient in both "sexual passion" and "intellectual curiosity"—may reflect the fact that Keats had been Morris's particular master, and Morris's dreamy monotony and artificiality were the tastes Yeats most needed to outgrow. His notorious depiction of Keats as "a schoolboy . . . With face and nose pressed to a sweet-shop window" is also to be considered in context; it comes in the doctrine-heavy verse debate, "Ego Dominus Tuus," and is spoken by the ascetic "Ille," who a few lines earlier has defined Dante's life as, simply, "lecherous." Such pronouncements served Yeats as counters in a self-argument

Shelley's poetry Yeats never denied the value of was its subjectivism, its creator's explicit trust in the workings of mind as source of everything genuine in poetry. In 1919, having achieved the new, calculatedly personal *longue haleine* of "In Memory of Major Robert Gregory" and "A Prayer for My Daughter," Yeats could write, as if in possession of a critical absolute, about "the rhetoric and vagueness of all Shelley that does not arise from personal feeling" ("If I Were Four-and-Twenty"). Correspondingly, a sense of disconnectedness and subjective absence made it easy for him, though grateful for Pound's bracing admonitions, to resist the expertly figured solutions of Pound's poetic style. Yeats subsequently remarked of Pound that his "conception of excellence . . . is of something so international that it is abstract and outside life" ("Pages from a Diary of 1930"), while Pound himself quoted Yeats as complaining that Pound's verse allowed him "no asylum for the affections" (letter of March 9, 1916: *Letters of Ezra Pound*, ed. D. D. Paige [1950]).

What is the governing theme in these various meditations and judgments? It seems to me the theme of authenticity; of a poetry, an art—a political faith, too, if it came to that—which would transform consciousness because it had behind it the definitive transactions and transformations of immediate experience. A diary entry of 1910 puts this in personal terms: "I

---

which never reached conclusion and was never meant to.

Elsewhere Yeats put Keats's odes alongside Wagner's dramas and Blake's pictures and poems as exemplary of the best in modern art ("Symbolism in Painting"); set Keats's poetry of vision over Burns's poetry of worldly talk (letter of August 5, 1913); told his father that Keats was "perhaps greater than Shelley and beyond words greater than Swinburne because he makes pictures one cannot forget and sets them as full of rhythm as a Chinese painting" (letter of March 14 [1916?]); and again contrasted Keats to Shelley (letter of October 17, 1918) in his having advanced to a "greater subjectivity of being, and to unity of that being." Possibly it was Keats's own compositional perfectionism, his apparent determination to resolve feeling into an entire coherence within each poem, that made Yeats wary of him, as exemplifying what is described in the Shelley essay as "the barrenness and shallowness of *a too conscious arrangement*" (my emphasis).

suppose that I may learn at last to keep to my own in every situation of life." All Yeats's poetry, and the bulk of his prose as well, turns on a lifelong inquiry into the forms and conditions of this decisive authenticity, this coalescence in a single moment or act (whether personal or world-historical) of the real affective world within and the real self-objectifying world without. "Unity of being" was one great name for it, yet a name, and concept, that in its static implications—pointing to a perfected condition and not the action of living forward under challenge—could lead Yeats into troubling excesses, as in the notorious lines in "Under Ben Bulben" about what occurs when "a man is fighting mad" and "completes his partial mind," or, during the catastrophe-threatened late 1930s, the eugenic harangues of *On the Boiler*, with their talk of the need for a new war to prevent decay of "the better stocks." More characteristically the unity imagined is one of strenuously opposed contraries. This is a state that living men can approach only through a passion to be faithful to both halves, both lived-through phases, of an ineluctably divided selfhood—faithful to all of imaginative life that is from beyond the individualized consciousness and that Yeats called the "primary"; faithful also to what he termed the "antithetical," all that develops out of conscious selfhood and is its most valued projection. (A total unity of being is conceivable only as obliteration, which is why for some men and women it may become an overmastering object of desire. In *A Vision* Yeats represented such absolute unity by the two humanly inaccessible phases of consummation: Phase 15, where "all effort has ceased," and Phase 1, where all is "supernatural" and "undifferentiated.")

Pragmatically, unity or authenticity of being takes form in Yeats's imagination as a convergence of action and agent (of "dance" and "dancer" in the figure Frank Kermode rightly took as typifying), and it is most imaginable where there has been a comparable convergence of every nurturing circumstance. In Yeats's ideal theater this meant plays in which each personage would "speak that language which is his and nobody else's"; speak it, moreover, "with so much of emotional

subtlety that the hearer may find it hard to know whether it is
the thought or the word that has moved him, or whether these
could be separated at all" ("Samhain: 1903—The Reform of
the Theatre"). Such plays in turn could grow only from an actual life shared by both performers and audience. In ordinary
understanding *authenticity* is most likely to go in company
with *heroism* and *nobility*, and much of Yeats's eloquence is
devoted to celebrating these traditional qualities, whether in
triumph and deserved acclaim or in defeat and a final, tragic
attenuation. (It had been "an early conviction of mine," he
wrote in *A Vision* [III, viii], "that the creative power of the lyric
poet depends upon his accepting some one of a few traditional
attitudes, lover, sage, hero, scorner of life.")

It is also possible that heroism and nobility were always, in
Yeats's deepest mind, epiphenomenal. This may be why an element of the forced and wishful hangs about their direct presentation.[15] Yeats loved in later life to look back on the reality of
"beautiful lofty things" (a title of the late 1930s) just as when
young he had taken for theme the loss to time and old age of
all rare virtues—and might it not be said that any theory of poetic value which leaves no room for an art merely of commem-
oration, a matching of language to the familiar occasions of respect or hospitality or worship or grief, is itself uncivilly
deficient? But what most of all brings definiteness and a witty
or impassioned trenchancy into Yeats's writing is the apprehension of *autonomy*, of acts and selves planted in their own
enabling character and history; planted there and unselfcon-
sciously putting forth new growth, new consequence, even
when at cross-purposes with their own first inclination or with
any hope of eventual equilibrium. Such autonomy is the more
compelling when it renews some long-nurtured custom or ex-

[15] To my taste now, almost all the more personalized Maud Gonne evoca-
tions fall into this class, even the middle lines in stanza IV of "Among School
Children," although here the superbly rapid and varied advance of the whole
poem more expertly absorbs them. For whatever reasons poems addressed to
Con Markiewicz, like "On a Political Prisoner," and to Olivia Shakespear,
most of all the beautiful "Speech After Long Silence," ring truer.

pectancy; when, that is, its claim is independent of merely personal preference but seems in the nature of things. It then becomes, we may say, virtue's own virtue. Where it materializes, it is the cause that virtue is in others; so it generates those "moment[s] of sudden intensity" (*Reveries*, xiii) that demonstrate—as we laugh, rejoice, start up in fright—that we, too, are alive and in life.

Yeats's own carefully worked autobiographical prose comes most to life in memorializing self-rooted, self-validating acts and persons that he had known in childhood and later in the public life of his time. (Anecdotes about himself, by contrast, are more often conventionalized admissions of some youthful inadequacy and tend to fix on moments of social chagrin—not the best subject for lyric celebration.) In public life autonomy of being shows in that generosity of force in certain particular men which compels others to follow them in defeat as well as in the promise of victory. Yeats remembered it in the austere, erratically impulsive John O'Leary, who had "moral genius," and of course in Parnell, but not in the popular orator John Taylor, whose private voice "had no emotional quality except in the expression of scorn" ("Ireland After Parnell," v). It is there in memories of certain forebears, especially Pollexfens, and of certain of their servants, too; it characterizes all who are "amusing or exciting to think about." (The memory of such persons is what constitutes "history," so his father's friend York Powell taught him to think: "Four Years," iii.) It is the quality Yeats means to isolate in speaking of men who are "creation's very self" ("Hodos Chameliontos," ix); who have "the faculty of experience" ("The Tragic Generation," xi); who can be full of the conflicts and contradictions that *are* consciousness, *are* passion ("Pages from a Diary of 1930," xxxix), yet remain free of jealousy, envy, resentment; who are, above all, "self-possessed." If for Yeats the character Hamlet remained exemplary from first to last—from Irving's performance "when I was ten or twelve" to the archetype of tragic pride and gaiety evoked in "Lapis Lazuli" (1936)—it was for that "heroic self-possession" which enabled him "to play with hostile minds" or else "look in the lion's face"; coincidentally,

it was for the "indifference and passion-conquering sweetness" such self-possession was grounded in (*Reveries*, ix,
xxvii).[16]

The ethos in question is unrepentantly aristocratic, and not
less so for appropriating the privileged increments of physical
vitality and beauty and of private freedom. Certainly it is central to all three of the published Robert Gregory poems, most
unconditionally perhaps in "An Irish Airman Foresees His
Death," where the hero acknowledges allegiance only to his
own district and rearing ("My country is Kiltartan's Cross")
and is indifferent to the eventuality of praise or blame, life or
death:

> No law, nor duty bade me fight,
> No public men, nor cheering crowds,
> A lonely impulse of delight
> Drove to this tumult in the clouds.

Yet it is an ethos in no way limited to birth and rank. Yeats,
writing from a sociohistoric time-warp relatively uncrossed by
modernity's alienations, can imagine the same "self-moving,

---

[16] In distinguishing his Pollexfen ancestry from the less flamboyant Middle-
tons, Yeats said of the latter that they were generally "liked" but "had not the
pride and reserve, the sense of decorum and order, *the instinctive playing before themselves* [my emphasis] that belongs to those who strike the popular
imagination" (*Reveries*, ii). As early as 1909 this sense of human consequence
had become doctrinal for him. "Active virtue," he wrote in a famous diary entry of that year, "is . . . theatrical, consciously dramatic, the wearing of a
mask. It is the condition of arduous full life" ("Estrangement," xxii).

In what seems to me the finest essay we have on Yeats's triumph in poetry,
Edwin Muir emphasized Yeats's own active fulfillment of this condition, re-
lating it to his calculated achievement of an appropriate audience. In maturity,
Muir wrote, Yeats "has made himself into a public figure, and speaks to an
audience. He had achieved this by dramatizing himself, and acting the role
which was really himself." In Muir's view the achievement is central to Yeats's
extraordinary power of appeal—and we may take it as a main reason why this
least modernist of modern poets still reaches out so directly. "Perhaps," Muir
continued, "this is the most real and intimate relation a poet can have to a public in our time, as a great faulty image, in which they can find their own faults
and their own hidden greatness . . ." ("W. B. Yeats," *The Estate of Poetry*
[1962], 51-52).

self-creating" temper of mind coming to the surface in every
class and reach of society: in the visions and recollections of a
Red Hanrahan, a Crazy Jane; in the performance of a plain fellow like the fiddler of Dooney, whose playing makes "[f]olk
dance like a wave of the sea," or of the holy con man Malachi
Stilt-Jack ('High Talk"); also in the schoolmasters, counting-
house clerks, and (some of them) bigoted, mannerless towns-
men of "Easter 1916," who in the crisis of their lives are
"changed, changed utterly." Indeed a comparable self-transformation is the privilege of every "girl or boy," to whom the
idea of "eternity" comes first as "passion" and who thus "[c]ry
at the onset of the sexual joy/ 'For ever and for ever' . . ."
("Supernatural Songs: VIII").

These are self-born life's human forms. A more absolute
manifestation belongs, for Yeats, to the spirit world itself,
which both mocks and tempts humankind with promises of an
immaterial ecstasy—"ecstasy/ No living man can drink from
the whole wine" ("All Soul's Night"). Human consciousness
can nevertheless gain knowledge of this transcendence and
does so whenever imagination rises "to that pitch where it
casts out/ All that is not itself" ("A Bronze Head"), though the
state in question be a vision of terror, a shattering of the soul.[17]
What is also certain is that all such states can pass from us as
abruptly and inexorably as they first blazingly materialize. The
confessional eloquence of, in particular, Yeats's final phase
turns repeatedly on the agony of their disintegration and loss,
and on the gnawing uncertainty of every grand claim about life
that has ever justified itself by way of their analogy:

[17] A version of this purity of, at once, being and consciousness is evoked in
the *Book of Thel* rhythms of one of Yeats's earliest successes, the charming
"Indian Upon God" (1886). Here a moorfowl, lotus, roebuck, and peacock
speak in series of a vision of all creation shaped entirely to their simple crea-
tureliness. Forty years later the same incarnate purity forms a visionary climax
in "Blood and the Moon" (1927), where the mind's passion finds within a still
divided universe a place for itself equal to its farthest reach: "The strength that
gives our blood and state magnanimity of its own desire; / Everything that is
not God consumed with intellectual fire."

All that I have said and done,
Now that I am old and ill,
Turns into a question. . . .

But hush, for I have lost the theme,
Its joy or night seem but a dream. . . .
("The Man and the Echo" [1938])

How does this metaphysic of virtue and consequence enter into Yeats's practice of the art of lyric? Any faithful reader of his work grows familiar with certain formulas and symbols that come to express it with singular directness, especially from *The Wild Swans at Coole* forward. Not least conspicuous is a set of syntactical reflexives which, as they recur, provide a virtual logistics of authenticity as Yeats imagined it. A striking instance is the argumentative climax of "A Prayer for My Daughter," where the soul is invited to the "radical" discovery that it is, after all, "self-delighting,/ Self-appeasing, self-affrighting,/ And that its own sweet will is Heaven's will"; clearly the spoken emphasis in this should fall on "self" and "own." In "Ego Dominus Tuus" Dante's supremacy is a matter of his having "utterly found himself"; in "Colonus' Praise" the masterliness of the mind of Athens derives from its being "self-sown, self-begotten"; in "Meditations in Time of Civil War: VII" a "self-delighting reverie" is the blessing first lost when crowd passion and senseless tumult take over. In "Two Songs from a Play" it is "man's own resinous heart" that feeds the fires mankind is, in its history, consumed by.[18]

[18] Correspondingly, in prose statements, an "Ireland of men's affections" is enjoined to be "self-moving, self-creating" ("The Stirring of the Bones," iv). In the "Introduction" to the enlarged *A Vision* of 1937 Yeats's first justification for the strange arguments to follow is that they are the reason his poetry, as in *The Tower* and *The Winding Stair*, has palpably grown "in self-possession and power." More or less the same clinching definition of artistic power is set out as early as "Samhain: 1908." It is a power "little affected" by external things since it is "self-contained, self-created, self-suffering. . . ." Our best ideas, the means by which we "discover ourselves," are true for us only as they are "images of our own power."

The major symbols for this self-realized dimension of created being appear to be the *swan*—with various more exotic or
unspecified birds representing more transcendental consum-
mations, as in the endings of "On a Picture of a Black Centaur" (1920) and "Cuchulain Comforted" (January 1939, two
weeks before Yeats's death)—and the *fountain*, or some overflowing basin, lake, or pool. More than once these two symbols come together in unforced brilliance. In "The Wild Swans
at Coole" (1916)—a poem upon which Yeats's new interest in
gyres and cycles leaves, as yet, only the faintest trace—the
nine-and-fifty swans the poet remembers as once suddenly
mounting and wheeling off "in great broken rings" and that
are now adrift in mysterious stillness, are placed upon an autumn lake's "brimming water"; and again in the more systematized argument of "Coole Park and Ballylee, 1931" the ascending swan, which "seems a concentration of the sky" (its
other element), rises up from a "flooded lake" described as receiving into itself a generative stream of moving waters. This
deeply traditional and brilliantly reworked symbol of the
brimming fountain is recovered perhaps most powerfully and
originally at the beginning of "Meditations in Time of Civil
War," in successive images of life raining down "until the basin
spills," of an "abounding, glittering jet" springing up again
"out of life's own self-delight," and of obscurely dark "rich
streams" which yield up the counter-symbol of an "empty sea-
shell."

But this is still in the realm of theme and statement. What is
the art itself which overcomes all that is grotesque, willful,
sometimes openly repellent, or that is sentimental and imaginatively self-indulgent, in the attitudes struck, the arguments
assertively delivered? It will help here to note the kind of discussion Yeats's poems attracted when he was merely, in a remarkably solid early consensus, the most satisfying lyric artist
within the whole post-Browning, post-Tennyson, post-Ros-
setti generation, the first of the younger poets (Ernest Rhys declared in 1895) "to emerge from the coteries and to reach the
centre." One particular emphasis in early reviews is on the nar-

rowness and simplicity of means in Yeats's verse and on, consequently, an underlying sameness of effect. This is made both a measure of his undeniable "individuality" and a source of concern as to whether he had not painted himself into a performative corner; whether (the Irish critic Darrell Figgis speculated in 1912) by "the continual chastening of his verse" he had attained "perfection of simplicity" only at the sacrifice of all weight or force of "vision." "He extracts from a simple and rather limited vocabulary effects of the rarest delicacy and distinction," the influential William Archer wrote in *Poets of the Younger Generation* (1902), going on at once to puzzle out the cost of this achievement:

> There is a certain appearance of mannerism ... in Mr. Yeats's individuality. One can scarcely turn a page of these books without coming upon the epithets "dim," "glimmering," "wandering," "pearl-pale," "dove-grey," "dew-dropping," and the like. His imagery is built up out of a very few simple elements, which he combines and re-combines unweariedly.

The acknowledged fineness, then, of the art in question has come about through a patient concentration on a limited vocabulary directed to a limited range of uses. The result is a highly personalized distinction which nevertheless is curiously like the impersonality, the self-enclosedness, of folk poetry— William Archer's next point, as it happens, in 1902 and also Forrest Reid's in 1915, in commenting on one new song in *Responsibilities* (1914) "which comes with all the authority of an old masterpiece that has sung its way triumphantly down the ages." There is little question that Yeats's special standing in modern poetry, even with commentators who claim to find both his temperament and his themes repugnant, turns on his celebrated act of re-creating himself, as he passed the age of fifty, in both craft and imagination. What these early commentaries appear to be telling us is that some such action of self-feeding growth and renewal was the secret of his distinction all along. It involved establishing a definite, even showy, personal manner and playing within it to this end or that, yet never getting mired down inside it. From first to last Yeats was a masterly impersonator, a speaker in identifiable voices and tongues (not least the voice of his own carefully tended passional self). All his hard effort of composition, revision, expressive and prosodic reconstruction, was to the end of giving verse-statement a self-completedness that would draw out and release to the full the energies of implication within its husbanded means.

Early on, this primarily meant turning over a limited repertory of words and images that came to him already stylized in late-Victorian convention and in the folk adaptations of the "Celtic twilight" interval. From *The Wind Among the Reeds* (1899) through *Responsibilities* (1914) it takes form as a building up, within sequences of short poems in a more colloquial syntax, of his own workshop of symbols and talismanic references; with *The Wild Swans at Coole* (the 1919 collection famously greeted by Middleton Murry as signaling the end of the line for a now unmistakably minor talent) this changes to a more systematic projection of what John Holloway has described as well as anyone, "a self-contained world of language within [each] poem" and within, we can add, the whole body of his poetry. Further, it is now a world of language in which, as William Pritchard nicely observes, "dream," "vision," "sing," and "world" have been joined without loss of coherence by "marmalade," "rhetorician," "sentimentalist," and "dissipation." The result is a continuum of discourse and redefinition which, after publication of *The Tower* (1928), led Edmund Wilson to remark that "Yeats' sense of reality today is inferior to that of no man alive" (*Axel's Castle* [1931], ch. II).

More and more one poem enlivens another, even as it pursues a separate argumentative course (the striking differences in angle of vision between "Sailing to Byzantium" in 1926 and "Byzantium" in 1930 were puzzling only at first). More and more frequently the poems open, or their climaxes are introduced, with some direct gesture of invocation. Their "forming

ritual," as John Holloway explains it, "is the solemnised call-
ing-up of objects by the poet to people the world of his imagination"—"I summon to the ancient winding stair," "I declare
this tower to be my symbol," "Before me floats an image," "O
Presences/ That passion, piety or affection knows"—and what
results is something inseparable from the whole enterprise of
creation and re-creation it coincidentally rehearses: "an always expanding network of transferring energies, of active in-
terrelatings," "a world . . . of vigorous action, of process and
event, and of emphatically transitive verbs."[19]

But it might also be said that the formal and prosodic mastery needed to support this enterprise was there from the start.
Hugh Kenner neatly points up this mastery by contrasting an
arch-Tennysonian verse sentence gracefully winding through a
passage in the *Idylls of the King* with "a boxed and bounded
Yeats sentence, in his mature manner as perfected by 1898" (*A
Colder Eye* [1983], 79); the example chosen is a little-re-
marked poem "The Fish"—one eight-line stanza, one shaped
syntactical unit—in order perhaps not to overdetermine the
case with the "Song of Wandering Aengus" from the next page
of *Collected Poems* (a poem leaving even Harold Bloom effectively speechless). For corroboration Kenner cites one of Ezra
Pound's root-of-the-matter judgments: "[Yeats] had made lyrics of a single sentence, with no word out of natural order."
Properly to complete stylistic arguments of this sort, we would
need to bring forward a whole set of intensifying and integrat-
ing devices that Yeats's best commentators have not missed the
chance to highlight: words not at all in natural order, articles
and possessives either omitted or replaced by demonstratives,
internal rhymes and terminal off-rhymes, extravagantly suspended subordinate clauses, breath-catching enjambments,

---

[19] "Style and World in 'The Tower,' " in *An Honoured Guest*, ed. Denis
Donoghue and J. R. Mulryne (1965). Yeats himself spoke with characteristic
extravagance of the effect he meant to imitate and re-produce, in the last sentence of his preface to *The Words Upon the Window-Pane* (1931): "All about
us there seems to start up a precise inexplicable teeming life, and the earth becomes once more, not in rhetorical metaphor, but in reality, sacred."

stanza resolutions of an Augustan point and force, or single
lines worthy of Pope himself in being "sweeping, witty and
grand" yet basically "colloquial" (Claude Rawson's judgment: *Times Literary Supplement*, March 14, 1975), and simply, at every turn, the ever-varying movement of packed phrasing across the grid of the chosen verse.

Individuality of voice, familiarity or remoteness (in either
case, a certain impersonality) of means, structures that summon and dedicate their own materials—these, along with an
insistent celebration of everything self-nurtured and self-delighting, are the confirming resources in Yeats's poetry. They
are how he worked to fulfill his mid-life resolve to make "a language to my liking" and to achieve with it both "a powerful
and passionate syntax"—"a passionate syntax for a passionate subject matter"—"and a complete coincidence between
period and stanza" ("A General Introduction for My Work"
[1937]). They seem to me best exemplified, as they would need
to be, in his most ambitious poems. Mastery of tone, or of a
dialectic of contrary tones, is indispensable in the triumphant
"Dialogue of Self and Soul," which Yeats worked at from July
through December of 1927. The first half of this poem is literally a confrontation of symbols: "Soul" (who begins and ends
it) fixing attention on tower and winding stair and on the
starry vision of "ancestral night" that is to flood down on consciousness, "Self" staying below and holding firm to earthly
thoughts of love and war as represented by a Japanese battle
sword and the embroidered silk "from some court lady's
dress." The two voices, though bound together in raptness of
contemplation, talk past each other as the poem advances. In
superbly self-contained stanzas each calls up and interprets its
own fulfilling symbols. "Soul," however, even as it talks "the
basin of the mind" into an overflowing fullness, talks itself into
silence. It thus leaves the stage to "Self," who completes the
poem; completes it, after contriving a singularly terrible image
of earthly life—blind men battering blind men in a filthy
ditch—by chanting out its great expanding prophecy of acceptance and blessedness:

When such as I cast out remorse
So great a sweetness flows into the breast,
We must laugh and we must sing,
We are blest by everything,
Everything we look upon is blest.[20]

Characteristically the argument of the "Dialogue" rises to a moment of passionate transformation. Perhaps less characteristically, the transcendence it speaks for is in and of the living present, specifically refusing the enchantments of the eternal. Passion and transformation (or transfiguration), states that earlier were ruefully lamented for their impermanence or their unattainability, more and more shape arguments and climaxes in the major later poems—as if answering to a summons in the programmatic essay *Per Amica Silentia Lunae* of 1917 (the first account of the system of understanding to be formalized in *A Vision*):

> I think that we who are poets and artists, not being permitted to shoot beyond the tangible, must go from desire to weariness and so to desire again, and live but for the moment when vision comes to our weariness like terrible lightning, in the humility of the brutes. ("Anima Hominis," xi)

"The subject of all art is passion," Yeats had declared in "Samhain: 1904—First Principles," and "what is passion"—he asked in a public letter to Lady Gregory in 1919, on "A People's Theatre"—"but the straining of man's being against some obstacle that obstructs its unity?" In "The Wild Swans at Coole" passion is still something yearned for, as symbolized in

---

[20] The dilemma "Soul" comes to may remind us that for Yeats a visionary not less than a political entrancement can turn "heart" or, here, "tongue" to "stone."

The one lapse in this splendid poem seems to me the line ending the second stanza of "Self" 's closing soliloquy: "If honour find him in the wintry blast"—in a moment of fatigue Yeats reverts to the wrong sort of Augustanism. The shift, on the other hand, from first-person singular to first-person plural in the end-stopped closing lines is as nice an example as one could wish of an art concealing its perfected artfulness.

the swans' alien beauty and freedom. In what became in *The Tower* the spacious political diptych "Meditation in Time of Civil War" and "Nineteen Hundred and Nineteen," passion too much wears the mask of destructive violence. It becomes the passion of "weasels fighting in a hole," or else, as a property of the soul, it dissolves—"[t]hrough too much business with the passing hour"—into mere "natural declension."[21] Only, for the most part, with the introduction of *A Vision*'s historical and mythic superforms does passion break through every barrier into a transfiguring dance of opposites—as it does in the climax of "News for the Delphic Oracle" when, to the "intolerable music" falling from Pan's cavern, nymphs and satyrs "copulate in the foam"; as it does supremely in the compact pageant-inquiry on the theme of Annunciation, "Leda and the Swan," a poem transcribed directly into the last chapter of *A Vision*.

"Byzantium" is perhaps the greatest, and riskiest, in this mode and the poem that most fully justifies Yeats's absorption in magic, alchemy, neo-Platonism, the religions of art and myth, the Byzantium construct and the rest. Here if anywhere Yeats tested poetically some of his most extravagant beliefs: that "mind [does] flow into mind," thereby becoming the theater of all meaning, and that the greatest art comes about "when a nature, that never ceases to judge itself, exhausts personal emotion . . . so completely that something impersonal, something that has nothing to do with action or desire, suddenly starts into its place" ("The Tragic Generation," xvi). "Byzantium" issues, at any rate, in one of the most concentrated and most obscure of all Yeatsian climaxes, as the extraordinary shadow play of descriptive fact and summoned spirits moves across the poet's entranced vision and in the last stanza springs loose into its own turbulent and ambiguous life (commentator

---

[21] Passion was not invariably heroic to Yeats. In one of the Irish Theatre reports he sourly remarks, with a writer's disgust at opinion-mongers, "there is nothing so passionate as a vested interest disguised as an intellectual conviction" ("Samhain: 1903"). And everyone remembers the "passionate intensity" that in "The Second Coming" belongs also to "the worst" of mankind.

after commentator finding the verb "break" untranslatably mysterious and unchallengeably powerful and right):

> Astraddle on the dolphin's mire and blood,
> Spirit after spirit! The smithies break the flood,
> The golden smithies of the Emperor!

There have been arguments in abundance about Yeats's "system" and the perhaps excessive dependence on its psychological-geometric vocabulary even of poems that like "Byzantium" are beyond question expertly wrought. I find good critical sense in the admonition of William Pritchard, who can be severe enough on this issue: rather than "assuming that by understanding the formulations of *A Vision* we will be able to read the later poems with success, we should . . . cast a cold eye on any language or concepts encountered which are comprehensible only through external reference" (*Lives of the Modern Poets* [1980], ch. II). But I think R. P. Blackmur's judgment equally true: "the system *is* dramatized, the typical figures *are* liberated into action" and, further, "seem most nearly individuals crying out, when inspection shows that they are in fact most nearly commentaries upon some notion or notions taken out of [the] system" ("W. B. Yeats: Between Myth and Philosophy" [1942]). To my own taste some of the purest moments of mastery in Yeats occur in certain late lyrics in which—with or without assistance from the system—that yearned-for humility of a wholly natural passion comes to the center again, or is recovered in passionate (not tranquil) memory. I find these the poems of Yeats's that, once taken into mind, never grow the least bit tiresome—although in one of them, the three-stanza lyric "Crazy Jane and Jack the Journeyman," the organizing image of a winding and unwinding *skein* comes straight from Yeats's visionary metaphysics:

> A lonely ghost the ghost is
> That to God shall come;
> I—love's skein upon the ground,
> My body in the tomb—

Shall leap into the light lost
In my mother's womb.

But were I left to lie alone
In an empty bed,
The skein so bound us ghost to ghost
When he turned his head
Passing on the road that night,
Mine would walk being dead.

A second—the *aubade*, "A Last Confession," in "A Woman Young and Old"—also builds on doctrines of the afterlife and on an ordered dialectic of spiritual and sensual, yet in its voicing keeps wholly to language authorized by popular tradition. The persona adopted is, again, a woman's. But, as Thomas Parkinson accurately comments, Yeats himself "stands behind these figures"; "it is in his loyalty to [them], his conviction of their rightness, that his employment of the persona differs from that of Pound and Eliot" (*W. B. Yeats: The Later Poetry* [1964], ch. I):

... when this soul, its body off,
Naked to naked goes,
He it has found shall find therein
What none other knows.

And give his own and take his own
And rule in his own right;
And though it loved in misery,
Close and cling so tight,
There's not a bird of day that dare
Extinguish that delight.

As much as "Byzantium" itself or "Among School Children" these late lyrics draw their clinching power from a dialectical abruptness, a quick reversal of the formative idea, when everything so far premised and elaborated suddenly yields to the most immediate sense of its human embodiment. It is on this ground, where natural virtue seems to speak out of its own rhythm of release, that Yeats most nearly approaches a standard of accomplishment which has been rather overlooked in the many informed accounts we now have of his consciousness of Romantic precedents or his Symbolist absorption in esoteric learning and a new hermeticism. I mean the standard of Shakespearean verse-argument.[22] "When I was a very young man, fresh from my first study of Elizabethan drama," Yeats wrote in *On the Boiler*,

> I began to puzzle my elders with the question: "Why has the audience deteriorated?" I would go on to explain that the modern theatre audience was as inferior to the Elizabethan as that was to the Greek; *I spoke of the difficult transition from topic to topic in Shakespearean dialogue.* . . . (emphasis added)

This same difficult rapidity of movement, when new feeling comes in aid or correction of established feeling and the advancing thought turns around on its determining axis, seems to me at the heart of Yeats's later, and greater, achievement in lyric. There is one obvious respect, of course, in which it comes short of the Shakespearean model. It works entirely in the mode of soliloquy, of subjective meditation and witness. It thus lacks, except by refraction, that richer interest that comes

[22] The index to Harold Bloom's *Yeats* (1970) prints forty-two lines of references to Blake, twelve lines for Keats, thirteen for Wordsworth, sixteen for Wallace Stevens, one for Shakespeare. Professor Bloom's only discussion of what Shakespeare might have meant to Yeats concerns the description in Phase 20 of *A Vision*, which is taken as demonstrating the "feeling of unrest" Shakespeare's art "always" induced in him. I think there is some deadness of ear in this. In *The Trembling of the Veil* (1922), when a quotation from *Hamlet* leaps out from the discussion of Celtic Revival aspiration—"We do it wrong, being so majestical, to offer it the show of violence"—isn't it the very trick of Yeats's own forensic eloquence that momentarily comes back to us? In opposition to William Morris's artificial style (in a language Morris's era delivered to him "exhausted from abstraction") Yeats cites "the language of Chaucer and Shakespeare" with its popular "warp" and learned "woof" ("Four Years," xii). Yeats's father had loved to read Shakespeare (and others) aloud, always selecting passages "from the play or poem at its most passionate moment" (*Reveries*, ix, xi, xv).

into Shakespeare precisely in dialogue. This is the interest that wells up in the dramatized action because, as V. G. Kiernan has written, its participants "are willing to be interested in each other"; because they "overflow"—Kiernan is speaking here of the comedies in particular—"with a golden readiness of fellow feeling for the world and everything in it, a readiness to be amused by it, to help it, to scold or reform it."[23] At its strongest, however, Yeats's lyric intelligence produces something comparable, when systematized thinking (and imagining) yields to the convulsions of actual existence but does so more powerfully by placing the poet himself, or his surrogate, directly within the poem's field of action as an agent of a particular kind, both suffering and passionately questioning its expanded burden.

I find such a moment in "Meditations in Time of Civil War"; and there are moments in our own desperate enough civil history when it represents what I value most in Yeats and what I would most hope for in any poetry. It opens out at the point of transition from section V into section VI. In section V ("The Road at My Door") the elaborately reared fabric of what has gone before in the poem—the symbols of fountain, tower, sword, and peacock; the prized remembrances of aristocratic and Homeric largesse, of Il Penseroso's Platonist and the Primum Mobile—give way to the plain talk of a countryside in armed turmoil, and the poet retreats into the role of disturbed citizen and property-holder, complaining a little petulantly to a uniformed lieutenant about storm damage to a favorite tree. He then turns back into his own house—but turns in thought into the re-emerging grip, the baffling and baffled creativity, of his whole anguished "dream," a dream of trouble and ruin and yet of a regenerative aftermath that despite everything is still promised:

> The bees build in the crevices
> Of loosening masonry, and there
> The mother birds bring grubs and flies.

---

[23] "Human Relationships in Shakespeare," in Arnold Kettle, ed., *Shakespeare in a Changing World* (1964); a reference I owe to Michael Ferber.

My wall is loosening; honey-bees,
Come build in the empty house of the stare.

We are closed in, and the key is turned
On our uncertainty; somewhere
A man is killed, or a house burned,
Yet no clear fact to be discerned:
Come build in the empty house of the stare.

A barricade of stone or of wood;
Some fourteen days of civil war;
Last night they trundled down the road
That dead young soldier in his blood:
Come build in the empty house of the stare.

We had fed the heart on fantasies,
The heart's grown brutal from the fare;
More substance in our enmities
Than in our love; O honey-bees,
Come build in the empty house of the stare.

It teaches us something of how this particular poem took form
if we recall that bees are a neo-Platonic symbol of wisdom and
also of self-possession (virtue's definitive quality), or if we remember the "Argument" of Blake's *Marriage of Heaven and
Hell*, telling how "the just man" is driven forth to where "on
the barren heath/ Sing the honey bees." It does not, though,
change understanding. The poem's forensic meanings are self-
delivered—in plain words, in the passive voice, and through
the barest abstractions: "A man is killed, or a house burned,/
Yet no clear fact to be discerned." If a poet of our virtue-de-
spairing century wanted to stand or fall on a single statement,
I can't imagine wishing for better than this.

~

". . . everything is all right and difficult. . . ."
—Frank O'Hara, "Ode to Michael Goldberg ('s Birth
   and Other Births)"

The "original, hydrogenic, anthropomorphic, fiscal, post-anti-esthetic, bland, unpicturesque, WilliamCarlos-Williamsian . . . definitely not nineteenth century . . . not even Partisan Review" poetry of Frank O'Hara (the self-characterization is in "Poem Read at Joan Mitchell's") reflects as continuously as Shelley's or Yeats's a rich awareness of the odds modern life keeps piling up against any "perfecting of its own nature in each thing" (the visible signature of virtue)—or in each man or woman, or in mankind collectively. It does this in arguments distinctive to its locale and epoch: New York ("most extravagant of cities" to Henry James) in the super-politicized but otherwise liberated and unbuttoned later twentieth century. So this poetry now and then explicitly reproduces the way in which, masking our most unreal terror, we casually mouth the names of those who have assumed command of modern megadeath, as if it were all a new species of media entertainment. For O'Hara politics was mostly a tiresome interruption, but he knew what he was doing in making "Khrushchev" the opening word of one of his most ebullient New York lyrics:

> Khrushchev is coming on the right day!
> the cool graced light
> is pushed off the enormous glass piers by hard wind
> and everything is tossing, hurrying on up
> this country
> has everything but *politesse*, a Puerto Rican cab driver
> says. . . .

Once touched off in this poem, legitimate anxiety about the recklessness of responsible statesmen hangs on through the brilliant city-morning scene and gives a sharper edge to the brisk repertory of Romantic attitudes: children and the beautiful young are innocent, art is the thing to get excited about, the world is more various than we commonly remember, love and friendship count most, nostalgia is comforting, selfhood always flirts dangerously with darkness but can steady itself by remembering its kinship with other men of the crowd—

                    . . . Ionesco is greater
than Beckett, Vincent said, that's what I think, blueberry
    blintzes
and Khrushchev was probably being carped at
                            in Washington, no *politesse*
Vincent tells me about his mother's trip to Sweden
                            Hans tells us
about his father's life in Sweden, it sounds like Grace
    Hartigan's
painting *Sweden*
  so I go home to bed and names drift through my head
Purgatorio Machado, Gerhard Schwartz and Gaspar
    Gonzales, all
            unknown figures of the early morning as I go to
            work

The September wind *is* "hard," hard as the life and probable
fortune of the great modern city whose buildings it transforms
into

    . . . ozone stalagmites
                    deposits of light

—but it is still the corresponding wind of Romantic, and Shelleyan, prophecy, and a benediction to those who can lift themselves to meet it:

        New York seems blinding and my tie is blowing up the
            street
    I wish it would blow off
                    though it is cold and somewhat warms my neck
    as the train bears Khrushchev on to Pennsylvania Station
        and the light seems eternal
        and joy seems inexorable
        I am foolish enough always to find it in wind.

O'Hara's writing is knotted tightly enough into its time and
place—Manhattan in the 1950s and early 1960s, when the
city's popular institutions still worked and its special pleasures

were commonly affordable—to need now as much scholarly annotation as Yeats's.[24] What is also true is that all its leading properties may be defined in terms of Romantic and late-Romantic (Surrealist, imagist, neo-Dada) precedent. It composes a very American and mid-twentieth-century Psalm of Life, though without Longfellow's earnestness and uniformity: a poetry of celebration and personal attachment, even if largely in the vein of parody and self-mockery. To be where "at least something's going on" is not quite all Frank O'Hara's aim in life (or in poetry), but aim enough when the result is also a willingness to "stand[] erect in the spirit's glare/ and wait[] for the joining of an opposite force's breath" ("In Favor of One's Time"); a willingness—not unlike the Self's in Yeats's "Dialogue" but deliberately understated—"calmly to face almost everything" ("Joe's Jacket").

Claims for O'Hara's weight and scope should be entered as discreetly as for others in his poetically favored but privately

---

[24] It would profit from annotation even among those whose commentaries have helped establish "The Day Lady Died," O'Hara's elegy for the singer Billie Holiday, as very nearly the surest American anthology selection of the past thirty years, yet who seem to have missed the clear logic linking all the random-seeming details of the poem's first four stanzas. Even Alan Feldman's discerning study speaks of this poem as written in opposition to "the elegiac tradition" and as being "full of irritating inconsequentialities." It is of course thoroughly traditional, a lament for an exemplary fellow artist which submits (as Milton in "Lycidas," Shelley in "Adonais") the poet's own imaginative identity to the ritual of grieving. And what is inconsequential about these details?—that he knows the exact departure and arrival times of the train taking him to dinner that night but does not know "the people who will feed me"; that only once has he ever heard his bank teller's given name and only once *not* been made to wait for his own identity and balance to be double-checked; that he accepts the task of finding out about "the poets/ in Ghana" however drably printed up—in addressing a life (Billie Holiday's) spent in solitude of spirit and ultimately in self-rejection, and a death that reaches its grievers only in the headlines of a newsstand tabloid. Aren't isolation and anonymity the consistent burden here? Doesn't, also, the serious work of choosing fine gifts for valued friends (Verlaine illustrated by Bonnard—!—or Lattimore's elegant Hesiod and three controversial off-Broadway plays; imported Italian liqueur and imported cigarettes) qualify and prepare him to be the right celebrant of Lady Day's heart-stopping gift as a blues interpreter?

watchful and circumspect generation. He does not—like Shelley, like Yeats—seek out heroic trials, or crave some posting of the odds beyond his own time's radical uncertainty and demoralization. He is quite unapologetic about wanting to live as long as possible inside a dream of life in which "all pain is extra" ("Ode (to Joseph Lesueur on the Arrow That Flieth By Day)"); a life resolutely devoted to love, art, festival, courtesy, though never to mere comfort or good taste. His effort is to appear to be writing from the very quick of continuous, unsegmented life, his own and the outreaching world's. "I don't have to make elaborately sounded structures," he announces in the first paragraph of "Personism: A Manifesto" (September 3, 1959); "I don't even like rhythm, assonance, all that stuff. You just go on your nerve"—a principle confirmed in the variousness of his self-dramatizations, in which reversals and self-evasions continually augment the illusion of human presence.

His vision seems sharpest a little off the center of things. "A step away" is best, distancing what matters most so as to get a truer purchase on it. (During the treacherous "confessional" interval in contemporary American poetry, Keats's negative capability became more needful than ever, and O'Hara—who alludes to it directly in "Personism"—effectively re-invented it as a working method.) "How I hate subject matter," he writes in a more contentious mood ("To Hell With It"), and there is now and then an over-indulgence in the clichés of post-Eliot, post-*Partisan Review* anti-intellectualism. Deciding, with fellow New Yorkers, that "we don't like Lionel Trilling" or even "Henry James so much" is good fun, especially when followed by "we like Herman Melville" and then, "we just want to be rich/ and walk on girders in our silver hats" ("Personal Poem"). But being against "ideas" simply because "ideas are obscure and nothing should be obscure tonight" intrudes something impertinent into a ceremony that does not need it ("Poem Read at Joan Mitchell's," celebrating a marriage), as if even marriage would not be a little better off for a few shared ideas; and the subordinate clause's turn of phrase in describing

the consequence of a too intense absorption in art at the expense of life—"it seems they were all cheated of some marvel-
ous experience/ which is not going to be wasted on me" ("Having a Coke With You")—has, even in context, an overtone of
aggressive self-approval. Such attitudes, we know, are in the
grand American tradition of come-off-it populism, but as
much as others they need to be captured afresh, as they are in
the detail of "A Young Poet" about "feel[ing] the noise of art
abate, in the silence of life," or in the direct Whitmanism of
"Poem: 'À la recherche de Gertrude Stein' " (cf. Whitman's
"Of the Terrible Doubt of Appearances"):

> sick logic and feeble reasoning are cured
> by the perfect symmetry of your arms and legs

   Disclaimers notwithstanding, O'Hara does write on subjects. Mostly they are conventionalized subjects matching the
conventionalized occasions that draw him out. He writes
small, direct love poems that on the whole (to borrow what
Artemus Ward said of George Washington) don't slop over,
even when sentimental.[25] He writes poems for and about artists, invariably expressing his gratitude. Painters—Jane Freilicher, Grace Hartigan, Red Grooms, Larry Rivers, Pollock,
De Kooning—are regularly greeted as collaborators and
kindred spirits; it is granted that musicians are sometimes
frightening because what they do can seem, in some moods,
"to punish [us]"; but miracle-working dancers, including the
one he is in love with, are only to be praised ("Ode to Tanaquil
Leclerc," the Vincent Warren poems). Also there are marriage
poems and party poems—occasions of refashioned community
and the breaking of bread, or bottles, with friends; poems hon-

[25] For O'Hara's own vision of the Matter of America—"the beautiful history"—and of the godfather of its republican self-renewal, there is the neatly
argued "On Seeing Larry Rivers' *Washington Crossing the Delaware* at the
Museum of Modern Art" ("See how free we are! as a nation of persons"). The
six-page discussion of this poem in James E. B. Breslin, *From Modern to Contemporary* (1984), and indeed the O'Hara chapter as a whole, suggest as well
as anyone has to date the complexity and suppleness of O'Hara's lyric style.

oring dead precursors ("Second Avenue: In Memory of Vladimir Mayakovsky"), dead movie stars ("For James Dean"), dead friends ("The 'Unfinished': In Memory of Bunny Lang"); poems for friends who may need cheering up ("Fantasy: dedicated to the health of Allen Ginsberg"); poems about Emily Dickinson's great subject of the seasons and their ruthless, life-nurturing changes ("Aus Einem April," "(July Is Over And There's Very Little Trace)"). There are Romantic voyage poems, such as an American Shelley would write:

>   a fleece of pure intention sailing like
> a pinto in a barque of slaves
>   who soon will turn upon their captors
> lower anchor, found a city riding there
>   of poverty and sweetness paralleled
>   among the races without time,
>   and one alone will speak of being
>   born in pain
> and he will be the wings of an extraordinary liberty.
>   ("Ode to Michael Goldberg")

And everywhere there are poems, and passages in poems, about the virtue of attaching oneself to the astonishing energy and variety (the *virtù*) of New York by day or night, "the feeling of life and incident pouring over the sleeping city" ("Joe's Jacket"). O'Hara has, on the surface, the look of a poet with eyes only for what is directly to hand and of merely personal moment; but he is in fact that rarity among his own contemporaries, a writer able to suggest—with what our most tactful writer of criticism, John Updike, pinpoints as the "openness, dailiness, intimacy, and odd control of it all"—the very substantial attraction and pleasure of modern big-city life, its inexhaustible power as a human environment to refresh and reawaken.

We see soon enough that "just going on nerve" is a controlled pose like any other. O'Hara's sense of design in poetry, of how to frame and when to break off, follows on a studious apprenticeship to French modernism in particular—Apolli-

naire, Eluard, Reverdy are major presences—and to the new
masters of painting and sculpture he knew and worked with
through the 1950s and early 1960s. (In the decade after 1955
O'Hara organized and wrote catalogues for contemporary ex-
hibitions at the Museum of Modern Art: Pollock, Motherwell,
David Smith, among others.) Yet he gives up a good deal in
pursuing the phantom of immediacy. He gives up not only the
counter-satisfactions of a sustained metrical eloquence but,
most of the time, the power that can come with the elaboration
of a single extended figure; the exception is, again, the cumulative figure of the city itself. And he is not consistently in command of his shape-changer's art. That "odd control" is not
always maintained. Sometimes, with confidence in your eventual rewards, you follow along through poems that sprawl and
sideslip and never do properly recover, to find at last that it
was almost (but not quite) for the sake of a single line, as in the
mock epithalamion read at Joan Mitchell's—"and there is no
noise like the rare silence when you both sleep. . . ."

There is also, with O'Hara, an antithetical muse to be reck-
oned with, a smotherer of everything wind-lifted and liberating, whose spectral presence looms up in several poems and
with whom, I think, he never did have it out to any conclusion.
This is the mother-figure who "flew in from Des Moines/ with
her dog" and ruined "the whole damn vacation" ("Summer
Breezes"). Even in the beguiling "Ave Maria"—"Mothers of
America/ let your kids go to the movies!/ get them out of the
house so they won't know what you're up to"—she is pictured
taking her final revenge when, the non-returning prodigal
son's advice having fallen on deaf ears,

                              . . . the family breaks up
      and your children grow old and blind in front of a TV set
                                                           seeing
         movies you wouldn't let them see when they were young

"All things are tragic/ when a mother watches!": so goes one
strange awkward dream poem ("There I could never be a
boy") in which the poet takes to himself the armored "speed
and strength" of a powerful horse—"a frightened black

mare," no less—"and she never threw me." There is, in short, a radically abridged family romance playing itself out through a considerable portion of O'Hara's writing. No doubt it too, as well as the collective apprehensiveness of the age, explains why his mask of self-limitation sometimes seems an anguished natural grimace.

But he is consistently a poet and gets his own back, family-romance-wise, in a brilliant condensation of Blake's "Mental Traveler" myth:

> I hardly ever think of June 27, 1926
> when I came moaning into my mother's world
> and tried to make it mine immediately
> by screaming, sucking, urinating
> and carrying on generally
> it was quite a day
> I wasn't proud of my penis yet, how did I know how to
>   act? . . .
>
> ("Ode to Michael Goldberg")

There is a rough wisdom, finally, in Frank O'Hara's lyric address to all that gathers in the recesses of our ordinary lives, and of all we do, all the shifts we are put to, both to embrace this hidden life and to keep from drowning there. A rueful wisdom about love, for example, as even in the ripest swell of it he can stand off—off from himself, too—without suspending delight:

> and each reason for love always
> a certain hostility, mistaken
> for wisdom
>   exceptional excitement
> which is finally simple blindness
> (but not to be sneezed at!) like
> a successful American satellite. . . .
>
> ("Ode to Michael Goldberg")

One other section of the same poem—a poem greeting new life by reviewing, synoptically, the testing places of his own already half-expended one—expresses with unusual force (despite one risky *boutade*) the sensibility and, among his contemporaries, uncommon personal honesty that in combination seem to me to have served poetry itself about as well as one may hope for nowadays:

> A couple of specifically anguished days
> make me now distrust sorrow, simple sorrow
> especially, like sorrow over death
>
> it makes you wonder who you are to be sorrowful
> over death, death belonging to another
> and suddenly inhabited by you without permission
>
> you moved in impulsively and took it up
> declaring your Squatters' Rights in howls
> or screaming with rage, like a parvenu in a Chinese
>   laundry
>
> disbelieving your own feelings is the worst
> and you suspect that you are jealous of this death

If it is indeed by way of an argument with our antithetical selves that poetry comes forth, an argument in which the responsive life in us—the accruent and ever-accruing virtue—discovers and confronts its most dogged adversaries, Frank O'Hara too belongs with the poets. As much as charm or good humor, celebration without self-deception is his lyric art's determining ethos. Coming to expression through attitudes of grateful acceptance in the least forgiving of modern cities, it seems to me a main reason for that art's uncommon trustworthiness.[26]

[26] Bibliographical note: Yeats, in the essays cited, is our best modern writer on Shelley, a poet who remains singularly resistant to critical categorization. The discussions of Shelley in T. S. Eliot, *The Use of Poetry and the Use of Criticism* (1933), and F. R. Leavis, *Revaluation* (1936), are documents in the vicissitudes of early twentieth-century critical debate. The best academic criticism of Shelley runs mostly to interpretive commentaries on individual longer poems; see collections edited by George M. Ridenour (1965) and R. B. Woodings (1969). Neville Rogers, *Shelley at Work* (revised edition, 1967), is richly informative on Shelley's compositional practice. Judith Chernaik's emphasis

on genre in *The Lyrics of Shelley* (1972) is valuable but restricts her to shorter poems. Book-length studies of the major poetry tend to concentrate on Shelley's intellectual adventuring (or "thought") and seem to me helpful according to their authors' grasp of what really creates poetic interest and satisfaction.

With Yeats hardly less than with Shakespeare there is so much genuinely illuminating commentary that any short list will misrepresent actual obligations. My ideas about Yeats's program for poetry remain indebted to Richard Ellmann, who first spelled things out in *Yeats: The Man and the Masks* (1948) and extended his presentation of unpublished materials in *The Identity of Yeats* (1954). T. R. Henn, *The Lonely Tower* (1950), keeps its panoramic value. In their several ways Thomas Parkinson, especially in *W. B. Yeats: The Later Poetry* (1964), Hugh Kenner in *A Colder Eye* (1983), and William H. Pritchard in *Lives of the Modern Poets* (1980), come nearest my own sense of why returning to Yeats is unfailingly exhilarating—and I would now add Seamus Heaney in his Harvard College lectures of March, 1985. Professor Pritchard's discriminating choice of materials for a Penguin critical anthology (1972) is my chief source for early reviews; this collection also reprints the most provocative later accounts, as by Edmund Wilson, William Empson, Blackmur, Auden, Eliot, John Wain, John Holloway, Donald Davie. Among other such collections John Unterecker's (1963) is exemplary in its range of viewpoints. Harold Bloom's textual command of the whole Yeatsian oeuvre and of Romantic poetry generally is unfailingly instructive, but the judgmental uses it serves in his *Yeats* (1970) seem to me too idiosyncratic to hold attention. The controversial new Macmillan edition of *W. B. Yeats: The Poems*, ed. Richard Finneran (1983), reestablishes the order Yeats himself seems to have intended for *Last Poems* (1983) and includes 130 additional pages of lyric verse, mostly from the plays. A. Norman Jeffares, *A New Commentary on the Collected Poems of W. B. Yeats* (1984), is, as revised, more indispensable than ever.

The Collected Poems of Frank O'Hara, ed. Donald Allen (1971), and *Poems Retrieved*, ed. Donald Allen (1977), are essential texts, though for new readers *The Selected Poems of Frank O'Hara*, ed. Donald Allen (1975), makes perhaps a better introduction and is, among its other merits, chronologically arranged. Prose pieces and interviews are collected in *Standing Still and Walking in New York*, ed. Donald Allen (1974), and in *Art Chronicles, 1954-1966* (1966). *Homage to Frank O'Hara*, ed. Bill Berkson and Joe LeSueur (1978), contains the recollections and tributes of friends. The most discerning book-length study seems to me Alan Feldman, *Frank O'Hara* (1979). Helen Vendler's *Parnassus* essay of 1972, reprinted in *Part of Nature, Part of Us* (1980), is characteristically organizing and perceptive, while James E. B. Breslin's long chapter in *From Modern to Contemporary* (1984) is perhaps the first commentary to build from the start on a recognition that moments of genuine power are not merely the odd accidents of O'Hara's "everywhere and nowhere" lyric presence but its scrupulously prepared result.

Afterword: On Some Arguments of Yves Bonnefoy

"The purpose of the writer is . . . not to assist in storing the passive mind with the various sorts of knowledge most in request, as if the human soul were a mere repository or banqueting-room, but to place it in such relations of circumstance as should gradually excite the germinal power that craves no knowledge but what it can take up into itself, what it can appropriate, and reproduce in fruits of its own."
—Coleridge, *The Friend*, "On Method"

What I have chiefly meant to do in the preceding chapters is—so far as mere commentary allows—to let the projected energy and abundance of particular writings speak out for themselves, to the end of inviting readers to meet them with a corresponding imaginative buoyancy. But what else does our critical concern with literature ever properly aim at? The point has been curiously at issue in recent times. Even within reader-centered theories, that predicated responsiveness is itself disregarded as a warrant of meaning or else written off as unqualified misapprehension. A core premise in much current theorizing appears to be that our minds as readers have no self-constituting strength or stability in receptive discrimination and therefore no power to hold contrary impressions in working balance. Moment by moment we are pictured as entirely vulnerable to manipulation and conceptual disorientation. It is as if we were strapped down without countervailing resources across some grid of signal wires any or all of which may at any time either go dangerously taut or else break loose altogether and, either way, leave us "in endless error hurled"—exactly where an earlier spell of deflationary self-analysis famously situated us.

As a reaction to conditions of life in the globalized later twentieth century, and specifically to the threat of political and cultural totalization, this premise does not lack support. But in thus universalizing an anxiety about semiotic manipulation a whole view of mind is predicated whose determining characteristic is an essential passivity and powerlessness. (The correspondence to modern fiction's recurrent nightmare of domination and control is eye-catching, or should be.) That human intelligence is itself constructively self-regulating, that it finds its health in negotiating contraries which it not only tolerates but actively invites, are possibilities notably underrepresented in current discussion. As regards literary theory, at any rate, the least realism about our actual experience as readers ought to be fundamentally reassuring. Even at our most changeable we do bring judgments down from one textual encounter to another; we do go on making some operative sense of things. Also we do collectively reach that measure of agreement which is minimally required for sustained dispute. Language, consciousness, human exchange generally: our own persistence in the world regularly confirms that all of these are working systems of remarkable tenacity and adaptive resilience, whether or not anyone accepts anyone else's theory of their principle of operation. I think it is only in the eye of a methodologically regressive positivism—the importance commonly assigned to attacks on simple referentiality presupposing a continuing belief in its primacy to organized understanding—that the arbitrariness of the linguistic sign, the indeterminacy of any projected address to experience, are scandals requiring all the world to change its ways.

The speculative situation seems to me (as a student of American instances) much like the one Emerson faced a century and a half ago in the pivotal sixth chapter of his 1836 manifesto *Nature*, when after many preliminary assurances he turned to confront the issue of the hour for the philosophic and religious culture he had grown up with. It is an issue worth formulating both in the terms Emerson applied to it, writing as a prophet of recovered human morale, and in our own narrower ones as commentators on textuality. Do the determining objects of consciousness—nature and creation for the mind of 1836; language and the structures of discourse for us—"enjoy a substantial existence without," or do they have their being only in some "apocalypse of the mind" where all is permitted and nothing can be confirmed or verified? To such questions Emerson's reply was, *what difference does it make?* "The relations of parts and the end of the whole remaining the same" (as pragmatically they do), "what is the difference" whether the line runs straight from word to thing, mind to reality, consciousness into text and text into consciousness, or is instead an arbitrary conspiracy and delusion? That conspiracy being coextensive with the terms on which life itself is given to us, it has as much and, in each instance, as little to do with action and judgment as does the force of gravity with the fitness of particular bodily motions. We take full note of it as a determining limit, like the need for sleep or the inevitability of dying, but otherwise go about our creaturely business, exercising our natural appetite for "secondary worlds" adequate to our own imaginative reach.

So this book's arguments round back to its first paragraphs and the opening claim for imaginative literature as, on balance, an augmentation of self-monitored, self-reflective life. Conveniently I find fresh support for such a claim in the poet Yves Bonnefoy's extraordinary Collège de France inaugural of December 1981.[1] Tactfully responsive to his double commission as successor to the chair of Roland Barthes but also as the first poet to be received into the Collège de France since Valéry, M. Bonnefoy spoke altogether respectfully of *nouvelle critique* and its motivations, yet felt compelled to question what progress had been made toward resolving the issues that creativity, too, must consciously answer to. So he opened by registering a

---

[1] Available in English in *New Literary History* (Spring 1984), but in a not always reliable translation.

regret that over many years the massive concentration on a semiologic fracture [*clivage*] in our existence in the world had
led to a turning away "from the direct study of poets." To M.
Bonnefoy this is a philosophic as well as aesthetic misfortune.
For it is in the effort and aspiration of poets, imaginative cre-
ators, that language works to recover a "freedom" which—
dream-aided, dream-resistant—moves always in advance of
the world's unfolding life.

To adapt Yves Bonnefoy's phrasing: we may so absorb our-
seles in the readily demonstrated deviation of signifier from
signified, and in corollary perceptions of ontological division,
that we forget the imaginative need this division brings about.
We thus betray the very power of origination by which—riding
loose as we may be in a flood of words—we know ourselves as
participants in the plenitude of existence; know ourselves, that
is, as predictable selves. But it is precisely this "excess of words
over meanings," these constellations of new tropes boiling up
out of the reservoir of the linguistic, that first turn the always-
being-formed self to the tasks of poetry. It is an excitement, a
passion, known as well to the reader, who also possesses imagination. And it is known especially to the young reader, who
discovers in the words of poetry, and in the things, beings, horizon and sky these words project, "a whole world given at a
stroke to his thirst." Such a reader, confronted even with a
Mallarmé, "does not read . . . as the poetic theorist or the se-
miotician asks him to !"

Thus the whole existence of both writer and reader conspires to seek what semiologic purity denies it: release into, en-
gagement with, a world known first of all through our desire
for it. The motive each acts from is not, by rigorous analysis,
to expose and clear away everything problematic (though a
Hart Crane spoke for all poets in making analysis half of the
always double work of imaginative creation). It is instead to
enter the transactive intensity that this very excess, this irre-
pressible projective energy, eternally signifies. It is thus, in M.
Bonnefoy's formulation, "to recover a hope." (A formulation
whose philosophic force William James would easily have

understood: though philosophy proper strangely ignores this, so James wrote in "The Sentiment of Rationality" [1880], "the fact is that our consciousness at a given moment is never free from the ingredient of expectancy.")

As much as anything it is the force of such hope that holds us to the poetic, to an imagining power that may indeed require an understanding of its own weakness and incompleteness in order to do us good. (So William James again: "It seems almost as if it were necessary to become worthless as a practical being if one is to hope to attain any breadth of insight into the impersonal world of worths as such": "On a Certain Blindness in Human Beings" [1889].) The literary work, so attended to, is not then a "text" but a "tongue," a speaking voice, and its service is not representation but re-institution—not least of itself as a force articulating a reality that registers with us (while we listen) as "substantial" and as "sufficient." To be sure, the inscribed result will be as partial as it is cognitively uncertain. It can only reproduce that "strictly limited particularity" characterizing any portion of existence we grow conscious of. (It will thus be, as Pasternak said of all art, "more one-sided than people think": *Safe Conduct*, II, vii.)

The newest new criticism has not been wrong in its governing perceptions, but though it understands the "contradictions" within the poetic, it misapprehends poetry's correlative "obstinacy" in self-renewal. *Nouvelle critique* repeatedly shows itself—in the overkill of its arguments—requiring a reductive fantasy of the *author* as someone who, on a certain day, self-deludedly pronounces his work finished and closed. But authors are not less aware than their deconstructors that "in the very heart of writing there is a putting in question of writing." What then is signified by their obstinate persistence? It is, M. Bonnefoy answers, that "they carry within themselves another idea of what counts, or simply of what *is*, than that issuing from the semiologue's inquest." They identify the poetic not with the manipulation of words—words that, as Eliot, too, made a point of reminding us, "decay with imprecision" and represent "only a different kind of failure"—but with the search, the human passion, for meaning.

In making his case M. Bonnefoy is driven to the extreme of imagining the task faced by a handful of survivors after some global catastrophe, survivors on whom the burden has fallen of reimagining existence itself. To such persons, exposure to their own re-emergent being would itself be an "origin." As the first fact about existence would thus be its self-generation out of an extreme negation, the first fact about the poetic is its persistence through all contradiction and against all demonstration of impossibility. Language may well be a prison house, but calling it that is meaningless unless we posit the presence within it "of someone who shakes [shakes down? *qui secoue*] the door." Further, the essential condition of poetry's inconceivable persistence is its naturalness. Like all art the poetic embodies, as coincidentally it symbolizes, whatever force inheres in us to bring whatever is near us into relation. (Czeslaw Milosz would complement this in affirming "that man is above all an organizer of space . . . and that this is in fact what is meant by imagination": *The Land of Ulro*, tr. Louis Iribarne [1984], 245.)

In order not simply to survive but to desire to survive—to survive as a force of desire—the human creature must continue to want and to need to make actable meanings out of life. If analysis of this desire and need lands us once more in an impasse, a conceptual *aporia*, the value of what poetic imaginations persist in doing is precisely in the different attitude with which the impasse is confronted. Against the arbitrary sliding-off of the sign from its referent, and equally against that presumption of presence within the sign which would bind us to it as "image" (i.e., as icon), poetry's task is to maintain its own openness, its reality to itself as a process of becoming. So it takes its place as first of all "an act of knowing."[2] Recognizing the push of every sign and image toward absoluteness, it also

---

[2] "La poésie n'est rien d'autre, au plus vif de son inquiétude, qu'un acte de connaissance."

recognizes in them the natural form—the power-to-itself; the *virtue*, in this book's major sense—of human desiring. Poetry, too, "denounces the Image," insight frozen into monumentality. But it does so by virtue of its natural love for images.

Thus, into the endless reciprocations of existence and illusion poetry introduces, dialectically, "this third term of compassion"—accepting the objects it predicates even as it refuses to come to rest in them. It acts to rehabilitate and replenish realities that a fixation on "immediacy" can always reveal as non-existent. Fully as iconoclastic as analysis, the poetic, the imaginative, refuses equally the dictates of iconoclasm. That which any scrutiny of texts can easily dissolve into meaningless signs, poetry conspires to readmit "into the unity of life." Out of all illusion and deficiency it ventures to disclose some part at least of an unfathomable plenitude. So conceived, it is always an impossibility, eluding what is prescribed for it precisely in the degree that the immediate eludes our words—until the moment it once again overtakes us and our unappeasable desiring.

With reassurance of the sort Yves Bonnefoy provides, I would contend once more than a criticism failing to acknowledge the authority of that overtaking is a criticism that forfeits its claim to relevance and truth.

Index

Page numbers for authors or texts discussed at length appear in italics.

Emerson, Ralph Waldo (*cont.*)
Poet," 79; *Representative Men*,
82; "Uriel," 79
Empson, William, 273n; "*Hamlet
When New*," 90n; *Some Versions
of Pastoral*, 77n; *The Structure of
Complex Words*, 23
Enright, D. J., on Musil, 161n
Euripides, *Antigone*, 12
Evans, Dame Edith, 102
Everett, Barbara, 90n, 104n

Faulkner, William, 10, 38, 83, 83-
84n; *The Sound and the Fury*, 32
The Federalist, 64n
Feldman, Alan, *Frank O'Hara*,
266n, 273n
feminism, 53, 89-90
Ferber, Michael, 262n
Fergusson, Francis, 43; *The Idea of
a Theater*, 90n
Feydeau, Ernest, *Fanny*, 29
Fielding, Henry, *Amelia*, 68; *Joseph
Andrews*, 5; *Tom Jones*, 68, 114
Figgis, Darrell, on Yeats, 253
Fitzgerald, F. Scott, *Tender Is the
Night*, 77n
Flaubert, Gustave, 133, 194; *L'Édu-
cation sentimentale*, 69; *Madame
Bovary*, 29, 36, 78
Fontane, Theodor, *Effi Briest*, 76
Forster, E. M., 72, 84
Foucault, Michel, 141n
Fourier, Charles, 80
Fox, George, 50n
Franz Joseph (Emperor), 167-168
Freilicher, Jane, 268
Freud, Sigmund, 31-32; *Beyond the
Pleasure Principle*, 51-52; *The
Psychopathology of Everyday
Life*, 32
Frisé, Adolf, 161n, 171, 178n
Frye, Northrop, 24, 24n, 234; *Anat-
omy of Criticism*, 19; "The Prob-

lem of Spiritual Authority in the
Nineteenth Century," 155
Fussell, Paul, 56n

Galileo Galilei, 59n
Gallie, W. B., *Peirce and Pragma-
tism*, 34n
Garber, Marjorie, *Coming of Age in
Shakespeare*, 120, 122-123n
Garrick, David, 102n, 103-104
Gaskell, Elizabeth, 69; *Mary Bar-
ton*, 70
Gay, John, *The Beggar's Opera*, 68
Geertz, Clifford, "Art as a Cultural
System," 33
Genette, Gerard, "Stendhal," 125n,
135n
Gernet, Louis, 46
Gibbon, Edward, *The Decline and
Fall of the Roman Empire*, 60-61
Gide, André, 3, 130, 180; *The
Counterfeiters*, 162; *La Sym-
phonie pastorale*, 77n
Gilbert, Felix, 43n
Gilman, Stephen, *The Tower as Em-
blem*, 154n
Ginsberg, Allen, "Howl," 58n
Giorgione, "La Tempesta," 54n
Gissing, George, *New Grub Street*,
73
Glanvill, Joseph, 59n
Gödel, Kurt, 36, 41-42n
Goethe, Johann Wolfgang von, 80,
131, 194-195; *The Elective Affini-
ties*, 66, 195-203, 205, 212;
Faust, 66, 195; *The Sorrows of
Young Werther*, 195; *Wilhelm
Meister's Apprenticeship*, 79, 89,
93n, 94; *Wilhelm Meisters Wan-
derjahre*, 64n, 200
Gogol, Nikolai, 16, 69, 79; *The In-
spector General*, 76n
Goldman, Lucien, 41

Goldsmith, Oliver, *The Vicar of Wakefield*, 71
Goncharov, Ivan Aleksandrovich, *Oblomov*, 77-78
Granville-Barker, Harley, *Prefaces to Shakespeare*, 118
Grass, Günter, 194
Gregory, Lady Augusta, 257
Grierson, Sir Herbert, 244
Grooms, Red, 268
Guys, Constantin, 83

Habermas, Jürgen, 31
Handke, Peter, 194; *A Sorrow Beyond Dreams*, 25
Hardy, Thomas, 66, 83, 83-84n, 233; *The Dynasts*, 83; *The Mayor of Casterbridge*, 76; *Tess of the D'Urbervilles*, 77n
Hartigan, Grace, 268
Hartman, Geoffrey, H., 31; *Beyond Formalism*, 27n, 31; "Toward Literary History," 26-27, 27n
Hatfield, Henry, *Goethe*, 196
Havelock, Eric A., 48n
Hawthorne, Nathaniel, *The Blithedale Romance*, 70, 78; *The Marble Faun*, 149; *The Scarlet Letter*, 77n
Hazlitt, William, on *All's Well That Ends Well*, 102n; on Shelley, 235n
Heaney, Seamus, 273n
Hegel, Georg Wilhelm Friedrich, 194; *Phenomenology of Mind*, 63
Henn, T. R., *The Lonely Tower*, 273n
Herbert, George, "Vertue," 57
Herbert, Zbigniew, "Elegy of Fortinbras," 90
Hermes Trismegistus, 108, 109n
Herodotus, 17
Hesiod, 266n; *Works and Days*, 17-18
Hesse, Hermann, 163, 195

Hickman, Hannah, *Robert Musil and the Culture of Vienna*, 160n
Higginson, Thomas Wentworth, 14
historicism, 65, 130
Hitler, Adolf, 203n, 219
Hölderlin, Johann Christian Friedrich, 79; *Hyperion*, 164
Holiday, Billie, 266n
Holloway, John, 273n; "Style and World in 'The Tower,' " 254-255
Holmes, Richard, 229
Homer, *The Iliad*, 46, 47, 49; *The Odyssey*, 17, 46, 47, 49n
Hopkins, Gerard Manley, 238; "God's Grandeur," 238n; "Spelt from Sybil's Leaves," 231n
Horace (Quintus Horatius Flaccus), 58
House, Humphry, on Shelley, 234
Hugo, Victor, 80
humanism, 25, 29, 39-40, 45
Hume, David, 8n, 226
Hunter, G. K., 90n

Ibsen, Henrik, 66
intentionality, 5-6, 6n
invention and inventiveness, 20-21, 28-29, 33-34, 38, 277-278
Irene (Samuel Johnson), 68
Irving, Sir Henry, 248

Jaccottet, Philippe, 161n
James, Alice, 141
James, D. G., *The Dream of Learning*, 90n
James, Henry, 83, 141, 267; *The American Scene*, 74n, 264; "The Art of Fiction," 12; *Essays in London*, 74n; *The Sacred Fount*, 66
James, William, 3; "On a Certain Blindness in Human Beings," 278;

Louis Philippe (King of the French), 136, 149

Lowell, Robert, 86; on Mallarmé, 81

Lucretius, *De Rerum Natura*, 21n, 234

Luft, David S., *Robert Musil and the Crisis of European Culture*, 160n

Lukacs, George, *The Historical Novel*, 69

Lyons, Bridget Gellert, *Voices of Melancholy*, 117n

Mach, Ernst, 166n, 178n

Machiavelli, Niccolo, 42, 92; *Discourses*, 47; Machiavellism, 97-98n, 114-115, 116-117n, 129, 143, 148, 154

MacIntyre, Alasdair, *After Virtue*, 45n

Madison, James, 64n

madness, 64n, 78ff.

Mailer, Norman, 86

Maistre, Joseph de, 76

Mallarmé, Stéphane, 81, 277

Mandelstam, Osip, 10

Mandeville, Bernard, *The Fable of the Bees*, 59-60

Mann, Thomas, 162n, 180, 195; *Death in Venice*, 184; *The Holy Sinner*, 54; *Joseph and His Brothers*, 159

Mao Tzedung, 72n; "The Ten Great Relationships," 34n

Martineau, Henri, 125n, 155n

Marvell, Andrew, 105; "The Unfortunate Lover," 122-123, 229, 234

Marx, Karl, 72n; Marxism, 25

Marx, Leo, *The Machine in the Garden*, 62n

Marx Brothers, 39

Mary (Mother of Jesus), 143

Masaryk, Thomas, 222

Matthiessen, F. O., 90n

Mauss, Marcel, 24

McCormick, John, on Musil, 160-161n, 165n

Meinecke, Friedrich, *Machiavellism*, 43, 43n

melancholy, 59; in *Hamlet*, 117-118, 118n

Melville, Herman, 72, 267; *Billy Budd*, 76; *Moby-Dick*, 11, 65-66, 94; *Pierre*, 94

Meredith, George, *The Egoist*, 69n

Michelangelo Buonarroti, 87n

Miller, J. Hillis, on *The Elective Affinities*, 195-196

Milosz, Czeslaw, *The Land of Ulro*, 279

Milton, John, 88; *Areopagitica*, 58; "Lycidas," 266n; *Paradise Lost*, 19n; "Il Penseroso," 59, 262; on Shakespeare, 87n

Mitchell, Charles, on *The Marble Faun*, 149

modernism, 9-10, 86, 133

Moers, Ellen, *Two Dreisers*, 37

Montaigne, Michel de, 137; "Of Virtue," 147

Montesquieu, Charles de Secondat, Baron de, *Considérations sur les causes de la grandeur des Romains et de leur décadence*, 60-61

Monty Python's Flying Circus, 39

More, Sir Thomas, 59n

Morris, William, 244, 244n, 261n

Motherwell, Robert, 270

Mozart, Wolfgang Amadeus, 127; *Così Fan Tutti*, 231

Mudrick, Marvin, "Character and Event in Fiction," 224

Muir, Edwin, "W. B. Yeats," 249n

Murdoch, Iris, 178; *The Black Prince*, 89

Murry, John Middleton, on Yeats, 254

Musil, Robert, 10, 20n, 80, *158-*

Foresees His Death," 249; "Lapis
Lazuli," 248; "A Last Confession," 260; "Leda and the Swan,"
258; "Long-Legged Fly," 86;
"The Man and the Echo," 250-
251; "Meditations in Time of
Civil War," 251-252, 258, 262-
263; "News for the Delphic Oracle," 258; "Nineteen Hundred
and Nineteen," 254; *On the
Boiler*, 246, 261; "On a Picture of
a Black Centaur," 252; "On a Political Prisoner," 247n; "A People's Theatre," 257; *Pere Amica
Silentia Lunae*, 158, 257; "The
Philosophy of Shelley's Poetry,"
226n, 232n, 234n, 242-244; "A
Prayer for My Daughter," 245,
251; "*Prometheus Unbound*,"
226n; "The Reform of the Theatre," 247; *Responsibilities*, 253,
254; "Sailing to Byzantium," 254;
"Samhain: 1908," 251n; "The
Second Coming," 258n; "Song of

Wandering Aengus," 255;
"Speech After Long Silence,"
247n; "The Stare's Nest By My
Window," 241-242, 262-263;
"Supernatural Songs: VIII," 250;
"Symbolism in Painting," 245n;
"The Symbolism of Poetry," 233,
242-243; "The Theatre, the Pul-
pit, and the Newspaper," 243;
The Tower, 251n, 254; "Two
Songs from a Play," 251; "Under
Ben Bulben," 246; *A Vision*, 25,
85, 146-147n, 246-247, 251n,
257-259, 261; *The Wild Swans at
Coole*, 251, 254; "The Wild
Swans at Coole," 252, 257; *The
Wind Among the Reeds*, 254; *The
Winding Stair*, 251n; *The Words
Upon the Window-Pane*, 255n;
on Pound, 245

Ziolkowski, Theodore, *Dimensions
of the Modern Novel*, 78n
Zola, Émile, 80; *Fécondité*, 37

Library of Congress Cataloging-in-Publication Data

Berthoff, Warner.
    Literature and the continuances of virtue.
    Bibliography: p.
    Includes index.
    1. Literature—Philosophy.   2. Ethics in
literature.   3. Virtue in literature.   I. Title.
PN49.B47   1986   801   86-15103
ISBN 0-691-06688-4 (alk. paper)